ISSUES IN THE LABOR-MANAGEMENT DIALOGUE:
CHURCH PERSPECTIVES

EDITED BY ADAM J. MAIDA, JCL, JD

THE CATHOLIC HEALTH ASSOCIATION OF THE UNITED STATES
ST. LOUIS, MO 63134

Copyright © 1982
by
The Catholic Health Association of the United States
St. Louis, MO 63134

Printed in the United States of America. All rights reserved. This book, or any part thereof, may not be reproduced without the written permission of the publisher.

Library of Congress Cataloging in Publication Data
Main entry under title:

Issues in the labor-management dialogue—church perspectives.

    1. Catholic health facilities—Personnel management. 2. Church and labor. 3. Collective bargaining—Health facilities—United States. 4. Trade-Unions —Health facilities—United States. I. Maida, Adam J.
RA 975.C37I87   261.8'5   81-21645
ISBN 0-87125-071-3   AACR2

CONTENTS

PREFACE

Questions on the labor relations of Catholic-sponsored institutions are of significant interest to those involved with the internal affairs of these facilities. On both sides of the labor-management issue in Catholic institutions, there are concerned people seeking guidance on unionization and on the more basic question of the quality of work itself. The urgency of this inquiry has been underscored by Pope John Paul II's recent encyclical, *Laborem Exercens,* which was released as this book was being prepared for publication.

This series of essays is an attempt to deal with the very serious questions surrounding the quality of work: What rights can workers legitimately expect to be recognized by their Catholic institutional employers? What institutional rights must the workers respect? What duties does the Catholic institution have toward its workers and do the workers have toward the institution? Can labor-management relations be structured, not in terms of rights and duties, but in terms of the justice and charity owed to fellow members of the Church community?

This is a book for reflection and discussion on these issues and on the related issues which their statement presupposes. It does not purport to provide final solutions to the complex human relations problems involved in this field. It is intended, rather, to provide a medium for study and analysis of those problems on a personal, an institutional, and a sponsorship level.

Before the reader are the independent viewpoints of a number of authors on the entire spectrum of labor-management issues in Church-sponsored institutions. Each author's opinion is, of course, his or her own, and not necessarily that of the other authors, the editor, or the publisher. Each author, in his or her own way, helps to sharpen the focus of the labor-management dialogue. The strength of the book, however, lies not so much in the individual merits of any one or more of the essays but in their collection. They should be considered as a whole, therefore, together with the discussion questions that follow each essay, as providing a means to analyze the critical "quality of work" issues at Catholic-sponsored institutions.

By participating in the reflective process which the essays encourage, the reader will be able to evolve, for his or her position in the Catholic-sponsored institution, a better-reasoned, a more Catholic-rooted approach to the institution's labor relations. To serve as a tool for this process is the book's raison d'etre.

Adam J. Maida

ACKNOWLEDGMENTS

This book is the work of many hands. The authors of the individual chapters are properly identified and to them goes my heart-felt thanks, for giving of themselves, their time and their talent, to help me assemble what will be, I hope, a seminal work on labor relations in Catholic-sponsored institutions. Besides the named authors, there are others whom I wish to acknowledge who have also contributed importantly to the idea of this book and who have aided its development at every stage. I would be remiss if I did not thank Jack Curley, president of The Catholic Health Association, for his support and understanding in the production of this book; Sr. Margaret John Kelly, DC, PhD, CHA vice-president, Mission Services, for her insight and suggestions on the work's shape and content; my associate counsel at the Diocese of Pittsburgh Legal Office, Nicholas P. Cafardi, whose advice and assistance I prize; and my secretaries, Catherine Figola and Marie Zagrocki for their tireless work in preparing this manuscript for publication.

Adam J. Maida
January 1, 1982

AUTHORS

Rev. William J. Byron, SJ, PhD, president, University of Scranton, Scranton, PA.

Charles Craypo, PhD, associate professor of economics, University of Notre Dame, Notre Dame, IN.

Sr. Melanie DiPietro, SC, JD, associate, Mansmann, Cindrich, and Huber, Pittsburgh, PA.

James A. Donahue, assistant professor of theological ethics, University of Santa Clara, Santa Clara, CA.

Rev. Thomas J. Harvey, STL, MSW, chairman, Committee on Pluralism, National Conference of Catholic Charities, Pittsburgh, PA, and pastor, St. Kilian Church, Mars, PA.

Rev. Jordon F. Hite, TOR, JCL, JD, provincial director of personnel, Third Order Regular of St. Francis, Loretto, PA.

Joe Holland, associate, Center of Concern, Washington, DC.

William E. Joy, MBA, JD, partner, Morgan, Brown, Kearns, and Joy, Attorneys-at-Law, Boston, MA.

Rev. Robert L. Kealy, STL, JD, director, The Center for Church/State Studies, DePaul University College of Law; judge, Archdiocese of Chicago Matrimonial Tribunal; and former chairman, Committee on Collective Bargaining, Canon Law Society of America.

Rev. Eugene F. Lauer, STD, visiting professor of religious studies, Seton Hill College, Greensburg, PA.

Rev. Donald G. McCarthy, PhD, director of education, Pope John XXIII Medical-Moral Research and Education Center, St. Louis, MO, and visiting professor of Christian Ethics, Mt. St. Mary Seminary, Cincinnati, OH.

Rev. Adam J. Maida, JCL, JD, general counsel and vice chancellor, Diocese of Pittsburgh, Pittsburgh, PA, and special counsel and canonist, The Catholic Health Association of the United States, St. Louis, MO.

James A. Serritella, JD, partner, Reuben & Proctor, Chicago, IL, and former member, Committee on Collective Bargaining, Canon Law Society of America

Rev. Patrick J. Sullivan, CSC, PhD, researcher in church labor-management relations, University of Notre Dame, Notre Dame, IN.

Leonard J. Weber, PhD, associate professor of philosophy and religion, Mercy College of Detroit, Detroit, MI.

INTRODUCTION

Pope John Paul II's recent encyclical *On Human Work* recognizes the movement of modern unions beyond industry to other sectors of society: "The experience of history teaches that [unions] are an indispensable element of social life, especially in modern industrial societies. Obviously, this does not mean that only industrial workers can set up associations of this type. Representatives of every profession can use them to insure their own rights." This book *Issues in the Labor-Management Dialogue: Church Perspectives,* deals with just the type of historical movement the Pope describes, namely, the movement of unions into a nonindustrial system previously unaffected by unions, the organizations that provide essential human services such as medical treatment and education. More specifically, this book tries to articulate, in the light of Catholic social teaching, those moral and ethical principles that are operative whenever a Catholic health care facility responds to a request from its employees to form a union.

The topic of unions in Catholic health care facilities is of rather recent origin, because, until 1974, health care facilities were exempt from many of the provisions of the labor laws of our country. In 1974, the National Labor Relations Act (NLRA) lifted these exemptions, and unions have made many attempts to represent the interests of various types of workers in health care facilities. But many Catholic facilities have resisted unionization attempts. To assist management in resisting unions, some facilities have had recourse to sophisticated labor counsel or to management consultants who have advised management not only about labor laws, but also about methods and tactics to win workers' support. Union sympathizers have characterized such "high-powered" tactics as unethical and immoral and as denials of the workers' rights upheld by popes from Leo XIII to John Paul II: "Workers' rights, together with the need for the workers themselves to secure them, give rise to yet another right: the right of association, that is to form associations for the purpose of defending the vital interests of those employed in the various professions.'' *(On Human Work)*

The consulting firms that advise management have, as their business, the goal of avoiding unionization. As a result, they, and the health care facilities that employ them, have been called ''union busters.'' The institutions' managers disclaim any immoral or unethical conduct; they prefer, instead, to view such consultation as helping them to instruct their supervisors on how to deal fairly with their employees as a simple expansion of their valid management rights.

Against this background, some Catholic facilities are being charged with a certain duplicity in their *modus vivendi* and *modus operandi*. On the one hand, they are charged with the mandate to be truly Christian and truly just in all their relationships with their employees and to be truly reflective of authentic Gospel values in their social and ethical teaching and activity. On the other hand, they are accused of violating basic human rights and the teachings they espouse by denying or effectively challenging the rights of unions to represent their employees.

It is in this ambiguous context that certain moral and ethical principles underlying Catholic social teaching need to be examined and objectively scrutinized. This can validly be done through scholarly analysis of the relevant social, moral, and ethical principles by experts in the various fields surrounding this debate. Such scholarly presentations can serve as invaluable resources to those who must make the difficult daily decisions in managing Catholic health care facilities.

This book is a collection of these scholarly essays. It presents the thoughts of theologians, historians, philosophers, priests, religious, sociologists, lawyers, and economists on the question of unions in Catholic health care facilities. Although the work has many authors with many backgrounds, it is not a disjointed assortment of essays. Instead, its purpose is to provide, through many mirrors, insight into a complex issue. This is not to say that the book offers one vision or one answer. It does not. What it does do, however, is to facilitate the reader's consideration of the many aspects of the unionization question. Such consideration can lead to the reader's broader understanding, since the book considers alternatives within the Catholic tradition for effective policy formulation.

Although the authors are many and their points for consideration numerous, the reader will find that their themes have much in common. The authors consider the history of the unionization question in health care facilities: how did Catholic facilities arrive where they are today?

They find the historical antecedents in the Industrial Revolution and the response of workers and the Church, to the social upheaval it caused. The authors examine the Church's teachings and their historical underpinnings, sometimes as reactions to historical movements and sometimes in the forefront of those movements. They apply these teachings to the current question: What does the Church teach concerning the unionization of the workers in its own apostolates?

One major consideration is, What does it mean to be a "Catholic" facility? Can an institution, in contrast to a person, *be* Catholic? How does an institution's Catholicity affect its actions? Are there some actions in which a Catholic institution cannot participate because of its Catholicity? Needless to say, the answer to such questions will provide many of the solutions in an institution's relationships with its workers.

Against this backdrop of an institution's Catholicity, the authors consider health care facilities' various organizational characteristics and the role professional managers and attorneys play in the facility. One major area of concern is the setting of priorities for the institution, that is, whether the institution's Catholic character or outside professionals set them. A critical factor in such decision making is the economic factor: How much will such a decision cost, and what effect will such costs have on the institution's provision of services or even its very existence?

The authors also consider the nature of unions and the role they play in labor-management relations. Unions' purposes and goals are explained and then questioned on their need or validity within a religious institution. The authors discuss the rights of workers that form the basis of unions, and they examine the effects of the assertion of workers' rights in such activities as strikes. The authors seek to find a solution to the difficult process of weighing the individual worker's rights against those of society in general. They also examine the role of religious membership in unions at their religiously sponsored institution: whether religious ought properly to belong to the union and what the consequences of their inclusion or exclusion are to the individual religious, the sponsoring body, the union, and the institution.

A final major topic of concern is alternatives to unions in Catholic hospitals. Not the least consideration here is whether it is morally permissible to avoid unionization, and, if so, how can a facility do so unobjectionably.

Although the preceding description provides the reader with an accurate overview, each author, of course, has his or her own niche, own ideas, and own concerns. In the first chapter, entitled "The Catholic

Vision of Work in the World," Fr. Donald G. McCarthy depicts the Catholic tradition of work especially highlighting work in the field of health care. He does this by considering the three key elements of the Catholic tradition of work: (1) the persons who do the work, (2) the significance of work, and (3) the economic relationships of work and workers.

The Catholic view of workers is one that exalts the inestimable dignity of the human person, gifted with knowledge, conscience, and freedom by the Creator, and seeking the common good through social structures and relationships. The significance of work in the Catholic tradition is found in the fact that man is the subject of work: human persons exercise dominion over the world through their work, thereby continuing the divine work of creation. In this view, labor belongs not to the state or to capital, but to the worker, whose individual wealth it is, and who is free to organize with other workers in order to assure to himself or herself the benefits of work. The Catholic vision of economic relationships seeks justice in those relationships, a justice in the distribution of wealth which in turn is based on love for the person. Following this discussion, Fr. McCarthy concludes with a picture of Catholic leadership "taking up and ...building" just solutions to labor-management conflicts within this tripartite Catholic perspective of human personhood, human work, and economic relationships.

In the next chapter "Unions and Catholic Health Care Facilities," Professor Charles Craypo and Fr. Patrick J. Sullivan provide an historical survey in which they examine the social and economic conditions that have made the health care system ripe for unionization. (In this context, they find that the failure of Catholic facilities to follow the Church's own teachings on social justice gives impetus to worker unionization drives.) The authors explain what functions unions traditionally perform, their goals, their internal workings, and their effects, both economic and noneconomic, on the institutions that they have organized. The authors look specifically at unions in the health care system, from the first health care unionizations in 1917 to the present. They focus on the individual unions involved in the current health care unionization drive, the historical background of each one, the results of their campaigns to organize health care employees, their economic effects on health care labor costs, and their effects on the administration of health care institutions.

Using this historical understanding as their foundation, the authors survey the current scene. They consider the recent trend in the health care system toward mergers and what effect that trend will have on labor-management relations. They survey the responses of administrators of Catholic institutions to unionization drives and conclude by providing some practical suggestions for health care administrators, organizers, and personnel.

Mr. William E. Joy, in his chapter, "The National Labor Relations Act: Ethical Considerations for Catholic Health Institutions," details the history of national labor legislation as a basis for an ethical examination of the impact of these laws. He begins with the 1935 Wagner Act and its genesis in New Deal economic thought and follows its transmogrification through the Taft-Hartley Act (1947), the Labor Management Reporting and Disclosure Act (1959), and the 1974 Amendments to the NLRA regarding health care facilities. As a source of ethical considerations, he traces the growth of the Church's teachings on the rights and duties of workers from *Rerum Novarum* through *Quadragesimo Anno,* Vatican II's *Gaudium et Spes* and John Paul II's *Laborem Exercens.* He also examines the nature of the modern Catholic health care institution, and the moral values inherent in its religious identity which will guide its actions. Finally, he seeks to put these two concepts—labor law and ethical considerations—together in a comparison of labor legislation and the rights and duties it creates with Catholic social teaching and its perception of those same rights and duties. He does this seriatim in an examination of the chronological phases of labor-management relations, beginning with the initial union organizing phase, possible legal challenges to such organizing, the consequential collective bargaining phase, the strikes that may occur, and finally ending with the on-going contract administration phase.

In the fourth chapter, "New Realities in Employment Matters: Counseling Catholic Health Care Institutions," Fr. Robert L. Kealy and Mr. James A. Serritella portray the tightrope tred by Catholic health care facilities. Religiously motivated institutions, they provide human services in a highly expensive, highly regulated system. They must do so economically in order to survive, but can they allow these economics to interfere with the institution's religious identity and the Church's teachings, especially those social justice teachings on the workers' right to organize?

In their essay, Fr. Kealy and Mr. Serritella examine the tensions in herent in the operation of a Catholic facility: social justice concerns vs. institutional concerns; managerial vs. religious conflict; civil law demands and alternative means of dealing with them. They address this conflict through a historical overview of the Church's teachings in the area of social justice, from Pope Leo XIII to John Paul II, including the statements of Vatican II and the 1971 Synod of Bishops. They follow this historical perspective by examining what it means to be a Catholic facility in this age of the multibillion dollar health care system and by clarifying the roles of boards, administrators, and consultants within this Catholic identity. The authors strongly suggest that it is the health care facility's Catholic identity that must define these roles, rather than the facility's allowing this identity to be defined by those who act on its behalf from their own disparate perspectives.

In the following chapter, "Service Strikes: The New Moral Dilemma," Fr. Eugene F. Lauer describes what it means to strike in the hospital or human services sector. We are used to hearing about strikes in the profit-making sector of the economy, with workers collectively withholding their labor to force capital to grant them a larger share of the profits as either wages or fringe benefits. But how does the industrial strike model fit the nonprofit sector? There, workers withhold not manufactured goods, but medical, educational, or counseling services.

Fr. Lauer examines this very difficult question, first by explaining the industrial strike model and then by examining how it "fits" the nonprofit provision of what he terms the *human services* sector. He highlights the difficult moral problems this model transfer creates, especially the effects of such strikes on the needy client and the worker's right to withhold his services balanced against the client's very human, sometimes life-threatening needs.

There are no easy answers to the difficult questions that this essay proposes, but by helping us to state the moral questions more clearly, and with a few proposals of his own, Fr. Lauer sets us on the road to a possible way of understanding, living with, and making morally valid decisions concerning strikes by personnel who provide essential human services.

In his chapter entitled, "Members of Religious Communities and Unions," Fr. Jordan F. Hite presents a case history of the National Labor Relations Board (NLRB) from 1971 until the present, considering its effects on the rights of religious "employees" at religiously sponsored institutions. The word "employees" has been placed in quotation marks because the developing labor law uses a different meaning for that word as it applies to religious workers at religious institutions than the word commonly has. More often than not, the law perceives religious not as employees, but as owners, when the institution at which they serve is one sponsored by their religious community. Fr. Hite examines this paradox in the relevant cases involving Catholic colleges, hospitals, and nursing homes that have occurred since 1971. He follows this case survey with a summary of the legal conclusions that can be drawn from the cases, conclusions which, within themselves, seem to depend not so much on logical consistency as on which legal tribunal decided the case.

After this survey of the relevant cases, Fr. Hite discusses their implication and the underlying issues which they present for religious in regard to labor organizations and their religiously sponsored institutions. He also scrutinizes the attitudes that are involved, on behalf of the individual religious, in deciding questions relevant to labor organizations and their membership therein, emphasizing the freedom of each religious to make such decisions guided by charity, the charism of the community, and a conscience fully informed by the Church's social justice teachings.

In the following chapter "Criteria for Union Membership: Are the Vows Relevant?" Sr. Melanie DiPietro continues this perspective of the individual religious. It is her thesis that religious, by acquiescing to NLRB misinterpretation of the meaning of the vows, both in regard to their own community life and in regard to their employment status in a separate corporation, suffer a loss of legal rights and, further, a weakening of their own viability as effective religious. Sr. Melanie goes on to present a perception of the vow and its meaning in the corporate, economic, and political structures in which religious must work. This perception evidences a need for a religious to protect his or her right of access to collective bargaining units.

She believes that the question of union representation and, specifically, of the eligibility of religious, requires a deeper reflection on the operation of the vows in the present corporate, economic, and political structures and on the function of poverty in this setting. Sr. Melanie suggests that the vow of poverty is really concerned with the direction, not the negation, of wealth and that the unionization question raises social justice concerns about the equitable distribution of resources within Church-related institutions. In the final section of her essay, Sr. Melanie, examining the Seton Hill case, sees the NLRB as failing to analyze the substantive relationships of religious either to the congregation or to the employer, thereby denying constitutional and statutory rights to a class of persons (religious) on the basis of religious association.

In the attempted unionization of Catholic health care facilities both labor and management assert that they are impelled to take a prounion or antiunion course because of their Catholicity. How can this be? Does not "Catholicity" imply a unity of belief that ought to translate into a unity of action by both sides? In his chapter, "Religious Institutions as Moral Agents: Toward an Ethics of Organizational Character," Professor James A. Donahue approaches this difficult dilemma without proposing any easy answers. What he does propose is an analytical framework, namely, the construct of an "organizational character" that both labor and management can use to resolve their conflicts.

It is Professor Donahue's thesis that, much as individuals have "character" as a basis for making moral judgments, so, too, Catholic health care institutions can be considered to have an organizational character that will form the basis for the organization's moral judgments. He first explains what makes up an individual's character and the basis of individual moral judgments in character and then examines an organization, the constitution of its "character," and how this character forms the basis for the organization's moral judgments. Although an organization is composed of many persons, its organizational character requires of its constituents a common basis or understanding, agreed upon beliefs, values, and convictions from which moral judgments can be made. But this common basis cannot be artificial or forced. It must be a mutual, albeit multifaceted, realization.

Quite often one looks at a situation to determine its content, never thinking that the way one looks at it affects its content. Professor Leonard J. Weber, in his chapter, "Labor Unions and Two Concepts of Social Justice," examines the way Americans look at the issue of social justice as it applies to the question of health care unionization. His presupposition is that those in charge of Catholic health care facilities wish to resolve the unionization question justly. The problem arises, however, in the two contrasting understandings of social justice to which the American Church has been subject. The first is mainstream American social justice. The second is the centuries-old Catholic tradition. Although the two understandings of social justice share many common values, in certain critical areas they are vastly different. The American view of social justice stresses individualism and the pursuit of self-interest. The Catholic tradition emphasizes achieving the common good through a necessary cooperation of individuals.

The problem, as Professor Weber points out, is that most people are used to seeing the unionization question through the window of the American view. Without entirely eschewing this viewpoint, since it is the basis from which American society and American laws act, he suggests that it be reconsidered from the Catholic understanding of social justice. Only in this fashion will Americans arrive at a method of dealing with the unionization of Catholic institutions that is also perceived to be just.

This Catholic understanding is one of many competing perceptions that form the basis of our modern pluralistic society. Father Thomas J. Harvey, in his chapter entitled, "The Catholic Health Care Facility: Roots in the Gospel and in the Nation," explores the situation of the Catholic health care institutions as it changed and maintained its Catholic identity in this pluralistic society. He attempts to isolate and describe the prevailing influences that have shaped American Catholic institutions, in order to offer a context in which the question of unionization in Catholic health care institutions can be addressed.

Fr. Harvey begins his contextual approach by explaining the development of American social policy toward health care institutions. He perceives, in this development, a vulnerability for Catholic institutions as a result of modern funding and labor patterns. He next considers the formulation of social policy by political consensus, as opposed to a rational formulation, and reviews the effects this political process has had on Catholic health care facilities. He also contrasts the development of educational policy with that of health care policy, to heighten our understanding of this political process. Finally, he questions whether Catholic health care institutions will approach the issue of labor organization from the Church's ideal or from the view of an institution which has been assimilated into the larger, secular society's organization, structures, and value base.

In the following chapter, "The Call for a Prophetic Catholic Health Care System," Mr. Joe Holland speaks forthrightly of the need for the Church to lead the way in asserting workers' rights, especially those workers in the Church's own apostolates. He locates the current crisis in labor-management relations in Catholic health care institutions within this larger historical context of the role of the worker and the poor in society.

Mr. Holland begins by examining the spontaneous ministry to the poor of the heroic founders of apostolic institutions during the laissez faire capitalism of the nineteenth century. He traces the development of this ministry into the twentieth century and its incorporation into the social welfare structure of modern society, in which the Church has become only one of many subsidized providers of health care. Mr. Holland characterizes the prevailing atmosphere as a movement away from social welfare and toward national security. In this shift, he sees society turning against the poor and the infirm.

In response to this societal antipathy, Mr. Holland believes that the

Church must reinvigorate its traditional defense of the poor and the worker through a pastoral strategy based on a "preferential option for the poor." Mr. Holland describes what such a pastoral strategy would mean for the Catholic health care system and its response to its own workers. He sees this course of action resulting in a prophetic health care system within a prophetic Church, in which both management and labor are similarly called to be prophetic in their ideas and actions.

In the book's final essay, "Catholicity and Creativity in the Collective Bargaining Process," Fr. William J. Byron examines what effect an institution's Catholic character has on its collective bargaining. The legally mandated areas of collective bargaining are job security, wages, and working conditions. Working conditions at a Catholic institution must, by definition, be consistent with employees' human dignity. Likewise, job security is a worker's unquestionable right. Fr. Byron thus concentrates his consideration on the remaining issue of wages or, as he characterizes it, *remuneration*. This is a difficult area for nonprofit institutions such as hospitals and schools because they have no "profits" out of which to pay wage increases. Every dollar of wage increases becomes a dollar of increased cost. How, then, does a Catholic institution handle the question of remuneration?

Fr. Byron suggests "opening up" the collective bargaining process to allow both workers and managers, inspired by their Catholicism, to be creative, thereby generating new options in collective bargaining. A major option that Fr. Byron suggests is "creative sharing," which involves worker participation in some fiscal decisions previously reserved for managers. This participation is not meant to usurp management's rights, but to allow workers and managers together to assess how the institution's income can be set to allow for fair worker compensation. Such creative sharing becomes a gain sharing in which the amount of income over costs can provide increased worker remuneration, together with the necessary capital surplus for an institution's future.

This proposal, as those of many of the other authors, appears to parallel what Pope John Paul II wrote in his encyclical, *On Human Work,* namely that "worker solidarity, together with a clearer and more committed realization by others of workers' rights, has in many cases brought about profound changes. Various forms of neocapitalism or collectivism have developed. Various new systems have been thought out. Workers can often share in running businesses and in controlling their productivity, and in fact do so. Through appropriate associations they exercise influence over conditions of work and pay and also over social legislation.''

This introduction is a brief description of what this book offers, by theme and by chapter. Before beginning the individual essays, the reader should consider how he or she wishes to use this work. There are at least three different ways this can be done.

The first is to read the work as a whole and thematically, identifying how each author treats the book's separate, major themes. This way will give the reader an overview of the entire situation, which can then provide a general basis for future policy considerations.

The second way to use this book is to read the separate essays that deal with one's individual areas of concern. Each essay has been described in a capsulized fashion that should allow the reader to decide what essays will help in a particular situation.

The third, and probably the most profitable, way to use this book is to begin by reading the questions that follow each essay. These questions are meant to immerse the reader into the book's considerations. After reading these questions, one should check any deemed relevant to a particular situation and proceed to read the individual essays with those questions in mind. The reader's own formulation of answers to the questions will provide a clearer understanding of the issues involved, so that when the reader as worker, administrator, professional consultant, corporate director or member, or religious sponsoring group member must make a critical decision in this area, he or she can do so with confidence.

This is really the book's purpose: to provide a practical tool for those in the health care profession who are called upon to participate in solving a difficult moral and ethical problem. The task is not an easy one, but, like all burdens assumed for a neighbor's sake, it is not borne alone: ''Come to me all you who labor and are burdened and I will give you rest.''

CHAPTER 1

THE CATHOLIC VISION OF WORK IN THE WORLD

Rev. Donald G. McCarthy, PhD

In the book of Joel the prophet, the Lord promises: ''I will pour out my spirit upon all mankind; your sons and daughters shall prophesy, your old men shall dream dreams, your young men shall see visions'' (Joel 3:1). This promised outpouring of the spirit, in Catholic belief, was eminently fulfilled on Pentecost when the Church began to undertake its prophetic mission.

The Church speaks prophetically to the world, drawing upon a vision of human life and destiny hidden from the naked eye. In that vision, the Church sees human successes and failures, triumphs and tragedies, more clearly and more penetratingly than the most advanced x-ray technology could hope to envision them. Guided by this vision, the Church approaches human problems with a missionary attitude. In his first encyclical, *Redemptor Hominis*, the present Holy Father, John Paul II, describes this attitude:

> The *missionary* attitude always begins with a feeling of deep esteem for ''what is in man'' (John 2:26), for what man has himself worked out in the depths of his spirit concerning the most profound and important problems. It is a question of respecting everything that has been brought about in him by the Spirit, which ''blows where it wills'' (John 3:8). The mission is never destruction, but instead is a taking up and fresh building, even if in practice there has not always been full correspondence with

Fr. McCarthy is director of education for the Pope John XXIII Medical-Moral Research and Education Center, St. Louis, MO, and visiting professor of Christian Ethics, St. Mary Seminary, Cincinnati, OH.

this high ideal. And we know well that the conversion that is begun by the mission is a work of grace, in which man must fully find himself again.[1]

The reference by the Pope to "a taking up and fresh building" and the conversion "in which man must fully find himself again" can apply very directly to the grave problem of humanizing and redeeming the world of work. In his third encyclical, *Laborem Exercens, (On Human Work)*, found in the appendix of this book, Pope John Paul II presents an all-embracing description of work as "any activity by man, whether manual or intellectual, whatever its nature or circumstances...any human activity that can and must be recognized as work."

This chapter will picture the Catholic vision of work in the world of contemporary human experience, with special concern for work performed in the public service of health care. In this picture, three key elements have a place: (1) the persons who work, (2) the significance of their work, and (3) the economic relationships they establish. The chapter will then conclude with a picture of Catholic leadership in the "taking up and fresh building" of just solutions to labor-management relationships.

The Persons Who Work

The Catholic vision of human persons, their unique and inestimable dignity, their individuality and eternal destiny, their equality and autonomy, does not belong exclusively to the Church or even to revealed religious belief. Yet it contrasts starkly with other views of the human person, particularly the determinist and materialist views, which refuse to recognize the spiritual dimensions of the person, exemplified in the exercise of freedom and the pursuit of truth. The Catholic vision of human persons and their relationships heavily influences the Church's vision of work in the world. Pope John XXIII spoke wisely of the various inadequate theories of the person in 1961 in *Mater et Magistra (Christianity and Social Progress)*:

Many systems of thought have been developed and committed to writing: some of these already have been dissipated as mist by the sun; others remain basically unchanged today; still others now elicit less and less response from men. The reason for this is that these popularized fancies neither encompass man, whole and entire, nor do they affect his inner being. Moreover, they fail to take into account the weaknesses of human nature, such as sickness and suffering: weaknesses that no economic or social system, no matter how advanced, can completely eliminate. Besides, men everywhere are moved by a profound and unconquerable sense of religion, which no force can ever destroy nor shrewdness suppress.[2]

Four years later, in the beautiful *Gaudium et Spes (Pastoral Constitution on the Church in the Modern World)*, the Fathers of the Second Vatican Council painted the Catholic picture of the human person. They spoke of the creation of human persons "to the image of God" set over all earthly creatures to rule and make use of them while glorifying God.[3] They quoted the exuberant Psalm 8, "Thou has made him little less than a God, and dost crown him with glory and honor." They cited the creation of male and female persons, making possible the partnership of man and woman as the "first form of communion between persons," since by innermost nature each person is a social being.

The Council Fathers went on to sketch in bold lines the essential features of human personhood:

Man is not deceived when he regards himself as superior to bodily things and as more than just a speck of nature or a nameless unit in the city of man. For by his power to know himself in the depths of his being he rises above the whole universe of mere objects. When he is drawn to think about his real self he turns to those deep recesses of his being where God who probes the heart awaits him, and where he himself decides his own destiny in the sight of God. So when he recognizes in himself a spiritual and immortal soul, he is not being led astray by false imaginings that are due to merely physical or social causes. On the contrary, he grasps what is profoundly true in this matter.[4]

The Church firmly believes and teaches that human persons are gifted with the intellectual power to understand what can be observed through the senses and thus to reach out to realities known only to the mind. They are also gifted with the power of conscience, calling them to love and to do what is good and to avoid what is evil. Through efforts to form a correct conscience, they search for truth and for the right solution to the many moral problems that arise in social relationships.[5]

The contemporary world includes views of human freedom, ranging from its complete negation in theories of determinism to freedom's elevation to an absolutely autonomous agency in the theories of atheistic existentialism. The Catholic vision of human freedom pictures it as endowed upon human persons as an exceptional sign of God's own image, enabling them to choose or reject the good that leads to God and always with responsibility to him for their use of his endowment.[6] As Pope John Paul II stated:

> Since man's true freedom is not found in everything that the various systems and individuals see and propagate as freedom, the Church, because of her divine mission, becomes all the more the guardian of this freedom, which is the condition and basis for the human person's true dignity.[7]

Pope Paul VI saw the authentic use of human freedom as leading to the fulfillment of the whole person and every person. He deplored a "narrow humanism, closed in on itself and not open to the values of the spirit and to God who is their source." He quoted with approval Henri de Lubac, the French Jesuit scholar, proclaiming that "a humanism closed off from other realities becomes inhuman."[8] Pope John XXIII earlier had said the same thing about a narrow, self-centered humanism:

> Separated from God, man becomes monstrous to himself and others. Consequently, mutual relationships between men absolutely require a right ordering of the human conscience in relation to God, the source of all truth, justice, and love.[9]

The vision of persons all created by the same heavenly Father and endowed with the same marvelous gifts of knowledge and freedom for their own self-perfection readily leads to the unifying concept of the "human family." The Fathers of the Second Vatican Council taught very simply, "In his fatherly care for all of us, God desired that all men should form one family and deal with each other in a spirit of brotherhood."[10] Furthermore, human persons cannot love God without loving his family, as St. John taught in his first Epistle: "One who has no love for the brother he has seen cannot love the God he has not seen."[11]

This "human family" model of looking at the entire human race, employed by the Second Vatican Council, firmly grounds principles of human equality and social justice. All members of that family have the same Father, all are called to the same eternal destiny, and all enjoy a morally equal dignity despite differences of physical capacity, intellectual powers, or social standing. The "common good," a concept at the heart of Catholic social and political thought, recognizes and protects the equal dignity and rights of all human family members. The Second Vatican Council described the common good as "the sum total of social conditions which allow people, either as groups or individuals, to reach their fulfillment more fully and more easily."[12]

The interdependence of human persons has widened with twentieth-century developments in communication, transportation, and economic interdependence. Although the strength of the ties between family members far outstrips that of those between members of the international human family, the latter concept is growing in meaningfulness. One speaks of brothers and sisters in Africa and Asia more readily now that at any previous point in history.

The growing interdependence of persons and groups of persons gives rise to organizations and associations of all kinds, from OPEC (the organization of petroleum-exporting countries) to Solidarity (the free Polish labor union). This trend of socialization brings many advantages for human fulfillment and the protection of human rights, but it cannot be considered an unmixed blessing: human persons are prone to sin, and social structures easily reflect that. The Catholic vision of human persons includes the original sin and its impact on all generations. Vatican II noted this succinctly, stating: "What Revelation makes known to us is confirmed by our own experience. For when man looks into his own heart he finds that he is drawn towards what is wrong and sunk in many evil ways that cannot come from his good creator."[13] Selfishness and pride are rooted deeply in fallen human nature, and they contaminate the atmosphere of society as well. When human persons interrelate, the temptation to selfish exploitation and discriminatory oppression can never be discounted.

Christ came into the human family to overcome sin and its effects. In him, God reconciled human persons to himself and to one another. Christ makes all things new; best of all, he renews human persons through the Spirit whom he has sent into the world. This holds true not only for Christians but for all persons of good will in whose hearts the Spirit's grace is active. Christ died to renew all people, and the Spirit offers to all people the possibility of participating in the redemption and renewal through Christ.

So the Church seeks to reach all people with the good news of the Redeemer. Thus Pope John Paul II in his first encyclical, *The Redeemer of Man,* proclaimed that the Church seeks to reach every single person on this planet, each person, "in all the unrepeatable reality of what he is and does," each person who is writing his personal history "through numerous bonds, contacts, situations, and social structures linking him with other men."[14] Hence the renewal of individual persons leads to a renewal of social structures and social relationships. The Church's vision of human persons transcends an individualistic morality and calls for an uprooting of social sin as well as individual sin. "Then, under the necessary help of divine grace,'' wrote the Council Fathers, ''there will arise a generation of new men, the molders of a new humanity.''[15]

The Significance of Work

In *Laborem Exercens (On Human Work),* Pope John Paul II links closely the notion of personhood and work:

> Man has to subdue the earth and dominate it, because as the ''image of God'' he is a person, that is to say, a subjective being capable of acting in a planned and rational way, capable of deciding about himself, and with a tendency to self-realization. *As a person, man is therefore the subject of work.* As a person he works, he performs various actions belonging to the work process; independently of their objective content, these actions must all serve to realize his humanity, to fulfill the calling to be a person that is his by reason of his very humanity.[16]

The Holy Father explains that, both objectively and subjectively, human persons express ''dominion'' over the world and its resources through their work. Remembering the *Genesis* account of the divine mandate directing human persons to ''fill the earth and subdue it'' (Gen. 1:28), Pope John Paul II teaches that original sin did not withdraw or cancel out God's intention that human persons subdue the earth. Hence, work remains a good thing for all people of all generations; it is not only useful, but corresponds to, expresses, and increases human dignity.

Pope John Paul II presents the core of this personalist view of work in one powerful sentence: ''Work is a good thing for man—a good thing for his humanity—because through work man not only *transforms nature,* adapting it to his own needs, but he also *achieves fulfillment* as a human being and indeed, in a sense, becomes 'more a human being'.''[17] In a faith perspective, human work becomes a continuation of the divine work of creation and a historical fulfilling of God's plan for the world. Christians are convinced that the achievements through human work are a sign of God's greatness, not conquests that rival or oppose God's creative plan. The decisive norm for the right use of human work can only be the authentic interests of the total human family, so that, collectively and individually, human persons may fulfill their total vocations as persons.[18]

Human work, of course, unites human persons and must be viewed in the context of the international human family discussed above. Pope Paul VI drew upon the writing of the French Dominican, Fr. M. D. Chenu, in expressing the unifying quality of work: ''When work is done in common—when hope, hardship, ambition and joy are shared—it brings together and firmly unites the wills, minds and hearts of men. In its accomplishment, men find themselves to be brothers."[19] Within this vision of the goodness and fulfilling capability of human work, one finds the central question of the value and recompense of human work. In his recent encyclical, *Laborem Exercens,* Pope John Paul II faces head on the practical materialism, widely accepted today, which considers human labor solely according to its economic purpose. In this model, labor and capital are two impersonal juxtaposed forces measured by purely economic standards. The Holy Father designates this a "nonhumanist" approach and says firmly:

It is obvious that materialism, including its dialectical form, is incapable of providing sufficient and definitive bases for thinking about human work, in order that the primacy of man over the capital instrument, the primacy of the person over things, may find in it adequate and irrefutable *confirmation and support.*[20]

The personalist perspective Pope John Paul II embraces refuses to juxtapose labor and capital and insists on the priority of labor over what we have grown accustomed to calling capital. He insists that capital, as we know it, both the natural resources placed at the disposal of human persons and the whole collection of means by which resources are transformed (and, in a sense, humanized), must be seen as the historical heritage of human labor and the result of work. Everything contained in the concept of capital is only a collection of things, man and woman alone are persons, and persons have priority over things. Hence, Pope John Paul II teaches as an essential element of the Catholic vision of work the principle of the priority of labor over capital.[21] Furthermore, the Holy Father takes pains to distinguish the Catholic vision of the relation of capital and labor both from that of the collectivism of Marxism and the rigid capitalism practiced by liberalism and political systems inspired by it. With reference to the latter, he rejects absolute ownership of the means of production, since the right to private property is subordinated to the right to common use, to the fact that goods are meant for everyone. Since capital increases through the work done over generations, the value of capital belongs at least partially to the workers who increase its value. Hence, the proposals for joint ownership of the means of production by investors and workers reflect and respond to the vision of moderate capitalism that Pope John Paul II presents.[22]

Workers need a direct and tangible means of benefiting by the principle of the common use of goods, the principle that theology traces to

God's original deeding of the world and its resources to the entire human family. Pope John Paul II teaches that wages and the social benefits of work are still, and always will be, a practical means whereby the vast majority of people can have access to those goods intended for common use, both the goods of nature and manufactured goods.[23] Catholic social doctrine since Pope Leo XIII's *Rerum Novarum* has upheld the right of workers to organize associations for the purpose of defending their vital interests. Pope John Paul II points out explicitly that "representatives of every profession can use them to insure their own rights."[24] He takes pains, however, to insist that unions and professional associations may not struggle to eliminate their opponent, because labor and capital are indispensable components and must remain cooperators in their common endeavor.

In summary, the Catholic vision of work sees it as the continuation of creation, a privilege and responsibility entrusted by God to his human family, one that unites them in common efforts and common use of the resources of nature and the means of production. Social justice demands that businesses and all agencies of work strive to enhance the personal good of workers since labor precedes capital. Nonetheless, the complexity of economic relationships renders this always an unfinished task.

Economic Relationships

Each new technological achievement in the advancing progress of human scientific inventiveness adds complexity to the world of work, because with technology's advance, the power and potential misuse of the instruments of work continually grow. The achievement of a just and right use of these instruments becomes an ever greater challenge. The Catholic vision of science and technology lauds each new achievement but constantly signals the potential abuses as well. In *Redemptor Hominis*, Pope John Paul II offers a criterion for the correct use of advancing technology:

> But the question keeps coming back with regard to what is most essential—whether in the context of this progress man, as man, is becoming truly better, that is to say more mature spiritually, more aware of the dignity of his humanity, more responsible, more open to others, especially the neediest and the weakest, and readier to give and to aid all.[25]

No one can answer these questions without serious reflection. In the realm of health care work, nurses are asking whether their role today in caring for the sick allows them to be more aware of the dignity of their own humanity, more responsible, and more open to others. Has the increase of skill and efficiency in nursing care through technological progress made nursing less human as a profession? What can be done to overcome the depersonalization that intrudes with increasing reliance on computers and electronic equipment?

When nurses and others in health care organize into associations, how do they determine their goals and objectives? The Fathers of the Second Vatican Council spoke frankly of the temptations that progress has introduced: "The hierarchy of values has been disordered, good and evil intermingle, and every man and every group is interested only in its own affairs, not in those of others."[26] Traditionally, Catholic teaching upholds the ideal of social justice as a norm to resolve the worker-management issues that continue to surface in the face of economic development and technical progress.

Yet justice alone may be inadequate. Pope John Paul II suggested this in his second encyclical, *Dives in Misericordia (Rich in Mercy)*.[27] He points out that appeals to justice alone can be corrupted by spite, hatred, and cruelty as individuals and groups struggle for justice. Past and present experience demonstrates that justice is not enough. Seeking justice alone can even lead to the negation and destruction of justice if a deeper human power, which is love, does not shape and mold the pursuit of justice. Thus, the Catholic vision of economic relationships insists that justice cannot be accomplished without love, and, of course, love without justice is vain and selfish. The 1971 Synod of Bishops' document, *Justice in the World,* focused on the task of integrating love with justice:

> According to the Christian message, therefore, a man's relationship to his neighbor is bound up with his relationship to God; his response to the love of God, saving us through Christ, is shown to be effective in his love and service of men. Christian love of neighbor and justice cannot be separated. For love implies an absolute demand for justice, namely a recognition of the dignity and rights of one's neighbor. Justice attains its inner fullness only in love. Because every man is truly a visible image of the invisible God and a brother of Christ, the Christian finds in every man God himself and God's absolute demand for justice and love.[28]

Pope John Paul II presented this same doctrine by linking justice with objective goods and love with persons.[29] He has clearly identified himself as a teacher of personalist humanism. The insistence that individuals and even groups of persons who act collectively, as unions and boards of

9

directors, must pursue justice *lovingly* reflects his humanism and the Church's vision of human affairs. The appeal to pursue justice in a loving way presumes the presence and action of the Spirit, sent into the world by Christ the Redeemer. Without confidence in the Spirit, the Catholic vision of work in the world would be an empty dream and a hopeless vision.

Conclusion

Catholic health care facilities are composed of dedicated, hard-working people. Each such facility constitutes the "world of work" for its own staff and employees. Everything said in this chapter about the Catholic vision of work in the world applies directly to each of these little worlds, not only the vision of persons and the significance of work in their lives, but the continual challenge in economic relationships. This entire book concerns those relationships.

Traditionally, the Church has sought to defend the rights and welfare of those oppressed by unjust working conditions. The 1971 Synod document, mentioned above, proclaimed this with powerful urgency: "Action on behalf of justice and participation in the transformation of the world fully appear to us as a constitutive dimension of the preaching of the Gospel."[30] The Synod subsequently reminded the entire Church that it must practice what it preaches:

> While the Church is bound to give witness to justice, she recognizes that anyone who ventures to speak to people about justice must first be just in their eyes. Hence we must undertake an examination of the modes of acting and of the possessions and life style found within the Church herself.
>
> Within the Church rights must be preserved. No one should be deprived of his ordinary rights because he is associated with the Church in one way or another. Those who serve the Church by their labor, including priests and religious, should receive a sufficient livelihood and enjoy that social security which is customary in their region. Lay people should be given fair wages and a system for promotion. We reiterate the recommendations that lay people should exercise more important functions with regard to Church property and should share in its administration.[31]

These practical goals can be translated from theory into practice. Creative ways can be found to implement the social justice doctrines of the Church in the new and changing conditions in the world of work. The prophet Joel promised dreams and visions that the Spirit would bring into the world. The Spirit expects, though, as an indispensable prerequisite, a true conversion of mind, will, and heart by all who would fulfill those dreams and visions.

1. Pope John Paul II, *Redemptor Hominis (Redeemer of Man),* Vatican translation, (Boston: Daughters of St. Paul, 1979), p. 22.
2. Pope John XXIII, *Mater et Magistra (Christianity and Social Progress),* (Washington: NCWC, 1961), #213.
3. Gen. 1:26, Wis. 2:23, Eccles. 17:3-10. See "The Church in the Modern World" *(Gaudium et Spes)* in *Vatican Council II, The Conciliar and Post Conciliar Documents,* ed. Austin Flannery, OP, (Collegeville, MN: The Liturgical Press, 1975).
4. *Gaudium et Spes* #14.
5. *Gaudium et Spes* #15 and #16.
6. *Gaudium et Spes* #17.
7. *Redemptor Hominis,* p. 23.
8. Pope Paul VI, *Populorum Progressio (On Promoting the Development of Peoples),* *The Pope Speaks,* XII (1967), pp. 144-172, #42.
9. *Mater et Magistra* #215.
10. *Gaudium et Spes* #24.
11. 1 John 4:20.
12. *Gaudium et Spes* #26.
13. *Gaudium et Spes* #13.
14. *Redemptor Hominis* #14.
15. *Gaudium et Spes* #30.
16. *Laborem Exercens* #6.
17. *Laborem Exercens* #9.
18. *Gaudium et Spes* #34, #35.
19. *Populorum Progressio* #27.
20. *Laborem Exercens* #13.
21. *Laborem Exercens* #12.
22. *Laborem Exercens* #14.
23. *Laborem Exercens* #19.
24. *Laborem Exercens* #20.
25. *Redemptor Hominis* #15.
26. *Gaudium et Spes* #37.
27. Pope John Paul II, *Dives in Misericordia, (Rich in Mercy)* in *Origins,* vol. 10, no. 26, Dec. 11, 1980, #12, p. 412.
28. *Justice in the World,* Synod of 1971, English translation published by National Conference of Catholic Bishops, Washington, DC, p. 42.
29. *Dives in Misericordia* #14.
30. *Justice in the World* p. 34.
31. *Justice in the World* p. 44.

DISCUSSION QUESTIONS

1. What is the missionary attitude with which the Church approaches human problems?

2. How does *Laborem Exercens* define human work?

3. What has been the Catholic vision of the human person?

4. How has this vision of the human person influenced the Church's vision of work in the world?

5. What are the essential features of human personhood as outlined by *Gaudium et Spes?*

6. What has been the Catholic view of human freedom?

7. What is the concept of the human family in Catholic thought?

8. How does this concept unify the strains of individual freedom, human equality, and social justice?

9. What is the effect of the growing interdependence of persons in the modern world?

10. How do social structures reflect the sinfulness of man, and what has been the Church's response to this sinfulness?

11. What is the significance of work within the Catholic tradition?

12. How does human work unite persons?

13. Why cannot human labor be viewed solely in economic terms?

14. What is the source of labor's priority over capital?

15. How does the Catholic view of the relation of capital and labor differ from the Marxist and the capitalist view?

16. Is ownership of private property an absolute right in the Catholic tradition?

17. Is private ownership of the means of production permissible in the Catholic tradition?

18. In the Catholic tradition, what is the correct use of advancing technology?

19. What ideal is normative for the resolving of worker/management issues?

20. Why is justice alone an inadequate norm for solving such issues?

21. How must individuals, unions, and boards of directors pursue justice?

CHAPTER 2

UNIONS AND CATHOLIC HEALTH CARE FACILITIES

Charles Craypo, PhD
Rev. Patrick J. Sullivan, CSC, PhD

Health care facilities are targets for unionization because of conditions both internal and external to the health care system. Internally, there are unavoidable sources of worker unrest; externally, there are forces compelling health care facility unions to expand their current representation and non-health-care-facility unions to begin organizing workers. To understand unions in Catholic facilities it is necessary to understand these conditions.

Internal Forces

It is axiomatic in labor relations that workers join unions to change things when they have become sufficiently unhappy with their employer and their jobs. This applies currently to health care workers in three ways: job distributions foster worker discontent; economic standards remain inadequate; the make-up of health care work forces compounds the other conditions and creates stressful labor relations.[1]

First, jobs in health care are distributed like an hourglass. Unlike jobs in other industries, where workers customarily advance from lower to higher level jobs, the largest number of health care jobs typically is found at the top and bottom of the occupational hierarchy. Physicians and other professionals are at the top. Aides, housekeepers, and kitchen help are at the bottom. A smaller number of technicians, maintenance workers, and nurses are in the middle. Licensing requirements, personnel practices, and social stereotyping segment the various levels and prevent workers at the lowest rungs from climbing the occupational ladder. The result is considerable frustration and dissatisfaction among workers

---

Dr. Craypo is associate professor of economics, University of Notre Dame, Notre Dame, IN.

Fr. Sullivan is researcher in church labor-management relations, University of Notre Dame, Notre Dame, IN.

at the bottom and a willingness to substitute collective action for individual effort to improve earnings and employment conditions.

Second, salaries for hourly health care workers lag behind those in other industries despite recent gains. In 1978, nonsupervisory health care workers averaged 85 percent of the weekly earnings of comparable workers in all industries; in addition, they received fringe benefits equivalent to 26 percent of their wage compensation, as compared to 37 percent for all workers. Combined with recent high rates of price inflation, this comparative disadvantage prompts these workers to find some means of forcing administrators to provide better wages and benefits.[2]

Third, occupational segregation of workers according to demographic characteristics creates tensions within institutions and adds to worker discontent. The highest paying and most responsible and rewarding jobs tend to be held by white, educated men. The lowest paying and least responsible and satisfying jobs are held by nonwhite, uneducated women. Union organizing drives frequently pit affluent, privileged professionals against poor, disadvantaged manual workers—a potentially explosive confrontation.

These internal forces were identified on several fronts: A St. Louis (MO) University professor of hospital administration in 1960 listed the reasons why employees elect to exercise their moral right to organize and bargain collectively. In addition to a conviction that their employers have failed them, they experience inequities (substandard wages and benefits), favoritism (disregard of seniority in promotions), and arbitrariness (a lack of method in handling their grievances).[3] Such employees are ripe for union persuasion.

One question posed by these characteristics of health care employment is whether the cohesiveness of a Catholic institution can overcome the divisiveness of hierarchical job structures, dissatisfaction with earnings and employment experiences, and contrasting worker demographics. But Catholic facilities have additional demographic features that are potentially divisive.

A 1957 article by John Cort, one of the *Commonweal* editors, entitled "Catholics and Social Justice,"[4] discussed unsavory working conditions, wages, and benefits in Catholic institutions, particularly health care agencies. Cort justified exposing such conditions and the record of administrative opposition to unionization efforts in terms of the need for a more open atmosphere in the Catholic press. Gone was the past reluctance to express things openly lest comfort be given to Church enemies, especially Communists, or lest the good already accomplished in spreading the social teachings and in inspiring labor and management with the spirit of social justice and charity be discredited.

Others, meanwhile, pointed to contradictions between Church teaching and Catholic institutional practices. William Consedine strongly reproached Catholic administrators at the 1957 Annual Catholic Hospital Association Convention.[5] Quoting John F. Cronin's *Catholic Social Principles,* he cited the poor record of Church institutions and observed that in economizing to carry out their primary purpose of health care, they often appeared to be applying the vow of poverty to their workers. He reminded administrators that a series of U.S. Bureau of Labor Statistics surveys of large metropolitan hospitals showed no instance of wages in Catholic institutions matching those in others. He recalled for them Pope Leo XIII's injunction to Catholic institutions not to look for the "best bargain" but for the "proper one" and also the mandate in Canon 1524 of the Code: "All and especially priests and religious and administrators of ecclesiastical goods, should give to their employees a fair and just wage."

External Forces

Conditions external to the system also prompt unions to try to organize health care workers. First, union bargaining strength depends in part on the establishment of effective wage and benefit patterns; second, erosion of union membership in other industries drives unions into compensating organizational efforts elsewhere. The former affects health care unions, and the latter involves unions not previously active in the health care system but whose established jurisdictional lines often are peripheral, such as the Teamsters. Negotiated wage and benefit patterns are important to health care facility unions because they enable them to extend their highest benefit contract to other area institutions.

To maximize its effectiveness at the bargaining table, a union needs to impose identical or very similar terms and conditions of employment upon all the employers in a given market area. As long as these employers pay the same labor costs, none has a particular incentive to oust or weaken the union for competitive reasons. When wide differentials exist among area facilities, some may be tempted to escape the union altogether or operate outside the union pattern. It is also easier for unions to negotiate labor cost increases when all employers are affected uniformly. This is not to say unionized facilities do not differ in how they use labor as a factor of production, but that the difference is a matter of degree. Standardized contracts thus minimize employer need to under-

16

mine or resist the union and put workers into competition with one another.

As for traditionally non-health-care unions, their current membership losses encourage many of them to look toward expanding and largely unorganized industries in search of new members. If a union is serious about representing health care workers, it will add the needed organizing and service staff in order to show competent results to both workers and employers. The Laborers' International Union, whose membership base has been diminished by technological and structural changes affecting the construction industry, is one such organization. The result of this clear trend is to raise the total level of union activity in the health care system and, inevitably, to increase the scope of union representation and collective bargaining.

What Unions Do
U.S. unions promote economic rather than political objectives. They are business unions, which means that their primary activities are negotiating and administering labor contracts. In doing so, they are pragmatic toward employers and labor relations. They try to improve their members' wages and benefits and to protect their jobs and economic security, but only to the extent permitted by an employer's ability to pay. They seldom choose to damage an employer economically because this would only jeopardize present and future members' employment opportunities. Exceptions to this rule of union behavior occur when a particular employer cannot match the industry standard and the union believes economic concessions in that instance would be futile. Such cases are few and far between. More typical is the response of the United Auto Workers union to Chrysler's financial crisis: making substantial concessions rather than hastening the firm's demise and the probable loss of tens of thousands of jobs. Another instance is the International Ladies Garment Workers Union, which has exercised restraint in bargaining with New York City garment firms in order to encourage them to stay in business in the metropolitan area where the degree of unionization has been greatest in the industry.

Consistent with this business union approach is the practice of organizing workers in particular industries and trades rather than along multicraft and interindustry lines. This explains why older unions are named after particular occupations, such as Bricklayers, Printers, Teamsters, Longshoremen, and Miners. They developed at a time when industry was structured around specific trades and in limited geographic locations. Younger unions are named after products (Steelworkers, Auto Workers, Aluminum Workers) because they emerged at a time when concentrated industries began mass producing and mass selling products and employing large numbers of workers on an industrial rather than a craft basis. Craft unions have since become more industrial in their membership policies. All unions generally are less committed now to particular industries than in the past; they are quite opportunistic in organizing new members. The United Auto Workers union has represented registered nurses in Michigan partly because it finds that location organizationally advantageous and feasible.

What do unions try to negotiate in labor contracts? The usual sequence of union bargaining demands is: union security, worker earnings and fringe benefits, working conditions, economic security, and job protection. Unions seldom try to negotiate contract language that displaces conventional authorities and decision-making responsibilities in the workplace. Business unionism responds to managerial initiatives; it does not usurp managerial perrogatives.[6] It negotiates in detail and with great attention the economic terms and conditions of employment, but only superficially and with general indifference the specific manner in which the employer uses labor as a factor of production.

Full-time union representatives mainly concern themselves with contract negotiations and top-level grievance handling. Normally, they try to avoid direct economic confrontations with an employer, especially when they are convinced the employer is dealing with the union in good faith. They see their labor relations function as renegotiating contracts and resolving administrative disputes without getting the members into work stoppages. Strike actions are reserved for situations in which employers refuse to meet area or industry standards, demand union bargaining concessions on previously negotiated standards, or try to undermine institutional union security.

What have been the outcomes of contract negotiations and the labor relations experiences of managers to date? First, unions have required managers to use labor more carefully and efficiently than they did before collective bargaining. The most comprehensive study of the impact of unions on management found that the primary effect of the industrial union movement of the period before and after World War II was to increase labor's productivity by raising its relative cost as a productive input.[7] Contemporary labor economists find that high levels of unionization still are associated with high levels of productivity.[8]

Second, unionized labor relations requires managers to submit to prescribed grievance procedures in disputes arising from perceived management violations of contract terms and language, legal statutes, or past practices. This is irritating and even costly to managers because it imposes an external accountability on what had been regarded previously as routine administrative decisions. Under most procedures the parties have several opportunities to resolve their differences at various levels of management and union authority. Two types of disputes are involved. One concerns the respective rights of the parties under the contract, such as the right of management to discipline a specific employee against the employee's right of due process and fair treatment. The other pertains to the opposing interests of the parties, as in a difference over the level of economic benefits paid workers. Most contracts specify that failure to reach agreement in rights disputes automatically results in neutral, binding arbitration to settle the issue. By contrast, interest disputes are seldom arbitrated but instead end with one or both parties making concessions or with impasses and work stoppages. Authorized strikes rarely occur during the life of the agreement because the prescribed grievance and arbitration clauses must be followed. Wildcat (unauthorized) stoppages usually occur when union members are dissatisfied with the actions of both the employer and the union.

What are unions' effects on the economic terms of employment? The first effect is to require the individual employer to meet area or industry standards of wage and benefit levels more exactly and promptly than might otherwise be the case. Even without unions, individual employers have to be competitive to attract and hold the desired work force. The union's effect is to institutionalize the competitive market process.[9] Second, labor economists believe that strong unions also increase the number and level of fringe benefits beyond what might be expected.[10] Third, nonunion employers feel the "threat" of unionization and therefore voluntarily meet prevailing union wage and benefit levels. This shields unionized workers from nonunion competition but also makes it harder for the union to organize the entire industry.

The main effect of collective bargaining on other than economic matters is to make it more difficult for managers to fire workers for alleged infractions of rules and regulations. Unions normally oppose disciplinary actions against members of the bargaining unit. Arbitrators are inclined to reinstate workers to their jobs with or without back pay unless management can show the misconduct was willful and sufficiently grave to warrant the "capital punishment" of labor relations. These tendencies force employers to exercise progressive discipline and keep careful records.

Nonetheless, unions have not been very successful in restricting employer use of property rights to erode workers' job or economic interests. They do not, for example, effectively prevent employers from contracting out work performed by union workers. Managers usually refuse to give in to union demands for specific contractual restrictions on their use of machinery or plant. Arbitrators are not inclined to impose such limitations in the absence of explicit contract language.[11] The result is that although collective bargaining affects the terms and conditions of employment, it generally does not deter the *way* in which an employer uses labor as a factor of production.

Separate data on the impact of unions on Catholic health care facilities are not available. It is generally believed, however, that negotiated settlements are not as favorable to unions in Catholic settings as elsewhere in the industry. Appendix A (see page 41) summarizes the terms and conditions provided in a representative Catholic health care facility labor contract.

Unions in Health Care Institutions

About one in five health care workers is presently covered by a collective bargaining contract. By contrast, about one in four eligible employees in American industry works under a union contract. Studies from a variety of sources reveal that unions are most likely to win certification elections in the following health care facilities: (1) public rather than private, (2) secular rather than denominational, (3) smaller rather than larger, (4) located in the Northeast and West, (5) when labor costs are a relatively high proportion of operating costs (suggesting that workers in poorly managed establishments are union prone), (6) when the contesting organization is a professional association rather than a labor union, (7) when the election unit includes one rather than two or more occupational groups, and (8) where there are already one or more certified unions in the institution.[12]

Historically, some facilities in California and Illinois were unionized as early as 1917, but the health care industry generally escaped the massive organizing drives that occurred during the 1930s—in part because it was exempted from newly enacted federal labor laws. Health care facilities were largely ignored by unions until the 1950s but then became serious targets during the 1960s. There have been historical exceptions, however. By the mid-1930s, 13 San Francisco area facilities were organized; three Minneapolis-St. Paul establishments were organized in 1941. The latter followed passage of the 1939 Minnesota Labor Relations Act. Each of these successful efforts was made by the

American Federation of Labor (AFL) or an affiliated national union and occurred in states where the union movement was generally strong.[13]

During the late 1950s the "Toledo Plan" was publicized as the solution to union initiatives. This referred to a joint union-industry settlement that ended a strike against several Toledo facilities, including three Catholic institutions. Under the agreement the unions publicly renounced strikes and abandoned efforts to win recognition rights for workers; in return, administrators agreed to recognize a "community board of appeals" for purposes of reviewing potentially disruptive grievances and complaints. This agreement was clearly a union defeat and revealed the overall weaknesses of health care unions at that time.[14]

Several successful union campaigns did occur, however, in Seattle; although one ended with the union being ousted after a violent 84-day strike. In early 1959 there was a massive and partially successful organizing drive among New York City institutions. At the same time hourly workers in two Chicago nonprofit facilities were organized, but after a five-month strike the union was defeated and decertified. Also in 1959, six health care facilities in Rochester, NY, forced an independent union to withdraw its demand for an election and instead endorse a "uniform personnel code."

Health care unions had more success in the next decade. Five New Jersey institutions were organized in the mid-1960s. Union drives in upstate New York were successful for the first time, mainly because protective labor laws were extended beyond New York City to include the entire state.

Following these drives, health care unions suffered a string of defeats due mainly to refusal of institution administrations voluntarily to recognize a dominant union as bargaining agent.[15] In 1964, of 7,127 health care institutions in the United States employing 1,886,839 full-time personnel with an annual $8 billion payroll, only 435 of them, or six percent, had one or more contracts with labor organizations. But by 1970 the ratio had more than doubled to 15 percent and by 1975 had risen to 20 percent. The proportions varied considerably among types of facilities however: three out of four federal institutions had one or more labor contracts, but that figure dropped to one in five for state and local facilities, one in six for private nonprofit facilities, and one in ten for investor-owned establishments.[16]

Changes in 1974 to bring private nonprofit institutions under federal labor law both helped and hindered union organization. They formalized union certification procedures and extended organizing rights and protections to health care workers. But these legal changes also deprived unions of informal tactics and pressures often used successfully in big cities and industrialized areas where unions are generally strong. They also permitted managers to frustrate unions by stalling elections through administrative law delays until after organizing drives had peaked. At least this is the position of union officials: "Organizing in the health care field is in chaos," said a spokesperson for the Service Employees International Union (SEIU) in the Chicago area. "The blame for this confusion lies primarily with the National Labor Relations Board [and] with a fair contribution by the diabolical action of management attorneys."[17]

Nevertheless, health care labor organizations won 57 percent of 841 elections during August 1974 to March 1978, compared to 47 percent before; traditional labor unions won 52 percent. They also won a higher proportion immediately following the 1974 revisions than in later years—70 percent in the first five months under the Act compared to 50 percent in the next 39 months. Second, union win-ratios were lower in church-affiliated institutions (41 percent) than in proprietary (60 percent) and secular voluntary (53 percent) institutions. Why this is the case is unclear. Perhaps it is explained by differences between employees in church and other health care institutions—greater resistance to unions in the former or different treatment of employees. Third, white-collar, often professional employees were more likely than blue-collar workers to vote for union representation, with labor organizations winning 58 percent of the elections involving the former and 42 percent of those including the latter. Labor was most successful in elections covering professional nurses.[18]

Aggregate health care union membership figures are not readily available, and individual unions may exaggerate their membership numbers for tactical purposes. A recent study estimates that 10 percent of private institutions' hourly production workers were covered by union contracts during 1968 to 1972 based on a survey of institutions employing 195,000 health care employees. More current accounts from union sources estimate that less than 12 percent of workers in private institutions are under union contract, although 23 percent of private-sector facilities are unionized, and 37 percent of public health care employees work under labor agreements.[19]

No single union has emerged as the undisputed leader in the health care industry, nor has any been given exclusive jurisdictional claim over the industry by the AFL-CIO. The result is a history of organizational rivalry among unions, between unions and professional associations, and between AFL-CIO affiliates and independents. Four unions have established themselves in the industry: SEIU; American Federation of State, County and Municipal Employees (AFSCME); Hospital and Health Care Employees, District 1199; and American Nurses Association (ANA). A host of other organizations have had some success and indicate increased levels of activity in the future, including the Teamsters (IBT), Laborers' International Union, United Food and Commercial Workers International Union (UFCW). A few years ago the American Federation of Teachers (AFT) announced its intent to organize nurses and later scored a substantial victory in the Wisconsin public health care sector.

SEIU is the oldest and largest health care union. Its Local 250 in San Francisco is the country's earliest ongoing health care workers' union. From a total SEIU membership of 625,000 in 1979, about half are in the health care industry, with perhaps 150,000 in health care facilities, three-quarters of them in private institutions. Its policy is to represent any and all occupational groups. Like other health care unions, its greatest organizing success has been in big cities. AFSCME had a 1979 membership of 1,020,000, perhaps one-quarter of whom were health care workers. It represents mainly public institutions. AFSCME was not very effective in the industry until passage of state laws in the 1960s gave public employees organizing rights and public employee unions bargaining rights.

District 1199 is also a more recent entry than SEIU. It originated in the 1950s as a union of professional pharmacists in New York City but evolved into an industrial-type health care union in several Eastern states. In 1969 it represented an estimated 20,000 health care workers, mainly in and around New York. By 1970 it had twice that number, and presently it represents more than 100,000. Recently, 1199 has been moving westward in its organizing activities. It is a nearly autonomous division of the Retail, Wholesale, and Department Store Union (RWDSU). Merger talks currently underway between SEIU and 1199 are logical from the union point of view and if successful will result in a formidable new union organizing presence in the health care industry.

ANA is a professional association for registered nurses that has only recently (partially and reluctantly) accepted collective bargaining as a means of resolving labor disputes. In 1979 the national ANA reported 187,000 members; ANA-negotiated contracts covered about 70,000 registered nurses at that time, up from 30,000 a decade earlier. Most are located in the industrialized, highly unionized states. Whether to adopt collective bargaining or remain a pure association is largely determined at state and local levels. Where state chapters are reluctant or ineffective in this regard, the regular trade unions organize nurses for collective bargaining purposes. In 1978 some 25,000 to 30,000 nurses were represented by non-ANA organizations.

Despite ANA rejection of unionization and collective bargaining, the economics committee of the Minnesota Nurses' Association initiated formal labor relations in health care institutions as early as 1938. During World War II other state affiliates negotiated with the Federal War Labor Board for wage increases. In 1946 the ANA inaugurated an "Economic Security Program" in response to the postwar earnings and occupational status problems of nurses, but in 1950 it adopted an official "no strike" policy. The Program has since been expanded to include formal association recognition and bargaining. Numerous strikes, threats of strikes, and other, more limited job actions have been used by ANA affiliates at state and local levels to win union recognition, make contractual gains in both economic areas and professional matters, and enforce existing contract provisions. Their success prompted Leo Osterhaus to anticipate that "nurses' associations may well set the pattern for other professional and quasiprofessional employees in the field."[20]

Among the lesser health care unions the IBT is perhaps the most unpredictable. Its involvement so far has been sporadic and uneven, varying from one locale to another depending on the opportunities, priorities, and objectives of particular local and regional leaders rather than on any declared policy of the international union. Where Teamsters do concern themselves directly or indirectly they introduce a power factor into the situation because of their control over the movements of materials in and out of facilities. During strikes by other unions at St. Luke's Hospital in Cleveland and Methodist Hospital in Gary, IN, for example, Teamster drivers assisted strikers by refusing to deliver food, drugs, and oxygen. Its strategic position makes IBT attitudes and intentions important. A determined Teamster effort would influence the future direction of health care labor relations.

Another union with potential impact on the industry is the United Food and Commercial Workers. UFCW was formed in 1979 through the merger of two food industry unions that already had some health care contracts. As one of the country's largest labor organizations, it has the financial and staff resources to launch a serious organization drive among health care institutions. Recent and continuing erosion of

UFCW's historic membership base in meatpacking, meatcutting, and retail food stores due to mechanization and operating consolidations is encouraging the union to look at other industries in which to make future organizational gains.

The election records of these and other labor organizations during August 1974 to March 1978 are summarized in Figure 1. Employee associations (mainly ANA), the SEIU, and 1199 together accounted for 64 percent of the 841 elections and 73 percent of the union wins. More than 123,000 hospital employees were covered by the 841 elections, and more than 45,000, or about 36 percent, were included in units won by the unions.

FIGURE 1: Labor Organization Success in NLRB Election Outcomes Involving Health Care Employees, August 1974 to March 1978

Labor Organization	Number of Elections	Union Wins	Union Losses	Union Wins(%)
Employee association (e.g., ANA)	246	161	85	65.4
SEIU	172	90	82	52.3
1199	116	65	51	56.0
IBT	56	21	35	37.5
AFSCME	38	18	20	47.4
UFCW (Retail Clerks)	36	13	23	36.1
Operating Engineers	28	11	17	39.3
Laborers	24	5	19	20.8
Others	125	51	74	40.8
Total	841	435	406	51.7

Source: John Delaney, "Patterns of Unions' Successes in Hospital Elections," *Hospital Progress,* February 1980, p. 39.

Most facilities that negotiate with unions do so independently of other negotiations and in single-unit bargaining structures. Both the union and management normally look to wider industry or area standards for their settlement patterns. They are followers rather than trend setters. By contrast, organized institutions in certain metropolitan areas, notably New York City, San Francisco, and Minneapolis-St. Paul, belong to multifacility bargaining associations that negotiate a single master contract applicable to all. At a lower level of consolidation, facilities in Chicago, Portland, OR, and many other metropolitan areas negotiate separate contracts but settle along pattern lines.[21] Where multiemployer bargaining structures occur, it is in response to management's fear of being singled out for union job actions and in that way "whipsawed" into accepting higher settlements than would otherwise be the case. Health care unions normally also prefer multiemployer contracts because they result in standard wages, benefits, and conditions among area hospitals.

Union Bargaining Power in Health Care Facilities

Health care unions have not been as successful at the bargaining table as have unions generally, either in economic or contract language matters. A number of trends and conditions account for this. First, fragmented union representation and bargaining structures weaken union bargaining power by isolating the ability of separate groups of workers and unions to bring economic pressure on managers. Failure of rival unions to cooperate with one another is a frequent complaint of union officials. Second, recent efforts at federal and state levels to contain rising health care costs prompt administrators to resist unions' economic demands. Third, the industry's method of payment, called "fee-for-service," makes it difficult for the parties to negotiate higher labor costs because this method does not reimburse costs. Moreover, physicians rather than administrators determine the extent of the system's usage. Thus, the economic bargaining settlement must take into account this inherently unreimbursed, uncontrollable financial element. Also contributing to health care union weakness are the low-income standing of unionized health care workers, which makes it difficult and risky for them to go out on strike, as well as community resentment of facility work stoppages and the paternalist tradition in health care management.

A survey of 816 negotiated hospital contracts during 1973 and 1974 shows that hospital unions did not match the economic gains of unions generally.[22] Hospital unions signed agreements of shorter duration than the standard three-year contract. This practice doubtless reflects management's unwillingness to enter into long-term pacts, either because it was unfamiliar with collective bargaining or reluctant to provide unions with long-term security. It also reflects a union refusal to accept three-year contracts that do not contain cost-of-living provisions to compensate workers for future inflation. Only six percent of the contracts contained such escalator clauses, one of the lowest ratios among all industries. Because protection against cost-of-living increases has been a principal objective of union members in recent years, a low ratio of health care contracts having escalator clauses indicates union bargaining weaknesses.

Other aspects of these contracts further support this conclusion. The ratios of coverage found in health care contracts in areas that are important to union and job security, member wages and benefits, and economic security are consistently below all industry contracts. About half the proportion of hospital agreements contained union shop provisions—under which bargaining unit workers must become union members after a specified period of time on the job—as those in industry generally. Twice as many had no form of worker obligation to the union. Restrictions on subcontracting of work were four times more frequent in all industries than in health care facilities. Union protections against crew-size changes that affect the number of jobs in the bargaining unit and prohibitions against supervisors performing work normally done within the bargaining unit were infrequent in health care facilities. Premium pay provisions were also much less frequent than in all other industries, as were fringe benefits involving time-paid-not-worked, such as paid holidays. Economic security benefits in these contracts were either virtually nonexistent or much less frequent than is generally the case in collective bargaining.

Union Impact on Health Care Facility Labor Costs

Labor economists have difficulty determining unions' net effect on health care facilities' labor costs. Conventional studies of union economic impact fail to distinguish clearly between direct and indirect, short term and long term, and wage and nonwage effects. A negotiated wage increase is clearly defined, for example, but the extent to which a voluntary wage increase by a nonunion institution is made in response to the threat of unionization is not as clear, even though this action is an indirect result of collective bargaining. Second, economists believe that a union's principal impact on wages occurs during the period immediately following unionization, but this has not been proved. Third, large negotiated wage increases may reflect union bargaining power and are commonly interpreted in that way. But, on the other hand, they may not. For example, a health care union may accept a substantial wage increase instead of holding out for some noneconomic objective, such as staffing procedures, which actually is more important to the membership than the magnitude of wage increases.

These qualifications notwithstanding, economists conclude that health care unions have not significantly increased health care labor costs. According to Fottler, labor accounts for approximately 65 percent of total facility costs, and nonprofessional workers on average account for about 36 percent of total labor costs. Nonprofessional labor costs therefore represent 23 percent, or roughly one-quarter, of total costs. If a union representing nonprofessional workers negotiates annual labor costs increases that are, say four percent above the increases that would have occurred through normal market forces in the absence of the union, then the net effect of collective bargaining on costs is one percent a year.[23]

David Dilts, another labor economist, reported that by 1978 the number of working days lost in health care facilities because of work stoppages had declined greatly from its high mark immediately following the 1974 National Labor Relations Act (NLRA) amendments. Moreover, he concluded, "wage rates, earnings differentials, and fringe benefits have not been significantly improved by unionization."[24]

In a recent econometric study of union impact on wages and fringe benefits of nonprofessional health care workers in three states—Illinois, Wisconsin, and Minnesota—Brian Becker found an overall union effect of six to seven percent on the total compensation cost of both union and nonunion employees.[25] On the basis of data provided by 144 hospitals in these states, Becker concluded that the greatest union wage impact involved the intra-institution compensation structure. Administrators are under considerable pressure to grant wage and salary increases to other occupational groups commensurate with negotiated percentage increases in order to avoid disturbing traditional compensation patterns. A significant threat to wages also existed among nonunion facilities included in the study. The total union impact in health care facilities however, was found to be less than in industry generally.

Becker attributed this below-average union performance to the fact that "management generally has the upper hand, and the unions have chosen not to take particularly militant positions at the bargaining table."[26] Specifically, in Minnesota it appeared that the large number of secondary wage-earning women from middle-income families among the unionized work force discouraged union militancy while reducing the pressure for large wage settlements. In Wisconsin the leading union traded strong union security provisions for low wage increases; in Chicago the mayor inhibited union strike activity.

Conservative economists, who generally minimize the economic value of unions to workers, contend that health care's rising cost is mainly due to the insurance-based fee-for-service system. They say that this payment method gives facilities a "cost pass through" mechanism to increase charges and reduces administrative resistance to union demands. In addition, they cite the rapid growth of federal health care programs for the elderly and the poor, which they claim allow administrators considerable labor cost flexibility. In this view, unions are simply the institutional vehicles that transform the excesses of these systems into rising health care labor costs.[27] Health care union officials disagree; 1199s organizing director argues that although the fee-for-service system does inflate costs—by increasing health expenditures $300,000 a year for each new practicing physician—the result is to squeeze financially both health care workers and consumers rather than to enhance union bargaining leverage, especially after initiation of cost containment programs during the 1970s.[28] Becker found, in fact, that negotiated increases were proportionately lower in facilities with the highest ratios of Medicare and Medicaid revenues. This may reflect the low average incomes of patients in these facilities. In any event, proposed cuts in federal government expenditures on health care would further reduce union bargaining ability.

Professional health care employee unions appear to have fared at least as well as nonprofessional ones. One study of nursing salaries found that a union's effect on beginning salaries for registered nurses was 4.6 to 7.4 percent.[29] Physicians and nurses are more inclined to bring professional issues into collective bargaining. Physicians' strikes and slowdowns have occurred in several big-city institutions over minimum professional staffing requirements and adequate medical equipment. In at least one instance, in Washington, DC, these demands were combined with others of a personal nature, such as private practice rights of employees. For one week in March 1981 some 2,500 interns and residents of New York City defied a court order and struck unsuccessfully over professional demands. Union activity among physicians can be expected to continue as increasing numbers of physicians become salaried employees of health care facilities.

Bargaining outcomes affecting nurses are comparable to those in other occupations and industries. Yet registered nurses attach importance to professional issues. Responses of 490 Canadian nurses to questions on their bargaining priorities show inservice education, continuing education, and orientation programs as three of their top four bargaining goals; the other was cost-of-living increments. "I admittedly enjoy the benefits the last bargaining gave to nurses," one of those surveyed wrote, "but I feel we must keep it in perspective. Contentment doesn't come with more and more money and better days off only."[30] Granted, the exigencies of the bargaining process may prevent these objectives from becoming reality, but such expressions do suggest a difference in the bargaining approaches of nonprofessional and professional health care employees.

Official surveys support the findings of labor economists regarding union impact on facilities' operating costs. Rising wages and labor-related costs were exonerated from responsibility for health care inflation in a 1975 report from the Council on Wage and Price Stability. The report covered the period in which health care unions made their greatest organizing and negotiating gains. It concluded that the effect of union activity on health care facilities, as a result of the 1974 NLRA amendments to extend the law to cover nonprofit facilities, was minimal. The conclusions are perhaps startling.

First, statistics from the NLRB make it clear "that the organizational results which most of the unions hoped for as a result of the passage of the NLRA amendments which included the health care industry have not been realized."

Second, data from the Council on Wage and Price Stability, as well as from health industry sources and independent accounts, indicate that unionization has not been the only cause of rising health care costs. The report says:

> In other words the rising level of hospital costs is not attributable as much to the changing wage rates or other input prices as it is to a changing product and the increased rate at which that product is consumed. The findings of this study clearly indicate that the problem of hospital cost inflation is endemic to the structure of the industry and to the incentives driving all those involved in hospital care—the doctors, the administrators, the nurses, the technicians, the semi-skilled and unskilled workers, the in-surers, and the patients. There is no one villain.[31]

There are, of course, exceptions to this general conclusion. The cost of health care delivery in New York City clearly was increased as a result of the multihospital contracts negotiated between 1970 and 1974.[32]

Another method of determining union impact on health care labor relations in addition to calculating wage and benefit influences is to ask administrators. Leo Osterhaus questioned managers in four metropolitan areas regarding union effects on 25 specific economic and noneconomic issues.[33] On wages, 15 of them said that unions had a definite upward impact, and 8 said that the same was true for fringe benefits. Six managers said the union presence prompted them to project costs and fix overall budgets two or three years in advance.

Adoption of written personnel policies accompanied health care unionization efforts in at least 10 instances. In the same number of cases the effect was to stabilize personnel procedures and make them consistent for all workers. Five administrators identified a change in institutional attitude from paternalism to recognition of employee needs and the value of participative management as the most significant impact of unions. Four thought the effect was to encourage managers to cooperate and join together in common defense. Four others thought their communication and public relations skills had improved because of union activity.

Osterhaus found that managers now had to develop personal expertise in labor relations procedures, acquire knowledge of relevant labor laws and regulations, and compete with industry in wages, benefits, and working conditions. Gradually they patterned their labor relations practices after the mutually accepting and cooperative relationship that often evolves in industry, an outcome Osterhaus approved of and encouraged.

Less positive regarding the union impact, A. Imberman, a management consultant, listed burdensome effects on management: strikes and strike threats, higher wages, formal seniority systems, compulsory grievance procedures, dues collection, required provision of institutional data, and possible union veto over administrative decisions.[34]

Norman Metzger, a hospital administrator, disagrees. His experience is that unions do affect management prerogatives and hospital costs but mostly in ways that are difficult to assess.[35] Contracts may limit the right to subcontract, make it expensive to work bargaining unit members at certain times, and curtail disciplinary action. Yet he says that "Rather than blame unionization for the problems of maldistribution of available funds, inflationary spiraling of costs, and incursions into management rights," as is typically done, "hospital administrators must take the initiative to correct abuses within the system that have led to or that are exacerbating these problems."

Health Care System Trends

Current developments in health care facilities' structures and operating methods and objectives are crucial to future labor relations. The trend toward corporate consolidation stems mainly from administrators' pursuit of cost economies, which are more easily available in multifacility systems in the form of, for example, tax incentives, increased purchasing power, less duplication of services, and centralized cash management. The health care industry's hospital segment is simultaneously contracting and becoming more concentrated. On the one hand, failure of numerous big-city nonprofit facilities and the closing since 1969 of more than 400 of the roughly 2,700 hospitals containing fewer than 100 beds signal contraction of institutions at the top and bottom of the size spectrum. On the other hand, the remaining facilities are merging at an increasing rate. Profit and nonprofit hospital chains are burgeoning—they currently lease or own at least 14 percent of that part of the health care system.[36]

A management consultant to health care institutions confirms this trend and predicts that health care conglomerates eventually will dominate a three-tiered industry structure. At the top will be 25 to 30 such complexes, each accounting for more than $1 billion in revenues annually. Structurally, these holding companies will consist of "one or more general hospitals, a philanthropic foundation, one or more nursing homes, a contract management company, a real estate corporation, professional office buildings, and a system of primary care centers."[37]

The middle-level structure will include free-standing facilities in suburbs and inner cities that have annual revenues between $5 and $500 million. The suburban facilities are likely to survive the financial squeeze occasioned by inadequate fee-for-service payments and rising equipment and personnel costs with which the conglomerate corporations are ideally suited to cope. The inner-city facilities are not so equipped and will either disappear or represent an inferior level of service associated with public-sector health care.

The third tier will be thousands of small (less than $1 million in revenues annually) multispecialty practices organized and maintained by professional groups and operated as the last vestige of the fee-for-service mode in private sector health care.

Operationally, the first tier will initiate a profound change in health care objectives, from primary concern with patient care to equal interest in patient care and in the financial capability and organizational flexibility of the large corporation. Management necessarily "will become more sophisticated" as top-down corporate decision making "will require balancing patient care and financial, political, legal, and social considerations." This means that physicians and other health care professionals will be subject to monitoring through statistical, systems control methods emanating from "senior executives far more concerned

32

about the corporate image and fiscal health than about the feelings of any dissident physician who could tarnish the organization.''[38]

Impact of Centralization Trend

What is the probable impact of this trend on labor relations? Centralized managerial control of large, diversified health care organizations will make it more difficult for unions to organize and bargain for workers. Conglomerate structures are the most difficult for unions to organize and in which to establish bargaining leverage.[39] Their considerable resources, organizational complexity, and operational secrecy enable them to outlast and frustrate unions.[40] Their size allows them either to develop in-house specialists or retain managerial consultants skilled in the practice of preventing unionization of employees and union negotiation of effective contracts.

On the other hand, centralized supervision of health care professionals, especially physicians, is almost a guarantee of increased unionization among salaried physicians. Their organization in turn makes unions and collective bargaining in health care institutions not only legitimate but actually imperative for other groups of workers, who will follow the professionals' example for both emulative and self-interested financial reasons. In industrial workplaces, it is frequently the skilled workers who initiate unionization efforts and pursue them through to success.

If unions did succeed in organizing these complexes and in somehow coordinating the various units in the bargaining process, then the multifacility structure would work to labor's advantage. Strikes and strike threats would become more effective because they jeopardize the entire operation. In addition, the combined system presumably has the ability to pay higher labor costs. Negotiated settlements in multiunit bargaining structures cover a broad range of employees and spread the pattern wide enough that wages and working conditions are standardized across a considerable range. Under these conditions, the administrators might in fact prefer labor stability with high standards than operational instability at the price of obtaining lower labor costs.

Catholic Response

During the 1970s health care administrators' general views toward unions and collective bargaining changed from reluctant acceptance to resistance. In 1967, Osterhaus observed that ''the majority of hospitals are conservative in their thought and action toward unions, but a trend

33

to a more liberal view is indicated."[41] On a scale of 1 to 3—(1) outright opposition, (2) tolerance, and (3) acceptance as an equal institution with management—he believed the weight of opinion was moving from 1 to 2. Recent events suggest a reversal of direction back toward 1; managers appear to be opting for union avoidance.

Our review of articles in *Hospital Progress* during 1955 to 1980 shows growing concern with employment-related aspects of health care administration. Although the articles cannot be described as being anti-union as such, with a few exceptions, clearly the tenor is that labor problems exist but voluntary improvements in personnel practices and monetary compensation can make unions unnecessary. More specifically, conferences sponsored by the Catholic Committee on Urban Ministry in San Francisco (1980) and at the University of Notre Dame (1981) revealed both puzzlement over and opposition to unionism among Catholic health care administrators. Concerns were that unions in health care facilities mean strikes, high labor costs, loss of managerial control, and complicated changes in administrative organization and procedure.

On the other hand, our survey of union literature indicates resentment at the perceived antiunion stance taken by health care facilities, especially church-affiliated institutions. Facilities are accused of resisting worker organization adamantly and relying heavily on management consultant firms to thwart unionization attempts—sometimes through calculated, deliberate labor law violations. Independent investigations often support these allegations.

In 1980 Fred Erman, a lawyer and Jesuit on the Holy Cross College faculty in Worcester, MA, reported his survey of NLRB cases alleging unfair labor practices in Catholic facilities.[42] He found 78 cases involving hospitals listed in the *Official Catholic Directory* and occurring from April 1976 through February 1980. In 71 of them, or 91 percent, the NLRB ruled in favor of the union and found unlawful activities by Catholic hospitals. Offenses include firing workers for their union activities or sympathies, threatening them about what will happen if the union wins the election, making reprisals against prounion employees, placing restrictions on worker activities during union certification campaigns, and refusing to bargain with unions that have been legally certified as exclusive bargaining agents for workers.

Erman believes these 78 cases necessarily understate the magnitude of Catholic health care's opposition to unions. Only final NLRB judgments and federal appeals court decisions are routinely published.

Therefore, cases were not included in which NLRB administrative judges found employer unfair practices and in which the institutions did not appeal those findings to the NLRB. Also omitted were instances of consent settlements, in which charges are resolved by employers agreeing to cease and desist certain activities and to compensate individual workers for losses without having to admit any wrongdoing. Finally, unions do not always have the time and resources to pursue their legal options. NLRB proceedings are time consuming and risky. Unions may prefer to go ahead with a scheduled certification election rather than lose organizing momentum or to abandon the effort altogether.

Erman attributes this startling number of labor law violations among Catholic facilities to the practice of relinquishing day-to-day management of labor relations to lay administrators who are trained in the union-avoidance principles of contemporary business schools but are unfamiliar with the charismatic meaning of a religious community and the Church's social teachings. This accounts for part rather than all of the explanation, however, because the NLRB case data show degrees of involvement by religious in the illegal acts ranging from total lack of knowledge to passive acquiescence to full collaboration.

Although Erman did not present any comparative figures for Catholic, as contrasted to all other private, nonprofit, health care facilities. His conclusions seem, however, to be borne out by the data: Delaney's analysis of union election successes in church-affiliated institutions—41 percent, as compared to 53 percent in secular voluntary and 60 percent in proprietary facilities. Also, a federal congressional report indicated management consultant firms continue to be the activating force in contested union hospital organizing drives.

Investigation of these firms by the House Subcommittee on Labor-Management Relations, fostered by their increasing involvement in union certification elections, resulted in a published report that concluded that "the strategies advocated and implemented by the consultants can have a troubling impact on labor-management relations far beyond the consultants' presence." The meaning of this is that the firm dominates the employer's antiunion campaign but stays in the background; "...the result can be lingering conflict and antagonism which is unproductive and debilitating for workers and management alike."[43] Often a legacy of worker bitterness and distrust follows, whether the union wins or loses.

The previously unchecked activities of management consultant firms are coming under federal administrative law review. In 1981 an NLRB regional office issued a complaint against one such firm alleging it had "complete control and use of supervisory personnel" at a facility in which the nurses voted down unionization but where the full NLRB had found illegal employer actions during the election campaign. Evidence indicated the outside firm "was given and exercised daily intimate and independent direction of the supervisory personnel" at the facility.[44] The outcome of this action is likely to establish the legal precedent for future use of management consultants in the industry.

Conclusion

Throughout this chapter we have presented as clearly and accurately as possible, the research findings we judged relevant to the phenomenon of "Unions and Catholic Health Care Facilities." We explained the internal and external forces in efforts to unionize, the functions and dysfunctions of unionization, the history and present status of most of the "health care" unions, the bargaining goals and accomplishments of such unions, the relative impact of labor costs and other managerial interests, the important trends in modern health care systems—especially mergers and centralization, and the response of many Catholic health care facilities to the unionization movement. Where we may appear to some as biased one way or the other, chalk it up to mutual biases. Although we searched sincerely and assiduously for all relevant data, we are ready to accept criticism and/or correction if presented with substantive evidence.

As faculty and researchers in a Catholic university, with consulting experience with unions and Catholic institutions, however, we would be remiss in our value commitments were we to conclude without some practical suggestions for busy and dedicated health care administrators, organizers or personnel. Pope John Paul II's recent (9/15/81) encyclical, *On Human Work,* provides a stimulus and introduction to our advice.

Pope John Paul II initiated this document, commemorating the 90th anniversary of Pope Leo XIII's *Rerum Novarum,* with a lengthy but important discussion of the Church's teaching on the nature and dignity of human work. Work is defined as any human activity, whether manual or intellectual, "whatever its nature or conditions." It is the Church's task to call attention to the dignity and rights of workers, to condemn situations violating the same, and to help guide the technological, economic, and political changes in human society. The sources of the dignity of work are primarily in the subjective (a person is doing the work) rather than objective (the kind of work done) dimension of work.

We are warned about treating work as a kind of "merchandise" or "force" and denigrating workers because the common scale of values deems what they do as the merest "service," very monotonous or alienating.

After tracing the causes and aims of worker solidarity in the late 19th century Pope John Paul II stated that such solidarity can be found among more recent groups of workers and must never be closed to dialogue and collaboration with others. Reaffirming the Church's firm commitment to the cause of worker solidarity if she is to be truly "the Church of the poor," he comments on the universal experience of toil:

> Toil is something...familiar to those doing physical work under sometimes exceptionally laborious conditions...to those at an intellectual workbench; to scientists; to those who bear the burden of grave responsibility for decisions that will have a vast impact on society...to doctors and nurses, who spend days and nights at their patient's bedside...

Proclaiming that the family is both a community made possible by work and the first school of work, the Pope calls the nation to which one belongs the great indirect "educator" and the historical and social incarnation of all generations. Both assertions call forth concrete and practical respect for family needs and the common good of the nation.

Pope John Paul II reaffirms strongly the many proposals of "experts in Catholic social teaching" and the "highest magisterium of the Church." Such proposals include joint ownership of the means of work, joint sharing by workers in the management and/or profits of business, and so-called share-holding by labor. In addition to reminders that the economic system and the production process benefit precisely when "personal values are fully respected," the Pope insists that every effort must be made to ensure that the human person can "presume his awareness of working for himself."

Finally, for our purposes, Pope John Paul II discusses the rights of workers. Among these rights are just wages, health care, limited working hours, days-off, vacations, pensions, insurance for old age and occupational accidents. The Pope says very pointedly,

> All these rights, together with the need for the workers themselves to secure them, give rise to yet another right: the right of association...for the purpose of defending the vital interests of those employed in the various professions. These associations are called labor or trade unions.
>
> Their task is to defend the existential interests of workers in all

sectors in which their rights are concerned. The experience of history teaches that organizations of this type are an indispensable element of social life, especially in modern industrialized societies...

Representatives of every profession can use them to ensure their own rights. Thus there are unions of agricultural workers and of white collar workers; there are also employers' associations...

Catholic social teaching does not hold that unions are no more than a reflection of the "class" structure of society and that they are a mouthpiece for a class struggle which inevitably governs social life. They are indeed a mouthpiece for social justice, for the rights of working people in accordance with their individual professions. However, this struggle should be seen as normal "for" the just good...which corresponds to the needs and merits of working people associated by profession; but it is not a struggle "against" others. Even if in the controversial questions the struggle takes on a character of opposition toward others, this is because it aims at the good of social justice, not for the sake of "struggle" or in order to eliminate the opponent.

...both those who work and those who manage the means of production or who own them must in some way be united in this community. In the light of this fundamental structure of all...[It] is clear that even if it is because of their work needs that people unite to secure their rights, their union remains a constructive factor of social order and solidarity and it is impossible to ignore it."

After maintaining the right, the widest possible types, the social indispensability, the social justice focus, and the ultimately cooperative aims of employer and professional associations and blue-collar and white-collar unions, Pope John Paul II stresses some necessary cautions. All parties should heed carefully!

Just efforts to secure the rights of workers who are united by the same profession should always take into account the limitations imposed by the general economic situation of the country. Union demands cannot be turned into a kind of group or class "egoism," although they can and should also aim at correcting—with a view to the common good of the whole society—everything defective in the system of ownership of the means of production or in the way these are managed. Social and economic life is certainly like a system of "connected vessels," and every social activity directed toward safeguarding the rights of particular groups should adapt itself to this system.

Speaking of the protection of the just rights of workers according to their individual professions, we must of course always keep in mind that which determines the subjective character of work in each profession, but at the same time, indeed before all else, we must keep in mind that which conditions the specific dignity of the subject of work. The activity of union organizations opens up many possibilities in this respect, including their efforts to foster their self education . . . It is always to be hoped that, thanks to the work of their unions, workers will not only have more, but above all, be more.

While admitting that it is a legitimate means, we must at the same time emphasize that a strike remains, in a sense, an extreme means. It must not be abused; it must not be abused especially for "political" purposes. Furthermore, it must never be forgotten that when essential community services are in question, they must in every case be ensured, if necessary by means of appropriate legislation. Abuse of the strike weapon can lead to the paralysis of the whole socioeconomic life, and this is contrary to the requirements of the common good of society, which also corresponds to the properly understood nature of work itself.

Finally, Pope John Paul II expounds a spirituality of human work. It is not only scripturally based and in tune with the best in developmental psychology, it, also, could resonate with the sincere use of modern management theory and the "community of faith" theme in many Catholic institutions.

The extension of the definition of "work" and "unions," the rejection of "class struggle" and "paternalism," the cautions about irresponsible demands for "more bread and butter" and indiscriminate use of "strike," the inseparability of "unions" and "capital," the "social justice" and "social stability" nature of unions—(blue or white-collar, professional or managerial)— challenge all Catholics, even The Catholic Health Association, an employer association, and Catholic trade unionists, members of blue or white-collar unions or professional associations.

For the long haul, we urge the commencement *soon* of a dialogue between representatives of CHA and some Catholic union officials, under the auspices of some Catholic agency or university. In the context of steel plant closings in places like Youngstown, UAW responses to the automotive industry crisis, and the PATCO strike against the government, both unions and CHA might look again. Worth considering with adaptations are issues such as conglomerate power and industrial democracy, essential and nonessential services rather than private and public employees' right to strike, amending emergency procedures in federal and local laws rather than recourse to compulsory arbitration or the "Toledo Plan." In the first few months of his pontificate, John Paul II negotiated with striking Vatican employees and cautioned striking hospital employees about the patients' needs. His words and example should beckon Catholic health care administrators and unionists to reason together. For the immediate decision making we offer a model.

In the real world context of increasing costs, accelerating multi-union campaigns, expensive and immoral pitches by unscrupulous management consultant groups, and intelligent labor-management relations, we propose a possible model of Catholic hospital responses. The model is an "ideal-type" or "construct," in social science terminology. It is based, however, on much experience. It exhibits the willingness and the ability of health care administrators to face reality with dignity and with a faithful outlook based on Catholic social justice principles.

This model is called "Mutual Respect" and its image is a handshake. Whether initially surprised, naive and ignorant, or not, the administration acknowledges it is being challenged by the union organizing campaign. It heeds the corroborative advice of others among its board members: we have not been paying the kinds of wages and benefits we should have in justice; working conditions and personnel policies need to be improved; we would rather not have a union but workers have the legal and moral right to decide, even if we do not think highly of the demands or tactics of the union involved; the hospital will not engage in any behavior that violates the letter or spirit of the law, for to do so would disregard the social justice teaching of the Catholic Church with which this hospital is affiliated.

With such clear motivation and policy clarifications, the administration, using its own staff or that of a reputable management consultant group, begins to analyze its problems and employees' needs, begins to exercise its rights and responsibilities in law and morality, and begins to communicate its sincere views and plans to the workers. It responds calmly and honestly to correct and incorrect union charges, objecting firmly and courageously to any unfair tactics of the union or its sympathizers in the community. It publicizes its policies and plans to the civic and ecclesial communities.

There will be mistakes and misgivings but not of the heart or will. There may be prolonged strikes or negotiations but little hardship or hardfeeling. There may be initial financial or administrative setbacks but enduring benefits and productivity. Win or lose, the employees and community will recall the dignity and respect that people received, will probably offer their loyalty and dedication to an institution that cares, and perhaps will accept additional and voluntary obligations on behalf of the hospital. The administration will have put its problems in perspective and its financial capability in a stronger position. It will have in its people a commitment and concern that redounds to more than its day-to-day operations. Such an administration will rarely be embarassed by its own statements about its mission and affiliation, its healing and its teaching—as a caring and Catholic institution.

Appendix A

The contract between a northeastern Catholic health care facility and an AFL-CIO affiliated union is typical of labor agreements in the industry. It was effective for nearly two years, from February 1978 through 1979. The specified purpose was that "of facilitating a peaceful adjustment of differences which may arise from time to time...while at the same time preserving to the hospital the prerogatives of its public trust." Included under the terms of the agreement were all hourly employees except clerical and technical; excluded were all professional and supervisory personnel as well as students and part-time workers. Management retained all rights and prerogatives except "where expressly prohibited" by the contract. There were few such restrictions. Subcontracting of work normally performed by members of the bargaining unit, for example, was permitted where "in the sole judgement of the hospital, it becomes necessary, due to economic or other reasons," to do so. A system of progressive discipline was carefully defined regarding violations of management's working rules and excessive absenteeism and tardiness.

Specified wage rates ranged from $3.53 per hour, effective January 1978 with a five percent increase over the previous rates, for helpers and attendants, to $5.37 per hour for senior maintenance repairmen. (The average hourly wage for nonsupervisory hospital employees nationally in January 1978 was $4.88.) No other wage increases were called for during the life of the agreement, but the union had the right to reopen the contract after one year for the purpose of negotiating wages and fringe benefits.

Other contract clauses provided for overtime and premium pay, two paid 10-minute shift breaks, elimination of split shifts, limited transfer rights of workers among shifts, 11 paid holidays, and paid vacations—from two weeks after one year of service up to five weeks after 20 years. Paid and unpaid leaves of absence were made available depending on the circumstances.

The union committed itself not to strike or not to permit unauthorized strikes, sitdowns, or other stoppages. In return, the hospital agreed not to lock out the workers and to allow one union steward on each shift to hear employee complaints and grievances. The grievance procedure consists of three steps culminating in binding arbitration.

Layoffs and rehires were to be made according to seniority but decisions involving promotion were not. Members of the bargaining unit were required to become union members after 30 days. The hospital also agreed to deduct monthly union dues and initiation fees from employees who authorized this in writing and to remit the monies to the union.

Finally, bargaining unit members were covered by medical and life insurance plans and were brought under the diocesan pension plan.

---

1. These conditions are identified and discussed in Richard U. Miller, "Hospitals," Gerald Somers, editor, *Collective Bargaining—Contemporary American Experience* (Madison, WI: Industrial Relations Research Association, 1980), pp. 375–381.
2. U.S. Department of Labor, Bureau of Labor Statistics, *Employment and Earnings, United States, 1909–78,* Bulletin 1312–11 (Washington, DC: GPO, 1979), p. 813.
3. Paul R. Donnelly, "General Personnel Administration," *Hospital Progress* (July 1960), pp. 84–85ff.
4. John Cort, *Commonweal,* April 12, 1957, pp. 33–35.
5. William Consedine, "Some Minimum Matters of Justice," *Hospital Progress* (October 1957), pp. 56–55ff.
6. The president of the Communications Workers of America, for example, has rejected suggestions that he try to obtain a seat on the boards of directors of major domestic telecommunications companies as a means of influencing company policy on the introduction of job-displacing technology.
7. Sumner Slichter, James Healy, and E. Robert Livernash, *The Impact of Collective Bargaining on Management* (Washington, DC: The Brookings Institution, 1960).
8. Charles Brown and James Medoff, "Trade Unions in the Production Process," *Journal of Political Economy* (1978), pp. 355–378. Workers productivity gains following unionization are not limited to manufacturing: in

1971 Coca-Cola Company recognized The United Farm Workers as bargaining agent for its Minute Maid orange grove workers in Florida; after a decade of collective bargaining experience, Coca-Cola's vice-president in charge of the food division concluded, "We were looking for increased productivity and [employee] loyalty; I think we've got what we wanted." Chester Goolrick, "To Johnny Crawford, Work Picking Oranges Goes Better With Coke." *The Wall Street Journal,* May 18, 1981, p. 20.

9. Harold M. Levinson, *Determining Forces in Collective Wage Bargaining* (New York: John Wiley, 1966).

10. For example, Robert MacDonald, *Collective Bargaining in the Automobile Industry* (New Haven: Yale University Press, 1963).

11. James Gross, "Value Judgments in the Decisions of Labor Arbitrators," *Industrial and Labor Relations Review* (October 1967), pp. 55–72.

12. John Delaney, "Patterns of Unions' Successes in Hospital Elections," *Hospital Progress* (February 1980), pp. 36–40.

13. Leo Osterhaus, "The Effect of Unions on Hospital Management: Part 2," *Hospital Progress* (July 1967), pp. 76–80ff.

14. Cort, pp. 33–35.

15. Osterhaus, pp. 76–80ff.

16. Miller, p. 391.

17. Ronald Peters, Helen Elkiss, and Helen Higgens, editors, *Unionization and The Health-Care Industry: Hospital and Nursing Home Employee Union Leaders' Conference Report,* Institute of Labor and Industrial Relations, University of Illinois at Champaign–Urbana (August 1980), p. 16.

18. Delaney, pp. 36–40.

19. Richard Freeman and James Medoff, "New Estimates of Private Sector Unionism in the United States," *Industrial and Labor Relations Review* (January 1979), p. 153; United States Congress, House of Representatives, *Pressures in Today's Workplace,* Oversight Hearings Before the Subcommittee on Labor-Management Relations of the Committee on Education and Labor, Volume III, Testimony of Robert Muehlenkamp, executive vice-president, Local 1199, (Washington, DC: GPO, 1980), p. 194.

20. Osterhaus, pp. 76–80ff.

21. Miller, pp. 409–414.

22. Bureau of National Affairs, *Daily Labor Report,* No. 116, June 15, 1976, p. A-4. Also see Hervey Juris, "Labor Agreements in the Hospital Industry: A Study of Collective Bargaining Outcomes," *Labor Law Journal* (August 1977), pp. 504–511.

23. Myron Fottler, "The Union Impact on Hospital Wages," *Industrial and Labor Relations Review* (April 1977), pp. 342–355.

24. David Dilts, "Unions and Health Care Cost Inflation," *Hospital Progress* (October 1978), pp. 53–58.

25. Brian Becker, "Union Impact on Wages and Fringe Benefits of Hospital Nonprofessionals," *Quarterly Review of Economics and Business* (Winter 1979), pp. 27–44.

26. Becker, p. 39. As a result of union reluctance to do so, health care managers sometimes assume a no-compromise position in initial contract negotiations following union certification in order to avoid reaching agreement and signing a union contract. For an example of this response, see *Nansemond Convalescent Center, Inc.*, 255 NLRB No. 89, 1981.

27. Martin Feldstein, *The Rising Cost of Hospital Care* (Washington, DC: Information Resources Press, 1971).

28. Peters, Elkiss, and Higgens, p. 8.

29. Charles Link and John Landen, "Monopsony and Union Power in the Market for Nurses," *Southern Economics Journal* (April 1975), pp. 649–659.

30. Allan Ponak, "Unionized Professionals and the Scope of Bargaining: A Study of Nurses," *Industrial and Labor Relations Review* (April 1981), pp. 405–416.

31. Martin Feldstein and Amy Taylor, *The Rapid Rise of Hospital Costs,* staff report (January 1977), Council on Wage and Price Stability, Washington, DC.

32. Norman Metzger, "Despite Unionization, Administrators Can Control Policy, Cost, Quality," *Hospital Progress* (September 1977), pp. 36–46.

33. Leo Osterhaus, "Union-Management Relations in 30 Hospitals Change Little in Three Years," *Hospital Progress* (October 1968), pp. 72–77.

34. A. Imberman, "Communications: An Effective Weapon Against Unionization," *Hospital Progress* (December 1973), pp. 54–57.

35. Norman Metzger, pp. 36–46.

36. Hospitals are being merged at a rate and in a manner reminiscent of earlier consolidations of manufacturing enterprises. Anticipated acquisition of Hospital Affiliates International, the hospital holding company of INA Corporation, an insurance-based conglomerate, by Hospital Corporation of America, will make HCA the nation's largest integrated health care management concern. HCA currently owns about 190 hospitals having a combined capacity of nearly 30,000 beds. Hospital Affiliates operates 154 hospitals with 11,700 beds and 19 nursing homes with 2,515 beds. (*The Wall Street Journal*, April 21, 1981, p. 6). Meanwhile, competitive bidding between two hospital holding companies, American Medical International, a billion-dollar-a-year chain of 64 hospitals that manages 30 others, and Humana, Inc., a Kentucky-based firm, drove up the offer price of Brookwood Health Services in one month from $77 to $145 million. American Medical recently had acquired Hyatt Medical Enterprises, an eight-hospital chain that managed 25 others. (*The Wall Street Journal*, April 7, 1981, p. 10 and April 17, 1981, p. 8.) Humana eventually merged with American Medical International for a $145 million investor tax-free exchange of shares. (*The Wall Street Journal*, May 11, 1981, p. 170.) For discussion of the merger trend in health care, see Richard Greene and Thomas Baker, "Paging Dr. Adam Smith," *Forbes*, April 13, 1981, pp. 152–157.

37. Richard Johnson, "Health Care 2000 AD: The Impact of Conglomerates," *Hospital Progress* (April 1981), p. 49.

38. *Ibid.*, p. 52.
39. See Larry Mishel, "Corporate Structure and Bargaining Power: The Coordinated Bargaining Experience," *Labor Studies Journal* (Winter 1979), pp. 308–332.
40. Charles Craypo, "Collective Bargaining in the Conglomerate, Multinational Firm: Litton's Shutdown of Royal Typewriter," *Industrial and Labor Relations Review* (October 1975), pp. 3–25.
41. Leo Osterhaus, "The Effect of Unions on Hospital Management," pp. 76–80ff.
42. "The Conflict Between Catholic Hospitals and Labor Unions," Center of Concern, Washington, DC, 1981.
43. United States Congress, House of Representatives, *Pressures in Today's Workplace,* Report of the Subcommittee of Labor-Management Relations of the Committee on Education and Labor, (Washington, DC: GPO, 1981), p. 26. Reports by avowedly pro-labor publications of additional experiences involving consulting firms and health care facilities include, Bruce Wexler, "Charity Begins At Home," *In These Times*, December 27, 1978–January 2, 1979, pp. 14 +; Ron Chernon, "The New Pinkertons," *Mother Jones* (May 1980); Kinsey Wilson and Steve Askin, "Congress, Labor Board Report Blast 'Anti-Union' Consulting Firms," *National Catholic Reporter*, April 17, 1981, pp. 1, 8–9. Our search of the health care labor relations literature revealed no articles that document illegal actions by health care unions, though such acts doubtless have occurred.
44. *AFL-CIO News,* March 7, 1981, p. 3. The case will be heard and decided by an NLRB administrative law judge. Either party can appeal that decision to the full NLRB, whose finding can be taken to a U.S. Court of Appeals.

DISCUSSION QUESTIONS

1. What *internal* conditions make health care facilities targets for unionization?

2. What *external* conditions make health care facilities targets for unionization?

3. Can the cohesiveness of a Catholic health care community overcome these conditions so as to make unions unnecessary?

4. How do goals of a union relate to the goals of the institution?

5. What issues are primary as unions and institutions negotiate labor contracts?

6. How does the existence of a union organization affect working conditions?

7. What are the economic effects of union recognition on the worker and the institution?

8. How do the unions involved in health care differ among themselves?

9. What is the difference between single employer and multi-employer bargaining units?

10. Why have health care unions not been as successful as other unions?

11. What factors have diminished the effectiveness of labor unions in health care facilities?

12. To what extent is health care cost inflation due to the insurance-based fee-for-service system which allows a simple pass through of rising labor costs?

13. What type of ripple effect can occur in an organization after a union is certified?

14. What are the current trends in health care facility ownership and management that will affect unionization?

15. What should be the response of the administrators of Catholic facilities to a union both before certification and after?

16. To what extent should their response be characterized by professional management goals and by Catholic social teachings?

17. What is the role of management consultant firms in Catholic facilities during union activity?

CHAPTER 3

THE NATIONAL LABOR RELATIONS ACT: ETHICAL CONSIDERATIONS FOR CATHOLIC HEALTH INSTITUTIONS

William Joy, MBA, JD

The 1974 Amendments to the National Labor Relations Act (NLRA) included all nonpublic health care employees under the act. In addition to granting these employees publicly protected rights to organize and bargain collectively, the amendments took cognizance of the specific nature of health care facilities and tailored certain amendments to this specific nature, i.e., procedural restrictions on the right to engage in economic sanctions, e.g., picketing and striking, and provisions for establishing boards of inquiry by the director of the Federal Mediation and Conciliation Service to assist in resolving disputes which will substantially interrupt the delivery of health care in the locality concerned.

For Catholic health care institutions, what moral criteria should be used to judge the morality of these amendments and what moral actions are consistent with Catholic teaching in the context of employees' exercising rights under the amended NLRA?

The NLRA
In General

The NLRA (popularly called the Wagner Act) was enacted in 1935. The basic rights guaranteed employees were set forth in Section 7, which then provided that:

> Employees shall have the right to self-organization, to form, join, or assist labor organizations, to bargain collectively through representatives of their own choosing, and to engage in other concerted activities for the purpose of collective bargaining or other mutual aid or protection.

Mr. Joy is a partner with Morgan, Brown, Kearns, and Joy Attorneys-At-Law, Boston, MA.

Five general types of unfair labor practices were proscribed, which applied to employers. None applied to unions. A procedure was provided to conduct elections and certify exclusive bargaining representatives and to investigate and prosecute unfair labor practice charges.

In 1947, Congress, in an attempt to redress a perceived imbalance, amended the NLRA in several ways with the Taft-Hartley Act. Among these amendments were the establishing of unfair labor practices against unions, guaranteeing employees the right not to engage in union activity, and placing certain limitations on bargaining units. In 1959, the act was further amended by the Labor Management Reporting and Disclosure Act, prohibiting certain types of hot-cargo contracts inter alia.

As Applied to Health Care Institutions

In 1974, Congress further amended the NLRA by placing nonpublic health care facility employees under the NLRA's jurisdiction. This was accomplished by deleting the exemption in Section 2(2) applicable to nonprofit health care facilities. These amendments had the effect of providing that: Employees of nonpublic health care facilities were given the right to organize and bargain collectively through representatives of their choosing. The National Labor Relations Board (NLRB) was admonished by Congress not to proliferate bargaining units. Certain procedural requirements were placed on the right to take economic actions such as picketing and strikes. For example, Section 8(d) and (g) of the NLRA provided for certain notices applicable to collective bargaining in health care institutions where bargaining is for an initial or a subsequent agreement.

Section 2 (14) defined the term "health care institutions" as follows:
The term "health care institution" shall include any hospital, convalescent hospital, health maintenance organization, health clinic, nursing home, extended care facility, or other institution devoted to the care of sick, infirm, or aged person.

The 1974 amendments also provided, in Section 213 (a), for the intervention of the Federal Mediation and Conciliation Service in collective bargaining disputes and the appointment of boards of inquiry prior to the taking of any economic action by unions in the health care field.

Ethical Norms for Catholics

In judging the morality of the NLRA amendments in so far as they involve health care facilities and in judging the morality of specific actions in relation to these amendments, definite criteria should be applied. One may look to the natural law as a guideline that looks at a human being as a rational being and develops from human nature what is natural and appropriate to the dignity of human beings and in harmony with their nature. Among the rights that derive from human nature are the rights to use the world's physical assets, to possess private property, and to associate freely with fellow human beings. For those in decision-making responsibilities in Catholic health care institutions, it is submitted that the following four papal pronouncements provide the best guidelines, since they deal with the totality of considerations involving employers' and employees' rights and duties. They deal not only with the natural law, but also with the experience of humankind, the wisdom of religious and secular experts, and the inspired writings of the Gospel.

Rerum Novarum

On May 15, 1891, Pope Leo XIII issued the encyclical *On the Condition of Workers*. this exceptional document was inspired by new developments in industry which affected the relations between employer and employee. It dealt in detail with the obligations of both, as well as with the state and religious institutions.

The encyclical gave unions a lofty place among associations of workers. Paragraph 69 states that:

> But associations of workers occupy first place, and they include within their circle nearly all the rest. The beneficent achievements of the guilds of artisans among our ancestors have long been well known. Truly, they yielded noteworthy advantages not only to artisans, but, as many monuments bear witness, brought glory and progress to the arts themselves. In our present age of greater culture, with its new customs and ways of living, and with the increased number of things required by daily life, it is most clearly necessary that workers' associations be adapted to meet the present need. It is gratifying that societies of this kind composed either of workers alone or of workers and employers together are being formed everywhere, and it is truly to be desired that they grow in number and in active vigor. Although we have spoken of them more than once, it seems well to show in this place that they are highly opportune and are formed by their own right, and, likewise, to show how they should be organized and what they should do.

Quadragesimo Anno

On May 15, 1931, on the fortieth anniversary of *Rerum Novarum,* Pope Pius XI issued his encyclical *Social Reconstruction.* It was felt that on this occasion, new needs of the age and the changed conditions of the society, plus a clarification concerning the correct interpretation of certain passages of *Rerum Novarum,* required the new encyclical. Again, the right to form associations of workers was clearly stated. In a reference to *Rerum Novarum* the encyclical stated:

Worthy of all praise, therefore, are the directions authoritatively promulgated by Leo XIII, which served to break down this opposition and dispel these suspicions. They have a still higher distinction, however: that of encouraging Christian working-men to form unions according to their several trades, and of teaching them how to do it.

Also, in a direct reference, it states:

Just as the citizens of the same municipality are wont to form associations with diverse aims, which various individuals are free to join or not, similarly, those who are engaged in the same trade or profession will form free associations among themselves, for purposes connected with their occupations.

Laborem Exercens

On September 14, 1981, Pope John Paul II issued his encyclical *On Human Work.* This was intended to be issued on May 15, 1981, on the ninetieth anniversary of *Rerum Novarum,* but the attempted assassination of Pope John Paul II prevented his completing it on that date. Again, as did his predecessors, he dealt with new and changing conditions in technical, economic, and political areas that will influence the world of work and production not less than the Industrial Revolution.

He stated the following on unions:

All these rights, together with the need for the workers themselves to secure them, *give rise to yet another right: the right of association,* that is, to form associations for the purpose of defending the vital interests of those employed in the various professions. These associations are called *labor or trade unions.* The vital interests of the workers are to a certain extent common for all of them; at the same time, however, each type of work, each profession, has its own specific character which should find a particular reflection in these organizations.

In a sense, unions go back to the medieval guilds of artisans, insofar as those organizations brought together people belonging to the same craft and thus on the basis of their work. However, unions differ from the guilds on this essential point: The modern unions grew up from the struggle of the workers—workers in general but especially the industrial workers—to protect their just rights vis-a-vis the entrepreneurs and the owners of the means of production. Their task is to defend the existential interests of workers in all sectors in which their rights are concerned. The experience of history teaches that organizations of this type are an indispensable element of social life, especially in modern industrialized societies. *Obviously, this does not mean that only industrial workers can set up associations of this type. Representatives of every profession can use them to ensure their own rights.* Thus there are unions of agricultural workers and of white-collar workers; there are also employers' associations. All, as has been said above, are further divided into groups or subgroups according to particular professional specializations.

Catholic social teaching does not hold that unions are no more than a reflection of the "class" structure of society and that they are a mouthpiece for a class struggle which inevitably governs social life. They are indeed a mouthpiece for the struggle for social justice, for the just rights of working people in accordance with their individual professions. However, this struggle should be seen as a normal endeavor "for" the just good: In the present case, for the good which corresponds to the needs and merits of working people associated by profession; but it is not a struggle "against" others. Even if in controversial questions the struggle takes on a character of opposition towards others, this is because it aims at the good of social justice, not for the sake of "struggle" or in order to eliminate the opponent. It is characteristic of work that it first and foremost unites people. In this consists its social power: the power to build a community. In the final analysis, both those who work and those who manage the means of production or who own them must in some way be united in this community. In the light of this fundamental structure of all work—in the light of the fact that, in the final analysis, labor and capital are indispensable components of the process of production in any social system—it is clear that, *even if it is because of their work needs that people unite to secure their rights, their union remains a constructive factor of social order and solidarity, and it is impossible to ignore it.* (Emphasis added.)

Vatican II Pastoral Constitution on the Church in the Modern World

On December 7, 1965, Pope Paul VI promulgated the *Pastoral Constitution on the Church in the Modern World.* This was issued after the Second Vatican Council.

In Paragraph 68 the following is set forth:

> Among the basic rights of the human person is to be numbered the right of freely founding unions for working people. These should be able truly to represent them and to contribute to the organizing of economic life in the right way. Included is the right of freely taking part in the activity of these unions without risk of reprisal. Through this orderly participation joined to progressive economic and social formation, all will grow day by day in the awareness of their own function and responsibility, and thus they will be brought to feel that they are comrades in the whole task of economic development and in the attainment of the universal common good according to their capacities and aptitudes.

Catholic Health Care Institutions' Specific Mission

The health care facility can take various forms. It can be a general hospital, a specialized hospital (which in some cases is a satellite of a general hospital), a nursing home, a convalescent home, an infirmary, or various extensions of the above.

Typically, a Catholic health care facility is one that is under the auspices of and administered by a Catholic institution, such as a diocese or a religious congregation. In each such facility there will typically be an administrative group, an employed group of professionals, an employed group of nonprofessionals, and patients. The primary reason for the facility's existence is to heal the patient. All else is subordinate to this primary purpose. Thus, the Catholic health care facility's mission is to heal in a context of a society or subsocieties that exists for this purpose.

In carrying out its duties to the patient, the Catholic health care facility must concern itself not only with quality patient care consistent with the most advanced scientific technologies, but also with the compassion toward the patient exemplified by Jesus Christ.

The NLRA Measured Against Ethical Norms for Catholic Health Care Institutions

The NLRA was passed in 1935 as part of the Roosevelt New Deal. It was an integral part of that administration's economic policy. It was felt that if workers organized and bargained collectively, this would elevate the level of wages and thus be another means of "priming the pump" under the Keynesian theory of economics. This is not to say, however, that the legislation did not have its humane considerations, such as protecting workers' rights and furnishing a framework for developing those rights.

The gist of the law was contained in Section 7, which guaranteed the rights of individuals to organize and bargain collectively through representatives of their own choosing and to engage in other mutual aid or protections. Five general types of unfair labor practices were proscribed. These applied only to employers. Basically, they prohibited interference, restraint, or coercion, domination or contribution of financial support, discrimination in hiring or tenure of employment, retaliation for using the processes of the NLRA, and failure to bargain in good faith. The NLRB was established in Washington, DC, and regional offices were set up in various parts of the country.

There are two types of procedures: the representation procedure and the unfair labor practice procedure. The former was designed to determine appropriate bargaining units and, after elections, to determine who was the certified bargaining agent for an appropriate group of employees. The second was the machinery used to determine whether an employer had committed an unfair labor practice as alleged by a union or an individual. Court review was provided in case of unfair labor practice proceedings. Representation matters could be challenged in court only through the vehicle of a refusal to bargain and a subsequent finding of an unfair labor practice by the employer.

In 1947 this act was amended by the Labor Management Relations Act of 1947 popularly known as the Taft-Hartley Act. Section 7 was amended to protect the right of individuals not to engage in collective bargaining and concerted activities. A corresponding set of unfair labor practices was included in Section 8(b) applicable to union conduct. Section 8(c) codified the right of free speech.

Also included in this legislation were certain provisions applicable to national emergency strikes, provisions providing for suits for violation of union contracts, prohibition against payment of anything of value by an employer to a union representative, the setting up of the Federal Mediation and Conciliation Service as an independent agency in the Executive Department of the government, and many others. Many observed that this legislation was an attempt to redress the imbalance that existed in labor-management relations as embodied in the Wagner Act. Expressions such as "the pendulum head had swung too far" were used.

In 1959 the Labor-Management Reporting and Disclosure Act was passed. This amended the NLRA inter alia by outlawing certain types of hot-cargo agreements, but, basically, the act's thrust was to set up a bill of rights for individual union members in relationship to their unions.

In 1974 the NLRA was again amended to place nonpublic health care facilities under the NLRB's jurisdiction. Certain safeguards were included, such as longer periods for required notices under Section 8(d) where collective bargaining on a contract was to begin for the first time or in the case of a renewal. Where economic sanctions such as strikes or picketing were to be used by a union, a 10-day notice was required except in the case of bargaining for a first contract, where the notice was 10 days following the 20-day notice required by Section F(d)(b). The purpose here was to give the health care facility an opportunity to prepare for such an eventuality by moving patients or otherwise providing for their care. The Federal Mediation and Conciliation Service, when given a notice of economic action, could set up a board of inquiry to report on the issues in the dispute. It is worthy of note that Congress expressed its view in the committee reports that the NLRB should take care not to proliferate bargaining units in the health care industry. The NLRB paid attention to this admonition for a time, then ignored it until the case of *NLRB* v. *Mercy Hospital Association,* in which the U.S. Supreme Court denied certiorari that in effect upheld a decision of the Court of Appeals for the Second Circuit that upheld a challenge of the NLRB on this issue, 445 U.S. 971, 103 LRRM 3082.

Since 1935 the NLRB has administered this act and its amendments. It has filled in the meaning of general terms such as interference, restraint, coercion, and good faith bargaining.

It is worthy of note that no scandal has ever touched the NLRB. The U.S. Court of Appeals and the U.S. Supreme Court have exercised a review authority to ensure compliance by the agency with congressional mandates and intent.

Measured against the ethical norms set forth in the three encyclicals and pastoral constitution cited above, it is submitted that the NLRA is a morally correct action by the government to protect and preserve employees' and employers' fundamental rights. Each of the three encyclicals and the pastoral constitution, although dealing with different conditions occurring at different times in history, has placed primary emphasis on workers' rights to associate through organizations such as unions. The NLRA clearly protects this right and, through its representation procedures, implements this right. Its thrust is that, given the right to bargain collectively through representatives of their own choosing, workers will have an opportunity to acquire a decent wage and to work under reasonable and human conditions. The unfair labor practices are designed to prohibit employers from interfering with these essential rights and also to prevent unions from interfering with employers' and employees' essential rights. The right of an employer or a union to communicate was also protected in Section 8(c) of the NLRA.

Practical Application of the NLRA to the Catholic Health Care Facility

Having previously addressed the moral criteria used to judge the morality of health care amendments to the NLRA, I will now address the moral actions that occur when employees, employers, and unions exercise their rights under the NLRA, with specific reference to Catholic health care facilities.

Union Organizational Activity

In order for a union to represent employees, it must first organize them. Organizational activity takes various forms, both covert and overt. The ultimate objective is to acquire sufficient evidence of designation of the union as the employee representative in an appropriate bargaining unit. Typically, a union will seek to acquire such evidence by obtaining authorization cards from employees, and, generally speaking, it seeks to obtain more than 50 percent of persons in an appropriate bargaining unit before it will request recognition without an election or seek a determination of representation through an election by the NLRB. (Note that a 30 percent showing of interest is all that is required to set the NLRB processes in motion.) Most unions feel, however, that unless they have a good margin beyond 50 percent signed up, their chances of winning an election are not great.

Frequently, unions will establish contacts among the employees and then build on these contacts through meetings off the employer's premises. As this activity progresses, at some point it surfaces and comes to the employer's attention. It is not at all uncommon for an employer to learn of such activity for the first time when he receives a claim of recognition from the union and a notice that a petition has been filed with the NLRB. In any event, the knowledge of such union activity is usually cause for considerable concern, particularly at a Catholic health care facility. Typical reactions are ''a union is totally out of place in a health care facility—somewhere along the line, the strike weapon will be used." Also, personal reactions may surface, such as resentment that employees were ungrateful in turning to an outside third party to represent them.

Usually, a petition is filed with the NLRB and a date for an election is established. Voting usually takes place on the employer's premises at a designated time; the voting is by secret ballot conducted by an agent of the NLRB.

The period preceding the election is one during which the parties may engage in a campaign. Essentially, the campaign is one of communications. Both the employer and the union have the right to communicate with the employees who will vote in the election and to state their positions on the various issues. The first amendment to the constitution and Section 8 (c) of the NLRA allow great latitude in communications. Prohibited are communications that involve threats, promises of reward or benefits, and inquiries into an employee's fears, union activities, sympathies, and internal union affairs. On the positive side, an employer may call the employee's attention to his past record of providing wages, fringe benefits, and working conditions. He may ask his employees to judge him on his record. He may state his preference to deal with employees without the intervention of a third party. He may point out the union's record in the matter of strikes at other locations and any evidence of union corruption.

Communications are usually by letter to the employee's home, by speeches to groups, and one-on-one dialogue between management representatives and the employee. In developing and implementing a communications program, an employer may have sufficient capabilities within his staff. On the other hand, he may prefer (or require) an outside consultant's services. In either case, the communication is made by representatives of management to the employees with the ultimate objective of getting the employees to vote no—against the union—in the election.

The health care facility's stance on union activity is complex and sensitive. Legally, the employer has the right to express his views within certain limitations, and he certainly has the right to express a preference to deal directly with the employees rather than with the intervention of a third party. Immediately, the question is raised, How does this square with the employees' right to organize into unions? It is clear that employees do have such a right, both legally and morally. It is also clear that the employer has the legal right to express opinions and, in fact, to state a preference for not having a union in his establishment. Such expressions appear to be morally permissible. Up to this point, nothing that has been said has denied the individual's right to exercise his freedom of choice on joining or not joining or voting or not voting for a union. As long as the employer conducts himself in such a fashion in a union organizational campaign, he operates within his legal and moral rights. If he engages in threats, retaliation, or promises of reward or benefits, however, he is clearly acting illegally and immorally. Between these two poles there is another area, sometimes difficult to establish, where through sophisticated psychological techniques employees are deprived of their free choice in an election. These situations occur by clever manipulation of an employee's doubt, anxiety, and, ultimately, fear, so that when he casts his vote he is not casting his vote with any degree of freedom—mentally or psychologically—although physically he appears to be doing so. Such activity clearly violates the right of freedom of association of workers based on their societal nature and their needs, befitting their dignity as human beings, such as adequate and proper conditions of employment.

The Papal pronouncements mentioned above dealt with conditions as they then existed and that had evolved over a certain period. The application of the principles set forth therein have to be applied to new, changed, or current conditions. At present, unions have a legally protected existence and an institutional character of their own. They have policies and practices that have been established and used and upon which judgments may be made on whether a particular union is good or bad for a given situation. It appears to be perfectly permissible to address these issues in a context of a union campaign in this day and age without denigrating the employee's right of association. The condition of workers in industrial nations is generally quite different today from what it was when *Rerum Novarum* was issued 90 years ago, and unions have achieved a national and international status unknown at that time.

Litigation

After an election, either party may file objections to NLRB, employer, or union conduct or unfair labor practice charges. To challenge the representation process, the employer may refuse to bargain with a certified union and then petition the appropriate U.S. Court of Appeals for review or await the NLRB's filing a petition for enforcement. These are permissible legal actions. Where substantial (as opposed to frivolous) issues are involved, employers not only have the right but the duty, in most cases, to take such action. It comports with preserving the purity of the process where the employees, unions, or individual's rights are being exercised. Obviously, frivolous litigation is improper, and courts have ample power to deal with this situation.

Collective Bargaining

Following certification (or recognition without certification), collective bargaining between the union and the employer ensues on the general subjects of wages, hours, and working conditions. The law requires good-faith bargaining on both sides. It does not compel an agreement. Surface bargaining (giving the appearance of bargaining in good faith but failing to do so by actual conduct) or deliberately engaging in bad-faith bargaining to delay agreement and ultimately to force the union out by a decertification petition or a strike is illegal. It would also appear to be morally wrong.

Strikes

Failing to reach agreement in negotiations, the union is free to strike. This poses special problems for Catholic health care facilities. Congress recognized the unique nature of health care facilities when it provided for advance notice of economic action and the provision for boards of inquiry. Strikes by health care workers are not uncommon. The encyclical *Laborem Exercens* addressed the use of the strike weapon as follows:

> One method used by unions in pursuing the just rights of their members is the strike or work stoppage, as a kind of ultimatum to the competent bodies, especially the employers. This method is recognized by Catholic social teaching as legitimate in the proper conditions and within just limits. In this connection workers should be assured the right to strike, without being subjected to personal penal sanctions for taking part in a strike. While admitting that it is a legitimate means, we must at the same time emphasize that a strike remains, in a sense, an extreme means. It must not be abused; it must not be abused especially for "political" purposes. *Furthermore it must never be forgotten that, when essential community services are in question, they must in every case be ensured, if necessary by means of appropriate legislation. Abuse of the strike weapon can lead to the paralysis of the whole of socioeconomic life, and this is contrary to the requirements of the common good of society, which also corresponds to the properly understood nature of work itself. (Emphasis added.)*

The morality of the strike weapon in a health care institution is one more directly involved with employees and their representatives. It is an extreme means. It withdraws aid from the sick and injured and directly involves obligations of charity and justice. It goes to the very core of the Catholic health care facility's healing mission. Each case, of course, must be viewed on its own facts and in its own frame of reference.

Given that health care is an essential community service that may be stopped by a strike, and where there is no appropriate legislation to ensure its continuity, does the Catholic health care facility have the moral right and duty to oppose unionization at the threshold to forestall such an eventuality? This is a legitimate question that can only be answered by examining a particular situation.

Ongoing Union-Management Relations

Once a contract has been reached in collective bargaining, the day-to-day administration of the contract and the interrelationship of the employer, the union, and its members commences. It is this ongoing relationship that is most important in the labor-management context for fulfilling the respective roles of the parties in carrying out their mission of healing. Most of the NLRA's provisions and the activities of the parties mentioned above are directed to coexistence under rules mutually agreed upon in a document constructed by the involved parties. This relationship involves application of the document to workers' daily work and remuneration. It also involves the mechanism for any disputes over its meaning and application that arise during its term. A grievance and arbitration procedure is the vehicle principally used for this purpose.

A proper recognition of and respect for the rights and obligations of each party in this day-to-day relationship comports with the moral obligation of each.

DISCUSSION QUESTIONS

1. What were the effects of the 1974 amendments to the NLRA on Catholic health care facilities?

2. What criteria should be used to judge the morality of the 1974 NLRA amendments?

3. What moral actions are consistent with Catholic teaching in the context of employees exercising rights under the amended NLRA?

4. What basic employee rights are guaranteed by the NLRA?

5. What antiunion employer practices are prohibited by the NLRA?

6. What basic employer rights were added to the NLRA by the Taft-Hartley amendments?

7. What national agency administers the NLRA?

8. What guidelines does the natural law offer in judging the morality of the NLRA amendments regarding health care facilities?

9. What guidelines do specific Church teachings (e.g. *Rerum Novarum, Quadregesimo Anno, Lumen Gentium, Laborem Exercens*) offer in the health care facility amendments to the NLRA?

10. What is the specific mission of Catholic health care facilities and how does this mission supply norms for judging the morality of the NLRA health care facility amendments?

11. What are the two types of NLRB procedures?

12. How does an employer challenge NLRB certification of a union?

13. What changes did the Taft-Hartley Act make in the original National Labor Relations (or Wagner) Act?

14. What changes did the Labor-Management Reporting and Disclosure (or Landrum-Griffin) Act make in the NLRA?

15. By what process does a union gain the legal right to represent workers?

16. How is the campaign preceding a union election conducted by the union and by the employer?

17. What type of employer statements and conduct are prohibited by the NLRA during a union election campaign?

18. What types of employer statements and conduct are legally permissible during the campaign?

19. Are there any types of legally permissible conduct which would be morally proscribed by the relevant Church teachings in a pre-union election campaign?

20. What moral criteria govern the employer's decision to challenge a union certification election?

21. What legal and moral criteria govern labor's and management's conduct of the collective bargaining process?

22. What moral criteria govern labor's decision to strike a health care facility?

23. Does the Catholic health care facility have a moral obligation to oppose unionization so as to preclude a possible strike at the facility?

24. What moral criteria govern labor's and management's conduct during the day-to-day administration of a union contract?

CHAPTER 4

NEW REALITIES IN EMPLOYMENT MATTERS: COUNSELING CATHOLIC HEALTH CARE INSTITUTIONS

Rev. Robert L. Kealy, STL, JD
James A. Serritella, JD

Two transitions have given urgency to employment matters at Catholic health care institutions. At one time the typical Catholic institution was staffed principally by religious, and personnel problems were mostly those of the internal administration of a religious community. Over the last 15 years that state of affairs has gradually changed, and now religious comprise only a very small portion of a Catholic health care institution's staff. Personnel problems have become those of any medium-sized employer.

In addition, before 1974 nonprofit health care institutions were exempt from National Labor Relations Board (NLRB) jurisdiction. Apart from the very few states that had labor boards with jurisdiction over nonprofit institutions, no civil authority could require such institutions to bargain collectively. In 1974, of course, the law was changed to give the NLRB jurisdiction over the nonprofit health care institution.

Thus, the Catholic health care institution became subject to the possibility of compulsory collective bargaining when the typical institution had lay employees in sufficient numbers to avail themselves of it. This coincidence of transitions has evoked a variety of responses. Some

---

Fr. Kealy is director of The Center for Church/State Studies, DePaul University College of Law, Chicago, IL. He is also judge on the Archdiocese of Chicago Matrimonial Tribunal and fomer chairman of the Committee on Collective Bargaining of the Canon Law Society of America.

Mr. Serritella is a partner in the law firm of Reuben & Proctor, Chicago, IL. He was a member of the Committee on Collective Bargaining of the Canon Law Society of America.

people are delighted that at last Catholic institutions can be compelled to follow the social mandates of the Catholic labor encyclicals. Others are angry that such institutions may be drawn into what they see as a union morass. Administrators, theologians, lawyers, and canonists have responded, and the available literature is replete with reactions of "moral" or "immoral," "constitutional" or "unconstitutional," "canonical" or "uncanonical," and "workable" or "unworkable." The voice of the lawyer has perhaps emerged from the debate the loudest for a number of reasons, not the least being that the law permeates virtually every aspect of the employment relationship.

This chapter is an effort to cut through this noisy debate and attempt to assist the various parties who must come to grips with these new realities in employment matters. We make no pretense of providing comprehensive answers. There are, frankly, many current situations that may lack answers. But we hope that by clearing away a bit of the clutter, the proper questions can be raised and the debate can be advanced.

The Debate

The debate over the new realities in employment matters at Catholic health care institutions can be viewed in the context of three apparent conflicts: (1) between the Church's social teachings as applied to commercial situations and Catholic health care facilities' special needs; (2) between Catholic health care institution's role as religious leader and its role as manager; and (3) the urgency of labor matters created by civil law imperatives and the need for Catholic institutions to explore alternatives. We will briefly address each of these apparent conflicts.

Catholic Social Teachings and The Catholic Health Care Institution

For almost 100 years the Catholic Church has marched at the forefront of the labor movement. In papal encyclicals and the documents of Vatican II the Church has unequivocally taught that workers have a natural right to organize associations of their own choosing and to bargain collectively to attain their just goals.

Although the Church has promoted workers' rights in commercial and industrial settings, it has not always applied all these principles to workers in its own institutions. One might legitimately ask whether the Church simply is not practicing what it preaches or whether it has a valid reason for its actions.

On the one hand, it seems that a Church institution should actively promote workers' rights. Resistance to unionization and collective bargaining would seem to contradict the Church's own teachings.

On the other hand, many administrators and, indeed, many employees fear a unionized health care institution. They worry about the new relationships between management and labor that the industrial model would bring. Would the "I" and "thou" of the typical management-labor relationship detract from the institution's religious mission? Would it harm team spirit? Would it help patients? How would it affect cost containment and continuity of services? Would it benefit the employees? Or is it even something the institution has the right to question?

Administrators will find little in the literature to assist them in making an objective analysis of their dilemma.

The Catholic Facility: Religious Leader or Manager?

The Catholic health care institution has a religious as well as a health services mission. The religious mission requires it to advocate by word and example the highest standards in employment matters taught by the Church.

At the same time, the institution must function as manager. That is, it must maximize economies and efficiencies across the board, including its relations with its employees. This effort is both complicated and rendered more compelling by the need to comply with the requirements of government regulators and third party payers.

The institution must deal at once with its broad theological mandate to exemplify Church teaching and its very focused obligation to manage. The world is quick to criticize hard management considerations as violations of the former and theological perspectives as violations of the latter. The clash of these two aspects of the Catholic health care institution places an understandable tension on the hospital administrator.

The new employment realities did not create this tension. They just made it more vivid. The tension was lodged in the institution's dual nature before the new employment realities emerged. When the union comes knocking, the hospital as religious leader feels obligated to open the door wide, while the hospital as manager feels the impulse to resist. The bottom line is at least moderate discomfort, whichever course the hospital chooses.

A major source of this discomfort is that the high social ideals have not been brought down to the nuts and bolts of employment relationships in a service institution. It is a bit of a jump from workers' natural right to organize to the possibility of a strike in the surgical intensive care unit or cost containment in the provision of an essential human service. As a result, even the most high-minded administrator would be hard pressed to reconcile the roles of religious leader and manager.

Creativity and Regulation

When employees petition the NLRB to conduct a representation election at a health care institution, the institution must respond promptly to the petition generally as well as to a number of very specific NLRB inquiries. The response will carry the institution along well-established channels to an election at which the employees will decide whether to have a union. Should they vote for a union, the institution's labor relations will be conducted according to the industrial model for the foreseeable future, that is, until such time as the employees vote otherwise. The rules of the NLRB move the whole process along with as much speed as a large bureaucracy can achieve. In short, there is little time to ferret out alternatives to the standard outcome of such an undertaking.

Once invoked, the NLRB, partly because of the operative law and partly because of established modes of operation, creates imperatives and well-established forms of action that the health care institution must accept or oppose under great time pressure. There is little opportunity to explore alternatives in a situation that many believe requires alternatives to the industrial model. Any alternatives must be thought out before the process is invoked at all.

Unfortunately, the debate has been caught in the moralistic or legalistic grooves of whether Catholic institutions should have unions at all and whether the NLRB can legitimately impose them. This probably occurs because of time pressures and the need to have lawyers respond to legal imperatives.

Addressing the Debate

It is useful to address the debate over the new realities in personnel matters by returning to basics. First, this involves focusing on the Catholic facility's fundamental objectives, namely, adherence to the Church's teachings on labor matters and maintenance of the institution's integrity. Then, it requires clarifying the roles of some persons involved with the institution.

The Church's Social Teachings

In formulating employee policies, a Catholic health care institution must adhere to the Church's teachings on labor matters. To understand the Church's teachings, the institution should analyze them in the context in which they were pronounced. Unfortunately, some people have criticized those who advocate examining the context and the history surrounding the teachings. But, since theologians and others are subjecting the Church's past pronouncements on morality to rigorous historical analysis, it is difficult to see why they should not do the same with the social teachings. Although we do not claim to speak as professional theologians, we hope that these ideas will spark further theological analysis.

One of the giants in the area of social concerns, Msgr. George Higgins, has noted recently[1] that official Church documents on socio-economic matters have in recent years become more inductive and more in the form of an invitation to dialogue, whereas in the past they were more deductive and dogmatic. In fact, it is no longer accurate to speak of Church social doctrine. More correctly, we should speak of Church social teaching. The basic principles enunciated in official Church pronouncements are conditioned by the times and circumstances and need to be updated and refined in the light of changing times and conditions.

Fr. John Coleman, SJ, recently addressed a convocation commemorating the anniversaries of *Rerum Novarum, Quadragesimo Anno,* and *Mater et Magistra.*[2] Fr. Coleman gave a thorough analysis of the social encyclicals in their historical context. His exposition shows that there is a unity in the social teachings in the sense that they form a social charter and tradition in their key principles and concepts, yet there are many inconsistencies in their presentation and application.

As evidence of the fact that unity does not leap off the pages of the encyclicals, Fr. Coleman points out that when *Mater et Magistra* was promulgated, both liberals and conservatives claimed to find confirmation of their position in it. While *The Wall Street Journal* saw *Populorum Progressio* as warmed-over Marxism, the right-wing authoritarian president of Brazil congratulated the Pope and claimed his regime embodied its principles!

Recognizing then that there is always a danger of selective perception in analyzing Church social teaching, we will proceed to isolate what we see as some of the key elements of the Church's social teaching and attempt to bring them to bear on the conditions in our Catholic health care institutions.

This historical analysis begins in 1891 when Pope Leo XIII startled the world with his encyclical *Rerum Novarum,* "On the Condition of the Working Classes." The Industrial Revolution had created a new labor structure in which millions of people were employed in factories and mines instead of on farms or at home. Child labor was common, and employers treated workers as chattel. Unadulterated capitalism preached that bottom-line economics should dictate policy, while Calvinistic determinism taught people to accept their lot in life. Because of these factors, supporters of unions had to fight for the most basic rights of workers, not to speak of the most basic rights of human beings.

During this social upheaval and brutish disregard for human dignity, Pope Leo issued the encyclical that Pope John XXIII later referred to as "the Magna Carta for the reconstruction of the economic and social order."[3] Pope Leo went right to the heart of the matter by upholding the right to private property, the right to a job, and the right to a just wage. He called for child labor laws and limits on hours worked. Most notably, he asserted that workers had a *natural right* to form workers' associations to work for justice and their mutual welfare. This right was based, he said, on the workers' right of free association. In Pope Leo's view, such an association should further not self-interest but commutative justice.

It was in the midst of worldwide depression, on the fortieth anniversary of *Rerum Novarum,* that Pope Pius XI issued the encyclical *Quadragesimo Anno,* "On Social Reconstruction." He asserted that workers have the right to organize in trade groupings and even broader associations and stated that these associations should be imbued with a spirit of justice, helping to "build up a juridical and social order able to pervade all economic activity."[4]

During the U.S. civil rights movement, and the emergence of the burgeoning third world countries, Pope John XXIII spoke about these issues in the encyclical *Mater et Magistra,* "On Recent Developments of the Social Question in the Light of Christian Teaching." In this, he taught that "work, inasmuch as it is an expression of the human person, can by no means be regarded as a mere commodity . . . [I]ts remuneration is not to be thought of in terms of merchandise, but rather according to the laws of justice and equity."[5] Pope John reaffirmed the "natural right to enter corporately into associations, whether these be composed of workers only or of workers and management, and also the right [of workers] . . . to act freely and on their own initiative within the above mentioned associations, without hindrance and as their needs dictate."[6]

The Second Vatican Council, in addressing the pastoral issues of the day, also spoke about labor. In a document entitled *Gaudium et Spes,* "The Pastoral Constitution on the Church in the Modern World," it reaffirmed the workers' right to organize.

As the principle of unionization became more accepted, Pope Paul VI, in his Apostolic letter *Octogesima Adveniens*, "A Call to Action," not only bolstered this right to unionize in the abstract but also supported the workers' right to unionize in practice. Pope Paul did mention, however, that this right had limits. Speaking of strikes, the Pope said:

> Here and there the temptation can arise of profiting from a position of force to impose, particularly by strikes—the right to which as a final means of defense remains certainly recognized—conditions which are too burdensome for the overall economy and for the social body, or to desire to obtain in this way demands of a directly political nature. When it is a question of public service, required for the life of an entire nation, it is necessary to be able to assess the limit beyond which the harm caused by the society becomes inadmissible.[7]

Finally as Church institutions hired more lay employees, the Synod of Bishops, meeting in 1971, issued the statement *Justice in the World,* which applied these principles to the Church's own employees. It reminded the Church that in order to preach justice, it had to practice justice in its own institutions.

Most recently, in the context of the great struggle in Poland of the Solidarity union and worldwide upheavals, Pope John Paul II has issued his encyclical *Laborem Exercens,* "On Human Work."

In this encyclical Pope John Paul stresses emphatically that the human being who is the worker must be our primary concern. He or she cannot be thought of only in terms of the work or service performed. Workers are not mere instruments; their rights and dignity cannot be surbordinated to economic concerns. We must maintain the primacy of persons over things.

The Pope tells us that the attainment of workers' rights cannot be achieved if economic systems are guided chiefly by the criterion of maximum profit. On the contrary, it is respect for the objective rights of workers that must be the fundamental criterion.

More specifically, the Pope writes that workers have the right to form associations to defend their vital interests and such associations are an indispensable element in modern industrial societies. The Pope, however, reminds us that labor and capital are not locked in a class struggle, but are mutually dependent and must be united in community. They must work together not only that workers have more, but that they be more, i.e., that they will be able to lead richer, more fully human lives.

The history of the Church's teachings on labor matters shows that most of the pronouncements speak about industrial workers. The Church saw that the industrial model usually pits management and labor against one another. Management tends to exploit workers to increase its profits, while workers want at least some of the profits for themselves. To combat the industrial managers' powers, the workers need the right to unionize.

In addition to describing workers' rights, the Church has also emphasized workers' responsibilities in labor matters. It has warned workers never to succumb to the temptation of naked self-interest. Instead, in seeking commutative justice, that is, a fair share of the company's earnings, workers must consider not only their own interests, but the interests of all, so that real justice can be accomplished. Moreover, the Church's teachings encourage workers' associations and management to cooperate with each other. Both should recognize their interdependence and treat each other with respect and reasonableness.

These documents also establish limits on the means that labor can use to accomplish its objectives. They condemn strikes that threaten the welfare of innocent parties or the commonwealth.

Although many Church writings balance the rights of workers and managers in industry, the Church did not even address the issue of workers in ecclesiastical or eleemosynary institutions until 1971, when the worldwide Synod of Bishops issued its statement. Even though this document did acknowledge the Church's obligation to treat its own workers justly, fairly, and humanely, it did not state that the teachings concerning collective bargaining applied to its own institutions.

This silence in advocating unions for religious institutions was not due to blindness or hypocrisy. Instead, it would seem to be attributable to an unarticulated belief that what might be appropriate in an industrial or commercial setting might not be appropriate for a religious institution, coupled with the fact that such institutions were staffed principally by religious. The religious, of course, were willing and able to sacrifice all to further the Church's religious mission.

Even with the increase in lay employees, who require adequate salaries to support themselves and their families, the Church apparently still has not adopted the industrial model for ecclesiastical institutions. For example, the Synod of Bishops, even though asserting the Church's obligation to treat its workers justly, did not directly speak of a church worker's right to organize for collective bargaining. The Synod only stated that "[n]o one should be deprived of his ordinary rights because he is associated with the Church in one way or another."[8]

This lack of any direct pronouncement on labor organizations in the ecclesiastical or eleemosynary setting most emphatically does not mean that the Church forbids or even discourages employees of Catholic institutions from organizing for collective bargaining. Clearly, the Church mandates that these institutions pursue social justice for their employees. The papal documents, however, do not appear to support one and only one vehicle to achieve social justice for these employees.

The Catholic Health Care Facility's Integrity

Employment in an ecclesiastical or eleemosynary setting raises issues not present in industrial or commercial settings. Catholic facilities were founded as charitable enterprises, supported principally by alms, to address serious human needs. Historically, there was little organized care for the sick, especially for the sick poor. The Catholic facilities responded, and their response went beyond providing mere physical health to care instead for the whole person.

But what does it mean to be a Catholic health care institution when the principal source of funds is no longer alms, but government assistance, insurance, or substantial payments by the recipients of the care? What does it mean to be a Catholic health care institution when there is a glut of beds in many areas and health care institutions (either sectarian or secular) compete with one another? What does it mean to be a Catholic health care institution when hospitals are operated as big businesses, with multimillion dollar expenditures and complex government regulations? What does it mean to be a Catholic health care institution when the number of religious on staff is declining and the number of laity and even non-Catholics on boards of directors is increasing?

The Catholic health care institution's need to address the new employment realities must be viewed in the context of its need to address its own new identity. Despite all the changes in this identity, the Catholic health care institution still stems from a humanitarian concern imbued with a spiritual perspective and is still directed toward a Christian concern for the whole person. This concern for the whole person is not seen only in the services offered by the pastoral care department, but more significantly by the Christian perspective that is meant to saturate the warp and woof of the entire institution. One might legitimately observe that the Catholic health care institution is a Christian health care community parallelling the Catholic schools' ''Christian educational community.''

Employees in a Catholic health care institution are sharers in this mission. This means that any vehicle they use to achieve social justice should not detract from their participation in the mission. On the other hand, although the mission, the Christian health care community, is the Catholic health care institution's reason for being, it should not be used as a mere ploy to deny employees the justice to which they are entitled.

Clarification of Roles

In going back to basics in the debate over the new realities in employment matters, it is critical to clarify the roles of certain key participants. This clarification is necessary because the true roles may be so taken for granted that they are fading into the background and the required relations are being unobtrusively rearranged.

• *The board of directors.* It is fundamental that the board of directors of a civil law corporation ultimately be responsible for establishing the corporation's policies and directing its management. It is not just another committee or advisory body. The board of directors of a civilly incorporated Catholic Church institution must establish policies and direct management in light of the relevant Church teachings.

• *The administration.* The administration in a civil law corporation is responsible for carrying out the policies and managerial directives established by the board of directors.

• *Outside professionals.* Health care institutions employ a variety of professionals, such as lawyers, accountants, and management consultants. These professionals have the responsibility of carrying out the policies and management directives established by the board and implemented by the administration.

We think there is great need to emphasize the diversity of these roles, because they frequently become confused, especially when the health care institution must deal with employment matters. When the union comes knocking there is an emergency meeting of the board in which attorneys and labor consultants are engaged and too frequently "turned loose to solve the problem." The attorneys and consultants, who are by profession completely result oriented and familiar principally with the standards of the industrial world, enthusiastically move out to make the problem "go away." Pointed questions are then raised by other concerned Catholics as to whether hospitals should oppose unions and whether they should use (the now, in some quarters, disreputable) "consultants" in doing so.

There are two sources of the problem. First, there is a lack of ideas on how the Catholic health care institution can carry out the directives of the social encyclicals and still maintain its functional integrity. There is no quick solution for this. Second, at a time when the institution is groping

71

for ideas, it is particularly counterproductive to depart from the basic organizational relationships (board-administration-professionals) and turn matters over to the professionals who, because of their own specialization, do not have the ability to deal with the theological-social issues. This is not the time for the board and administration to walk away from their leadership obligations.

Dealing with the new realities in personnel matters, especially in the highly charged circumstances of a union election campaign, requires close coordination of board, administration, and professionals. Persons in each group must interact with the others according to the groups' respective roles. The board should lay down policies containing the general parameters of what is expected of all participants. Administration should make sure that these policies are properly implemented, and the professionals should assist.

In this last connection, it is important to make clear who is doing what. If a consultant has been engaged to assist in a representation election, the consultant must do so according to the policies laid down by the board as implemented by administration. If a lawyer has been engaged, the lawyer's role is to make sure that both the administration and the consultant act within the law. Although both the consultant and the lawyer contribute to policy, neither should set policy, especially because of the board's failure to do so.

These relations among the participants, of course, hold true in the institution's day-to-day operations as well as in crisis situations. In fact, departure from the proper relations in day-to-day activities makes it impossible to respond to a crisis in a manner consistent with the institution's philosophy and outlook.

Therefore, the answer to the frequently asked question "How should the good *Catholic* lawyer (or labor consultant) advise the Catholic hospital on the new realities in personnel relations?" is that the Catholic lawyer should advise the hospital in the same way that the good Jewish or Protestant lawyer or consultant should advise. The lawyer and consultant do not set the institution's course of action. They use their professional expertise to assist the board of directors in formulating policy and the administration in implementing it.

This is not to say that lawyers and consultants are all the same. They are not. Some are better able to understand the religious health care institution's special policy objectives. Some have greater skill in implementing these objectives. Some are more creative. Importantly, some are more careful not to intrude on the board's and administration's policy-making responsibilities. It is the task of boards and administrations to select the best professionals from this point of view, professionals with an "ecclesiastical ear." Once the selection has been made, the board and administration still must guide and direct these professionals' activities to make sure that they do not depart from the institution's policies.

There is a further point to be made. If cases like *NLRB v. The Catholic Bishop of Chicago* and *NLRB v. Yeshiva University* mean anything, they mean that there is room for new creative solutions to the new realities in nonindustrial employment settings. In those two cases, the U.S. Supreme Court held that Church-affiliated elementary and secondary schools are not subject to the NLRB jurisdiction and the faculty members at the university were managerial employees excluded from NLRB coverage. More pertinently, in other cases dealing with hospitals, the courts have left open the possibility of patterns of employee participation other than the industrial model. Rather than "turn the professionals loose" to "solve the union problem," boards and administrators should be directing them to search for ways of achieving social justice that are compatible with the health care environment's special needs.

In putting forth these suggestions, we do not mean to undermine the professional judgment of the lawyers or consultants, only to help direct that judgment properly. These professionals do not feel called upon to make business or financial decisions for commercial enterprises. There is no good reason for them to be making theological or administrative decisions for religious institutions. Their professional expertise relates to law or a specific brand of consulting. They are rank amateurs at everything else. This whole discussion of roles hinges upon the board's establishing policies to govern the conduct of the institution's administration and professional advisers. The content of these policies is critical to the institution's addressing the new employment realities in a manner consistent with the Church's teachings on labor matters and the needs of these kinds of institutions.

The social encyclicals do not contain a mandate that there be one and only one vehicle for achieving social justice in ecclesiastical or eleemosynary institutions. These institutions really do have dimensions that commercial and industrial enterprises lack. Nonetheless, one cannot legitimately point to these dimensions as an excuse to avoid the mandates to accord employees social justice. It is beyond this chapter's scope to discuss alternatives to the industrial model in great detail, but examples worth considering include the formation of an employee council to deal with a variety of issues including issues related to employment, or, employee participation on boards and advisory committees.

The Necessity for New Ideas

This is a time for plain talk. The increased number of lay employees and the 1974 National Labor Relations Act amendments have created a new reality for Catholic health care institutions. They have brought employees' needs and employees' rights to the forefront. This state of affairs is going to exist for a long time.

There are no neatly packaged formulas for dealing with this new reality. Boards and administrations cannot avoid the hard questions by pointing to the social encyclicals or their institutions' mission or even by referring the whole matter to professionals. If they try to do so, they will find themselves impaled on either the theological or managerial aspects of their institutions. Anyone offering such quick and easy solutions is selling snake oil.

There is a clear need for new ideas to deal with the new reality. Although the social encyclicals, the institution's mission, and the use of professionals do not provide complete solutions, they are excellent starting points for development of these new ideas. Any new ideas must be tested against the theological traditions and functional integrity on which these institutions are built. Critically, the inquiry should not be used as strategem to delay or deny social justice.

Before creative thought can begin, those in the Catholic health care system must transfer the debate from the simplistic question of whether Catholic facilities should have unions to more useful areas of inquiry. A key issue is how can Catholic facilities improve communication to accord employees real input on their employment status and still maintain the institution's integrity. Unions or organizations of differing kinds will be more or less useful in differing situations. Solutions are not going to be found among platitudes and generalities but among the specifics of specific institutions.

Now is the time for inquiry and experimentation. While this enterprise is going forward, we should expect and tolerate differing solutions in various institutions, maybe even in various parts of the same institution. We should also learn to live with the possibility that there may be more than one acceptable long term solution.

---

1. Msgr. George G. Higgins, "Issues of Justice and Peace," *Chicago Studies,* Vol. 20, No. 2 (Summer, 1981), pp. 191-206.

2. Rev. John Coleman, SJ, quoted in *Origins,* Vol. 11, No. 3, June 4, 1981.
3. Pope John XXIII, *Mater et Magistra* (Boston: St. Paul Editions, Daughters of St. Paul, 1961), p. 10.
4. Pope Pius XI, *Quadragesimo Anno* (Boston: St. Paul Editions, Daughters of St. Paul, 1931), p. 45.
5. Pope John XXIII, *Mater et Magistra* (Boston: St. Paul Editions, Daughters of St. Paul, 1961), p. 15.
6. Pope John XXIII, *Mater et Magistra,* p. 15.
7. Pope Paul VI, *Octogesima Adveniens* (Boston: St. Paul Editions, Daughters of St. Paul, 1971), p. 15.
8. Synod of Bishops, *Justice in the World* (Washington: United States Catholic Conference, 1972), p. 44.

DISCUSSION QUESTIONS

1. What are the problems of applying the social teachings of the Church, written for the industrial sector, to religiously sponsored health care institutions?

2. Do we, or should we, prefer managerial concerns (economics of labor and scale, for example) to theological concerns in an effort to sponsor effective apostolates, such as health care institutions?

3. Trace the historical context of the Church's teaching on social justice.

4. Give examples of how changes in culture have caused changes in Church teaching.

5. What are the factors operative in the limitations of workers' rights?

6. What do the Church's teachings say specifically about workers in charitable or ecclesiastical institutions?

7. How does the Catholic health care facility's identity as an institution of apostolic charity affect the role of the worker in that institution?

8. What is the role of the board of directors in the Catholic health care facility?

9. What is the role of the administration in the Catholic health care facility?

10. What is the role of outside professionals, such as lawyers, accountants, and management consultants in the Catholic health care facility?

11. How should the institution's identity as a Catholic health care facility affect the actions and the advice of professional consultants and attorneys?

12. What alternatives exist to the classic labor-management conflict in the nonindustrial, charitable provision of services employment setting?

CHAPTER **5**

SERVICE STRIKES: THE NEW MORAL DILEMMA

Rev. Eugene F. Lauer, STD

When the first strikes by U.S. "service" employees took place in the early 1960s, many Americans experienced ambivalent feelings. We have a proud tradition of being "for the working person," for the "underdog" in our democratic society. Teachers, nurses, hospital aides, and other public service employees were traditionally paid less than workers in industry. It seemed only just that they gain more control over their economic fate and have more power to shape the policies that controlled their work situations.

On the other hand, there was an uneasy sense that something was not quite right about a teacher refusing to teach because of a salary dispute with the local school board; there was a certain hesitation about completely supporting a nurse who refused to care for patients until a new fringe-benefit package had been negotiated. There was a feeling that, in the matter of striking, a teacher, nurse, or hospital aide was essentially different from an assembly-line worker in an automobile plant.

This ambivalence, to my knowledge, has never been resolved. Each time service employees strike, they receive strong support when it is emphasized that they are still treated less equitably than their counterparts in industry. And they receive equally strong disapproval when one sees innocent clients deprived of a valuable human service.

In this chapter I will attempt to bring some clarity to this ambivalent state of feelings of the past two decades. I contend that the lack of clarity about service strikes comes from the following fact: The idea of a strike was transferred from the arena of profit-making industry to the arena of nonprofit human services without an ideological transition.

Fr. Lauer is visiting professor of religious studies, Seton Hill College, Greensburg, PA.

Is a cessation of work by a person who is involved in the manufacture of structural steel the same reality as cessation of work by a guidance counselor? Should the same terms be used to describe both events? Can the same principles be used to determine the justice of the two realities, or are they so different that each must be approached with its own unique principles? At the very least, there are *some* major differences in the two phenomena that must be taken into account in determining an ethic for a service strike.

The Anatomy of an Industrial Strike

To expose these differences clearly, let us first review the nature and purpose of the industrial strike, as it developed from the beginning of the Industrial Revolution. Workers organized and went on strike, that is, stopped working as a group, to pressure their employers into meeting their demands for higher wages and better working conditions. The logical construct of their action was simple and direct. When they stopped working, no further goods were produced. The owners could make no profit on their investment because they had no goods to sell.

In such a situation, it was clear that the persons responsible for the low wages and poor working conditions were directly pressured by the work stoppage. In effect, the workers were saying, ''If you don't pay us just wages, we will see to it that you make no profit.'' Most human beings will respond with admiration to such a direct confrontation. The workers felt that they had reasonable demands, that the owners were the ones responsible for meeting those demands, and the owners would be directly addressed—and inconvenienced or even made to suffer—by the work stoppage.

It would be accurate to conclude that consumers are indirectly inconvenienced, by a strike. If a product is not manufactured, it is not available for general purchase and use by the public. In a free-enterprise society such as ours, however, the real inconvenience or negative impact is minimal, perhaps nonexistent. Other companies, whose employees are not on strike, manufacture similar products (unless it is a national strike). In effect, this continuation of production by other companies actually helps the strikers. The public remains unaffected and perhaps supportive of the strikers, and the other companies continue to make a profit; *only* the investors and owners of the striking company are negatively affected. These investors see that the public can manage without them, they see their competitors making money, and they see that the primary reason for the original investment, to make a profit, is directly thwarted. They alone feel the pressure of the work stoppage.

I admit that this is a simplistic explanation, but it does describe the primary effect of a strike. The complexities of industry today do not allow most strikes to be so clear cut in their process and effects. Nonetheless, I maintain that the essentials of this description are verified in almost every successful industrial strike.

When management prepares by stockpiling and making short term investments, admittedly the situation changes and the force of a strike is diffused, since the company continues to make a profit. But this only confirms one of my major points, that the attack on profit making was and is the major legitimate pressure of a strike. Take away their profits, and the owners are literally *forced* to deal more directly and authentically with their employees.

The Anatomy of a Service Strike

When profit is removed, the rationale for setting up the work system (school, hospital, counseling center) changes. To describe the nature of the change as precisely as I can, I will use as my term of comparison the situation that is the direct opposite of the profit-making investment situation, the *client-centered, nonprofit, directly delivered, necessary human service* (nursing, teaching, counseling). There are service areas that stand "in between" (public transportation, mail service, and so on) that are not so clearly distinguished from the industrial arena. I think that it is sufficiently clear to say that some principles from both forums will apply to such services. For the moment, let me concentrate on the area of sharpest distinction.

By *client-centered,* I mean a service in which the client's welfare is the dominant concern in setting up the service. No product is involved, and no business goals are set. The primary goal is to provide a specific kind of help to human beings who need it.

I specify here *nonprofit* because some services are set up as profit-making businesses (e.g., some business and technical schools). I purposely intend to exclude such enterprises from this discussion, because they are at least somewhat (if not primarily) accountable to the principles that apply to profit-making industry. Public schools, public hospitals, church-related schools and hospitals, public counseling agencies, homes for the handicapped, and church-related long-term care facilities generally belong in the category of the non-profit-making client-centered services.

By *necessary* I mean those services that are either by their nature or by the developed needs of society crucial and essential for living a reasonably fulfilling human life in any given society. Health care is necessary by its very nature; education has become necessary because of our society's development; counseling can be necessary to cope with various physical, spiritual, and emotional crises.

By *directly delivered* I mean a service in which the worker is in actual contact with the client. A physician, a teacher, a nurse, or a counselor works by communicating the benefit of a special skill directly to the client. I am not including *indirect services* such as maintenance personnel at health care institutions and schools, people involved in transportation to such institutions, and so on.

The Specific Differences
The Client's Position

The most significant difference between an industrial strike and a service strike is that, in industry, the direct pressure of the work stoppage is placed on the owner or manager. In a service strike, the direct pressure is placed on the client. To put it another way, the service strike can be effective only if the client's needs are not being fulfilled. Should someone else give the same care to the client that the striker was giving, that person could be named a *strike breaker*. He or she would be diffusing the pressure of the strike by seeing to it that the client's life could go on as normal, as though there were no strike.

This difference points to a weakness in the use of strikes by service personnel. The strikers themselves *do not want the client to be hurt*. They desire, rather, to cause enough inconvenience to pressure the school board or the hospital board into resolving the dispute. Hence, some leaders of service unions have distinguished the client's *welfare* from the client's *health and safety*. The strike does intend to disturb the client's *welfare,* but never his or her health or safety. *Welfare* means those valuable effects of a service that help a person to grow, to learn, and to enjoy life fully: good education, supervised recreation, participation in the arts, regular medical check-ups, and so forth. These benefits, if withheld, can be recovered later. Withholding them causes no permanent damage to the client.

Health and safety can be understood here in the normal usage of these terms, but with one important modification. They include those benefits from human services that, if withheld, are not recoverable or are recoverable only with some enduring impact on the client (for example, a broken bone that is not attended to, a severe depression that is not treated). Hence, critical to the distinction between the client's *welfare* and *health and safety* is the idea of *recoverability*.

Admittedly, this distinction is not always immediately apparent in a situation; its intent, however, is clear. The strike is intended to disrupt the normal, comfortable pattern of things, to shock the community (and even the client!) into an awareness of the service's value, and to force everyone involved to reevaluate whether the service workers are being treated fairly in the delivery system.

Having made this distinction, let me return to the observation of why this fact is a weakness in the use of strikes by service personnel. Since the strikers are genuinely concerned about their clients' health and safety, they may cause only a limited amount of inconvenience (and, therefore, only a limited amount of pressure) in their strike. They must cease their pressure once their clients' health or safety seems to be affected. (I might add here that if, after many months, the strike is still only an inconvenience to the client's general welfare, the public might begin to wonder about the value of the service.)

Hence, the effectiveness of service strikes is limited from the start. The strikers know that the strike can only go "so far"; then, the strikers themselves are pressured to end it, lest they be accused of wanting to inflict harm on their clients. The longer the strike lasts, the more pressure there is on the striker to perform the service, and the greater the client's need becomes. The industrial striker experiences no such limitations. Work can be stopped for many months (presumably preventing a profit on the industrial investment) and thus the pressure on the capitalist becomes more intense.

When one views how the pressure in the situation is constructed, a second weakness emerges in the use of strikes by service personnel. The strike is intended to pressure the school board, the hospital board, or the like. But the client is the one who feels the pressure directly. The board experiences it only indirectly, presumably because it also cares about the client and wishes to see the services resumed. The client is literally caught in the middle and, although most important, is powerless.

It is the client's powerlessness that causes a very practical moral-ethical reflection. Can it be just to place a client who is receiving a necessary service into a position where there is no opportunity to receive the service? It has been considered "strike breaking" for anyone else to supply the service. Hence, the service union would be in a position of saying to the client not only, "We will not serve you in this dispute," but also "You will be acting in an antagonistic way if you seek the service from anyone else."

The client's powerlessness is further emphasized by the fact that the client cannot resolve the dispute. Resolution is in the hands of the strikers and management. The client remains powerlessly "in between" until the two sides can reach an agreement.

Finally, the third significant difference between industrial strikes and service strikes is that when workers stop manufacturing a product in an industrial strike, they cause no direct tension with the person who would buy or use that product. The purchaser of an automobile or an electric appliance generally does not know the worker who manufactured it. In a service strike, the client not only knows the service worker but has probably come to feel that the worker is genuinely concerned about his or her needs. Almost always, there is a sense of an authentically developed personal relationship. Work stoppages in human services may cast some cloud on these personal relationships, even when it is clear that the strike's *intent* is to pressure the third party employer, not the client.

The Striker's Position

Several service union leaders whom I interviewed expressed very clearly the position the service striker is in. The striker is weighing personal needs against the client's needs. The strikers are judging that their need for just compensation, just working conditions, or whatever is greater than the client's need to receive the service.

The distinction that I made before is useful here. Members of service unions feel justified in placing their own welfare on the same plane as their clients', but they will not give it greater value than their clients' health and safety. Hence, the strikers admittedly place a direct pressure on the client whose welfare is hindered by the lack of a service in the interest of promoting the strikers' welfare.

According to our traditional understanding of equity, this seems to be a just action. Some would argue—as one union leader did eloquently in an interview—that it is extremely beneficial for the self-esteem of service workers to emphasize their own needs and to see them as valuable and worth fighting for. It is both unfair and unrealistic to act as though only the client has needs.

One professional arbitrator whom I interviewed suggested that there was a historical reason why the public mentality does not easily allow service workers to put their own needs on the same level as client needs. In the not too distant past, many, if not most, of the services now supplied by professionals were done by clergy and religious; they had taken a vow of poverty and were not supposed to be interested in their own personal property, but were supposed to give their lives totally for others with no concern for self. When a service worker bargains for the betterment of his or her own position, society has a beneath-the-surface feeling that this is an "indecent" way to behave. But, is it not just to say that client and service worker both, as human beings, have genuine needs? That it is fair to evaluate those needs in any conflict situation and decide which are presently greater?

A second observation about the striker's position shows yet another significant difference between a service strike and an industrial strike, one that leads to a complication regarding the solidarity of a striking service union. In an industrial strike, the striker is generally faced with the choice of siding with fellow workers or with management. In such a situation, it is easy to develop a solidarity and, often, to demand it if management is clearly unjust.

In a service strike, a third party, the client, is immediately involved. In fact, the client is more directly involved than management, since the client feels the direct effect of the work stoppage. The striker, therefore, is in the midst of a more complex decision-making process in terms of solidarity with fellow workers. A striker could agree perfectly with all the union's positions, feel that management is indeed unjust, and still have such a concern for the client that he or she would want to serve the client's needs, for example, by tutoring high school seniors or by serving old people in a long-term care facility. Individual strikers might authentically make the decision that such service is necessary from the very nature of their profession, no matter where the issues of wages and working conditions stood. The industrial striker faces no such conflict.

This specific difference leads to the question: Does the individual striker have the right to independent ideals, even if it causes serious cracks in the union's solidarity? Is it just for individual service workers to decide to serve clients during a strike, even when the union's demands are obviously just? I will answer this question a little further on in the chapter.

Management's Role

The first and most significant observation to be made about management in service strikes is that it has invested no money in the enterprise and is not involved to make a profit. Its involvement (at least from the *nature* of "boards," although not necessarily always the *fact*) stems from an interest in promoting the service involved, in overseeing the process of the delivery of a service, and in integrating all the facets of the service in such a way that public interest is served.

Because of the different role of management, the primary and immediate pressure of a strike as developed in industry is instantly removed. The immediate pressure felt by the capitalist, that profits will be endangered, is not present in a service strike. In fact, the board feels no direct pressure of any kind.

Indirectly the board will feel pressure from the general public if the public concludes that the board is at fault in the strike. The board may also feel some pressure from the families of clients who are upset by the withdrawal of the services. But neither pressure is direct and neither is certain to occur. The public and the families of clients may decide that the union is at fault and support the board. The only certain and direct pressure is what the client experiences: A needed service is not available.

The construction of the pressure here leads to an unfortunate conclusion, one that tends to weaken a service strike's value. A well-disposed, genuinely interested, caring board will feel more pressure from a strike than a manipulative, uncaring board. The well-disposed group will work much harder to restore the service and to evaluate the union's demands. The manipulative group will care less about the clients, be less ready to face the demands, do everything in its power to impugn the union. Hence, the pressure tactic, the strike, will tend to affect good people and will have far less value with people who need to be affected the most!

Is There an Alternative to Striking?

Many of the service union people whom I interviewed readily admitted the shortcomings involved in striking. They generally added, however, that strikes are somewhat effective and that presently there is ''no other way'' to exert pressure—albeit indirect pressure—on the boards responsible for the less than adequate salaries, working conditions, and so on that service workers experience.

In my analysis, there are two challenges that this attitude must face. The first is that such an attitude *could* mean a willingness to use unethical measures to bring about just results, if no ethical means existed. I am not here presuming what the entire paper intends to discuss, that is, the morality of service strikes. I am only pointing out that if circumstances in any crisis were such that only one means of pressure were available to a group of good, well-intentioned people and that means were immoral, then the group would have no right to choose it. In a "values" approach to morality, the end does not justify the means. The means must be evaluated in terms of its inherent moral value, even if it is the only means available.

The second challenge is more psychological than philosophical or theological. It is well explained by a conversation that I once had with a retired construction worker who was reminiscing about his days working on the first U.S. "skyscrapers" built in the early 1900s. "We had a rule of thumb," he said, "that there would probably be one serious accident to a worker per story of the building. Twenty stores to a building? You're going to have 20 serious injuries, including some deaths." He explained that the cost of building safer scaffolding and taking more extensive safety measures was considered prohibitive by management. But then came unions and a more humanitarian way of regarding the workers. No longer could management balance human lives with costs as starkly as one story—one accident.

The kind of thinking this story implies could also be applied to the "no other way" mentality in service strikes. Perhaps service workers, like all other human beings, will not reach for another way, will not strain to fashion one, until they are forced to do so. Human nature has a tendency to follow "the pathway of least resistance," just as material creation does. Hence, if strikes seem to be effective in capitalist-industrial confrontations, it is easy for people to conclude that this ready-made and tested format may be used in any area of work. And, if it has in some instances provided service workers with better wages and working conditions, there is a further tendency among people to say, "Why stop something that seems to be working? Go with a winner!" It is difficult to get people to evaluate the morality of something that seems, at least on the surface, to have some good practical effects.

The more a process is used, the more acceptable it becomes. After only 20 years of service strikes, they seem to be in some sense already "ordinary" parts of America. We assume that they will take place. The more frequently we do something, the less argument we need to judge it ethical. It is important, therefore, to cut through the mentality of "no other way" to discover if service strikes are ethical and, if so, to face the equally important question of their value in resolving service worker-management conflicts.

Binding Arbitration as an Alternative

The one well-known "other way" to handle a worker-management conflict without striking is binding arbitration. How valuable is binding arbitration in preventing service strikes? Is it sufficiently valuable that both the service workers' union and management should use it to avert strikes? Let us analyze the dynamics of the binding arbitration process to see how it may help to resolve some of the tensions among service workers, clients, and management.

Binding arbitration's most obvious value in a confrontation between service workers and management is that it allows the innocent party, the client, to be free of any disruption in service. The client's needs continue to be met by the service workers while the dispute is being settled. There is no tension in the service worker-client relationship. A (presumably) objective and just-minded third party sees to it that the workers' rights and needs are adequately addressed.

But those drawbacks to binding arbitration, which have been noted when the process has been used in industrial confrontation, are also present when the process is used in service confrontations. Binding arbitration puts any worker in the position of having to be "cared for" by a third party. Rather than allowing the service workers to "fight their own battles," this process allows the workers to state their needs and their positions and then to step aside and let others make the final decisions that they, the workers, are bound to accept. The strength, self-esteem, and sense of unity that come from personally facing confrontation are absent, or at least diluted, in a union that is committed to binding arbitration.

A second criticism of binding arbitration applies specifically to service work. The monies involved in a service workers-management confrontation do not ordinarily come from private capital investments. They usually come from taxes, from voluntary contributions of persons or philanthropic institutions, or from fees paid directly by the clients. It would seem that the parties responsible for the ministration of these monies are absolving themselves of their responsibilities by inviting a third party to make a final judgment for them. A school board, a hospital board, or a state legislature has a fundamental duty to its constituents to use wisely and effectively the monies entrusted to it to deliver various services. To concede this duty to another party could be seen as a yielding of responsible stewardship.

In summary, we may conclude that binding arbitration can be sometimes valuable for resolving service worker-managment conflicts. Because of the defects in the process that have been pointed out above, however, one could hardly conclude that it is the ideal way to resolve a dispute and that it must always be used in place of a strike. Human ingenuity should be able to devise even more appropriate and effective ways of procuring justice for service workers, other than strikes and binding arbitration.

Future Directions

I would like to summarize the observations that I have made about service strikes under two headings: an evaluation of such strikes' morality or ethics and an evaluation of their human value.

From my analyses of the nature of the conflict between service workers and management, I would conclude that a service strike that disturbs only the clients' "present welfare" is an ethical means for bringing about just treatment of service workers. I emphasize in this conclusion the word *welfare*. Strikes that would endanger clients' health or safety would be a direct violation of the Christian principle of authentic concern (love) for one's neighbor. To harm others to gain even what is just for oneself contradicts basic charity.

There is a further clarification to be made about clients' *welfare*. I have carefully stated that strikes that disturb clients' *present welfare* may be judged ethical and moral. I mean to exclude strikes that would permanently inhibit some human development in the client, for example, a school strike that would cause students to lose college scholarships, or a public agency's strike that would stop an urgent counseling process. I admit that, practically speaking, it is very difficult to make this distinction about a client's welfare in each individual case. I defend, however, the distinction by pointing to the fact that the development of some people is permanently stunted because of delay in receiving a necessary human service. To delay a service purposely and consciously in such a situation would be contrary to the mandates of Christian charity.

On the other hand, it is basically just and honest for service workers to weigh their needs and just deserts (their *ordinary welfare*) against their clients' needs. The Christian command to "love thy neighbor" includes self as an object of "neighborly love." To develop oneself into an image of God is a divine command. To care for oneself is a basic duty, rooted in the Judaeo-Christian teaching that all creation, including self, is good and that all creation is a reflection of the divine. As we have an obligation to discover and bring out the divine reflections in all of God's reality, so we have a duty to bring out that "divinity" in self. This is not a vain task. It is a God-recognizing task.

In more traditional moral theology terms, one's self is one of the recipients of distributive justice. To form a sound and just society, all people should strive to distribute the goods of society equitably to all the members of society (including themselves); all have the duty to see to it that everyone's needs are met, including their own. To judge one's own needs to be greater than another person's in any individual situation need not be selfish, but simply a fact.

Finally, Christian theology contains no obligation to altruism. It is a simplistic explanation of the Sermon on the Mount to assert that the needs of others must always come before one's own, no matter what those needs are. It is genuinely Christian to be discerning about fulfilling others' needs.

A service strike based on the fact that workers' ordinary welfare is presently more important than clients' ordinary welfare can be an ethical means for bringing about just treatment for the workers. The human *value* of service strikes is quite a different issue. Here my conclusion addresses the effectiveness of such strikes in the light of their overall impact on clients, the public, service delivery systems, and the workers themselves. I conclude that a service strike is so limited in its application and that there are so many conditions on the procedure of the strike that such strikes will always be an anemic means for dealing with service worker-management conflicts. Put in another way, a strike ill fits the kind of human dynamic that is present in the delivery of client-centered, nonprofit, directly delivered human services. From my analysis of the differences between industrial strikes and service strikes, I conclude that four prominent limitations and conditions on service strikes render them ill fitting in the service work arena.

- *A strike by a service workers' union can never go ''all-out'' in its struggle for justice.* As soon as it nears endangering the health or safety of the clients involved or even begins to cause some irrecoverable damage to their welfare, the strikers must pull back and see to it that the clients' needs are met. From the first moment that the workers cease work, this dilemma impedes them, because the pressure of the strike is directly on the clients and only indirectly on the ''culprit.''

- *The public's sympathy will always be with the innocent client who stands powerless in the middle of the conflict.* The client did not cause the injustice; the client cannot correct the injustice (at least not directly). A means of pressure that must always have an innocent party trapped inside the conflict will never, practically speaking, have a sufficient clarity about it for society to agree wholeheartedly that it is just. By its very nature (not by circumstances) a service strike will always have a haze surrounding it, a cloud of unclarity diluting its forcefulness.

• *Service strikes will generally cause some disruption to the human relationship between the client and the worker.* The client depends on the worker's competence and skill and recognizes a genuine concern in the worker as the service is delivered. It is humanly impossible for all clients (in their dependent role of client) to feel that the worker's needs are not primary, that the service must therefore cease, that the cessation of the service is the "only way" to handle a conflict with management. To expect every client-worker relationship to resume smoothly after a strike is unrealistic.

• *It is not just to expect that all members of a service workers' union be obliged to place their needs before clients' needs.* Although we have argued that there is no obligation in Christianity to be altruistic, we can argue with equal force that there is no obligation *not to be.* Individual service workers, or even groups of workers, can justly maintain that their primary motivation for entering their particular service field is to serve and that everything else is secondary. They have a right to their idealism (especially if they are suggesting other ways to pressure management that do not involve the client). A solidarity of service workers in strikes cannot exist in the same way that it does with industrial unions. There could hardly be an altruistic reason for an assembly-line worker in an automobile plant to return to work during a strike. There can often be an altruistic reason for a teacher to tutor a student during a strike as college board examinations draw near or for a nurse to care for an aging and very ill patient during a strike.

It would thus seem that the healthiest direction for service unions to take would be to devise methods of confrontation that directly pressure management without involving the powerless client.

DISCUSSION QUESTIONS

1. What is the basis of the ambivalency felt concerning strikes in the public-service sector?

2. What is the nature and purpose of an industrial strike?

3. What is the primary effect of an industrial strike?

4. What are the characteristics of work in the service sector?

5. What distinction do service-strikers make between a client's welfare and his or her health or safety?

6. What limits does a client's health or safety place on a service strike?

7. How do these limits compare with those that may exist in the industrial strike model?

8. Is it just for social service workers to weigh their needs against those of the client?

9. How are worker solidarity and personal ideals in a social service strike affected by the presence of the client?

10. What is the role of management in social service strikes?

11. What alternatives to the social service strike exist to exert pressure on management regarding wages and working conditions?

12. To what extent must social service workers examine the morality of the "means," i.e., the strike, in seeking to reach the just end of a fair wage and working conditions?

13. Is binding arbitration an effective means to prevent service strikes?

14. What are the benefits and drawbacks of binding arbitration in the social services sector?

15. Of what effect is the distinction between a client's welfare and safety in evaluating the morality of a social service strike?

16. What obligation exists in Christian theology to give the needs of others priority over our own?

17. What difference exists between the ethics of service strikes and the value of service strikes?

CHAPTER **6**

MEMBERS OF RELIGIOUS COMMUNITIES AND UNIONS

Rev. Jordan F. Hite, TOR, JD, JCL

Whether religious should participate in the labor relations process is a question of recent origin. The area I will address in this chapter is not the individual religious who was a union member before entering religious life and retains membership while continuing similar employment as a religious, nor the religious who joins a labor organization as a result of his or her employment. The primary focus here is on the religious employed at a health care facility operated by a religious community who may be employed in areas of work in which some employees are seeking representation by a labor organization.

This chapter will chart the development of the National Labor Relations Act (NLRA) from 1971 to the present, summarize the conclusions that can be drawn, and discuss the implications, underlying issues, and attitudes that do or should form a part of the decision-making process for religious on labor organizations and the institutions at which they are employed. Since other chapters in this book focus on the facilities religious institutes operate, this chapter will focus on individual religious, although some overlapping of concerns may be expected.

From 1971 to 1981 a series of 10 cases has been decided by the National Labor Relations Board (NLRB),[1] two of which have been reviewed by the courts. The cases have involved colleges, hospitals, and nursing homes. They will be discussed in chronological order, although notice should be taken of those which terminated with the NLRB decision and those which were reviewed by the courts. The nature of the institution (college, hospital, or nursing home) has not been an important factor in decisions thus far.

Fr. Hite is provincial director of personnel, Third Order Regular of St. Francis, Loretto, Pa.

Legal History

The initial decision by the NLRB was in 1971 in the case of *Fordham University*.[2] Fordham is affiliated with the Society of Jesus. It is incorporated, but the NLRB opinion does not describe Fordham's corporate structure. The university had 70 Jesuits on the faculty. The petitioning labor organization argued for the inclusion of the Jesuits in the bargaining unit. Fordham did not argue for or against this inclusion. Jesuits were hired by the same process used for all other faculty, and their salaries and terms of employment were determined in the same manner as for other faculty. If a Jesuit left the community, he could remain a faculty member, continue at his former salary, and accept tenure even over the objection of the Jesuit community.

Based on these facts, the NLRB held that the Jesuits would be included in the bargaining unit because no evidence showed that membership in the Jesuits was in any way inconsistent with collective bargaining in regard to a Jesuit's salary or other terms or conditions of employment.

Two years later the NLRB, in *Seton Hill College*,[3] decided the first case in which the union seeking to represent employees of an institution operated by a religious community argued to exclude the members of the religious community from voting in the representation election. Legal title to the property of Seton Hill was held by the Sisters of Charity. The college was incorporated and had a 99-year lease to the college property, for which it paid $1 per year. The college bylaws provided that it was to be governed by a board of trustees of between 20 and 30 members; 50 percent of the board was to be sisters who had professed perpetual vows, and 50 percent was to be selected from laypersons. The mother general of the sisters was a board member.

The procedure for hiring a member of the community as a faculty member was that the Mother General would receive a request from the college for a faculty member and would then refer sisters to the college as prospective faculty members. At this point, the sisters followed the same process for employment as the lay faculty. All hiring was approved by the president of the college, who was also a member of the community. All faculty, including sisters, were paid according to the same salary scale; all signed a standard employment contract, and all had similar teaching assignments.

According to the NLRB, sister faculty members were unlike members of the lay faculty because they professed vows of poverty and obedience. The vow of obedience was to the mother general and included a sister's assignment. Unlike the lay faculty, a sister did not receive her salary individually; it was paid to the community. As the NLRB described it, "pursuant to the vow of poverty undertaken by each sister, her wages less living expenses, are paid directly to the order." Although the NLRB's wording seems to indicate that the salaries are paid this way because of the vow of poverty, there is nothing about the vow that requires the particular manner of payment described. The community, by contractual agreement, returned to the college, in the form of an annual gift, that part of the salaries not used by the sisters for living expenses. The sisters also had a separate medical insurance and pension plan.

The NLRB held that although the work and the working conditions of both the lay faculty and the sisters were identical, their interests were different. The sisters' relationship to the college was seen as more complex than that of the lay faculty, which was seen as only an employer-employee relationship. A sister is an employee and an employer at the same time because the college is owned and administered by the community. A sister has vowed obedience to the mother general, who is also a member of the board. Thus, if a sister were a member of the bargaining unit, she would be subject to conflicting loyalties. The NLRB also stated that the sisters would not be as interested in salaries as lay faculty because they had no families to support and that the vow of poverty removes interest in economic reward. In addition, the sisters contracted to return a substantial part of their "nominal wages" to the college. All the above plus the separate fringe benefits program was held by the NLRB as sufficient to find that the groups had different interests and should not be part of the same faculty bargaining unit. The NLRB added a note to its decision stating that *Seton Hill* overruled *Fordham University* to the extent that the latter was inconsistent with *Seton Hill.*

Five days after *Seton Hill,* the NLRB issued a decision in *Carroll Manor Nursing Home.*[4] This time the employer was a nursing home owned and operated by the Carmelite Sisters in Maryland. The facts showed that the sisters who worked for the nursing home were all members of the community that owned the home. The sisters did the same work and worked the same hours as the lay employees but were on a separate payroll. The sisters were paid monthly, and their total monthly salary of $3,000 was reflected by a bookkeeping entry, rather than by a cash payment to the individual sister. The salary was held in a common fund and given to the sisters according to their personal needs. Any money not used for living expenses was forwarded to the motherhouse. The NLRB noted that the sisters professed vows of poverty and obedience, but did not discuss them at all. Whether the NLRB thought the foregoing facts were a result of the vows of poverty and obedience is not discernible from its opinion.

The NLRB held that "on the basis of the foregoing, we find that the sisters have special interests resulting in a special employment relationship clearly different from that of other employees. Accordingly, we exclude them from the unit," citing *Seton Hill* as authority for its ruling.

In 1975 the NLRB decided the case of *Saint Anthony Center*,[5] 1 of 14 health care facilities owned and operated by the Sisters of Charity of the Incarnate Word. All 14 facilities, including Saint Anthony Center, are subject to a parent corporation that has the superior general as president of the board of directors. The top management official of each institution is a member of the Sisters of Charity who is nominated to the position by the superior general. The parent corporation reserves control of certain operations of each of the facilities. The controlled operations include approval of certain capital and real estate transactions, making contracts in excess of a specific amount, and changing employee benefits. In addition, the parent corporation evaluates and approves each institution's budget.

The terms of the sisters' employment were set out in a separate contract between Saint Anthony Center and the Sisters of Charity. The sisters were not paid individually; they lived in a convent in the center, and the discipline of sister-employees was taken through different administrative channels. The sisters were excluded from the bargaining unit because they had different economic interests and different terms of employment and because of the conflicting loyalties that could result from "simultaneous membership" in the employee bargaining unit and the religious community that owns and operates Saint Anthony Center.

In 1976 the NLRB decided the cases of *Saint Rose de Lima Hospital, Incorporated*[6] and *D'Youville College*.[7] In *Saint Rose de Lima* the hospital board of trustees consisted of five Sisters of Saint Dominic and four laypersons. The hospital administrator was a member of the Sisters of Saint Dominic and also a member of the board. Two sisters were employed as registered nurses by the hospital. The petitioning labor organization argued that the sister-nurses should be excluded from the bargaining unit, and the NLRB accepted the argument based on the authority of *Seton Hill* and *Saint Anthony Center*.

In *D'Youville College* the NLRB overruled a regional director who had excluded four Grey Nun faculty from the bargaining unit based on *Seton Hill*. The NLRB found *D'Youville* different from *Seton Hill* in two significant regards:

- D'Youville's corporate structure provided that no more than one-third of the board of trustees could be members of any religious institutes, including the Grey Nuns, and thus they did not own or administer the college as in *Seton Hill*. Therefore, there was no basis for holding that the four nuns were in any manner affiliated with the college except in their capacity as faculty members.
- In *D'Youville* the petitioning union specifically included the religious in the bargaining unit. Thus, although the NLRB noted the nuns had taken a vow of poverty and retained only necessary living expenses while returning the remainder to the college as a gift, much like the sisters in *Seton Hill,* the fact that the petitioning faculty had agreed to include the Grey Nuns in the unit along with the fact that there was no law or other over-riding policy consideration precluding such an inclusion, the NLRB accepted the Grey Nuns in the unit.

Between 1975 and 1977 the cases of *Niagara University*[8] and *Saint Francis College*[9] were decided by the NLRB and then appealed to a U.S. Court of Appeals.

In *Niagara University* v. *NLRB,* Niagara petitioned the Second Circuit Court of Appeals to review an NLRB order to bargain, contending that the NLRB erred in excluding 17 Eastern Province Vincentians from the bargaining unit. Niagara had a full-time faculty of 134 laypeople and 21 religious. The religious included 18 Vincentians, 17 of whom were members of the Eastern Province, which was associated with Niagara; the remainder were sisters from various communities. Niagara was governed by a 17-member board of trustees, of which not more than one third was to be Vincentians. The provincial of the Eastern Province of the Vincentians was required by university statute to be an ex-officio member of the board of trustees.

Both religious and lay faculty were employed at a common salary scale and had the same conditions of employment. The application of policies concerning probation, leave, promotion, academic freedom, university life, insurance, and retirement programs were the same for all. The Vincentians professed vows of poverty, chastity, obedience, and stability. The Vincentians did not sign a written contract, were not eligible for tenure, and could be reassigned by their superior at any time. Their salaries were paid directly to the community, and the community provided them with a monthly personal allowance.

The first issue dealt with by the court was the NLRB's contention that an identity of interest existed between the Vincentians and Niagara University similar to that in *Seton Hill*. The court, however, found that *Niagara* and *Seton Hill* were not alike because the Sisters of Charity held legal title to the property used by Seton Hill College, while the university corporation held legal title to the Niagara University property. In addition, the Vincentians could never constitute more than one third of the Niagara board of trustees. Therefore, the court held that there was no identity of interest between the Vincentian faculty and the university.

The second reason the NLRB offered for the exclusion of the Vincentians was their vow of poverty. The court held that there was no necessary connection between the vow of poverty and interest or lack of interest in salary. The language here is important, because it says that there is no real difference in these cases between unmarried lay professors who may choose to live an austere life and contribute a large portion of their salaries to charity and religious who do the same thing. Thus, the manner in which a person decides to spend his or her income was deemed irrelevant for both lay and religious faculty.

A third issue, which was decided by the NLRB and examined by the court, concerned the vow of obedience. The union argued that the vow of obedience disqualified all religious faculty from inclusion in the bargaining unit. The court rejected that argument, saying that the obligations of the vow of obedience are concerned with matters of religion and not with an individual's professional conduct as a professor nor with faculty activities concerning labor unions or other professional organizations.

The final question left for the Court of Appeals to decide was whether the fact that the Vincentians made a gift to the university precluded the Vincentian faculty from being members of the bargaining unit. The NLRB argued that, in essence, the Vincentians were making a salary "kickback" to their employer.

The court rejected the NLRB's argument by distinguishing the *Seton Hill* decision. In *Seton Hill* the sisters had a contractual obligation to return a portion of their salaries to the employer-college. The Eastern Province of the Vincentians, however, made a gift to the university, but there was no contract to return any portion of the salaries to Niagara. Since there was no obligation, there was no relationship between the Eastern Province Vincentians and the university that would distinguish them from lay faculty. This meant that the only remaining reason for excluding the Vincentians was the lay faculty's desire to exclude the religious, which the court found an insuffient rationale for exclusion.

About a month later, the Third Circuit Court of Appeals reached a decision in *NLRB* v. *Saint Francis College*. The record showed that Saint

Francis College was founded by the Franciscans and was controlled by the Franciscans until 1966, when laypersons were elected to the board of trustees; at that time, the college and the Franciscans began operating as two distinct, nonprofit entities. The Franciscans did not own the college, but the bylaws provided for a 15-member board of trustees, 8 of whom, including the chairman, must be Franciscans.

The Franciscan faculty members were hired in the same manner and by the same standards, were subject to the same salary scale, and worked under the same conditions as other faculty members. The Franciscans had their salaries sent directly to the monastery in which they lived, although there was testimony that a Franciscan could have had his salary sent to him individually if he so desired.

The monastery paid its members' living expenses from the total income of all the friars in residence, which included the earnings of friars not employed at the college. After the payment of living expenses, the monastery made a number of donations, with Saint Francis College as a prime beneficiary, although there was no contract obligating the Franciscans to donate any portion of the friars' salaries to the college.

Regarding fringe benefits, the college paid premiums for medical insurance for the lay faculty, who also participated in short-term income disability and pension plans. The Franciscans participated in the short-term income disability plan but not in the others.

Based on this evidence, the Franciscans were excluded from the bargaining unit by the decision of the NLRB's regional director, and the NLRB affirmed this decision. The exclusion again was based on the *Seton Hill* precedent.

The court dealt with two NLRB arguments in support of its position. First, the Franciscans were, in effect, paid substantially less than lay employees and received different fringe benefits. Thus, the Franciscans' economic interests differed significantly from those of the lay faculty. Second, the Franciscan faculty had a ''special and complex relationship'' with the college that would present a conflict of loyalties for the Franciscans.

In contending that the Franciscans' economic interests were significantly different from those of the lay faculty, the NLRB relied first on *Nazareth Regional High School*,[10] in which the Second Circuit Court upheld the exclusion of religious faculty members because they were paid at a substantially lower rate than the lay faculty. The NLRB argued that the Franciscans had the ''economic benefit'' of much less than they were paid because of their vow of poverty. It also argued that, because the monastery made a donation to the college of close to 50 percent of the Franciscan faculty salaries, the college was really only paying the Franciscans about half the salary it paid to lay faculty. The court dismissed this argument summarily, noting that the evidence was clear that the Franciscans did receive a full salary, thus making the *Nazareth* decision inapplicable. The court said that if it is irrelevant what the individual Franciscans do with their salaries, it must also be irrelevant that the monastery, to which they give their salaries, chooses to make a substantial gift to the employer-college. The court noted that the Franciscans themselves did not directly return a part of their salaries to the college. Rather, the monastery donated a portion of its income, which included earnings from outside sources. In addition, the monastery's donation was a gift, not an obligation. The court added that even if faculty members did return part of their salaries directly to the college, this would not be cause to exclude them from the bargaining unit. Thus, in this matter related to the vow of poverty, the court found no legal effect of the vow that would exclude religious from a bargaining unit.[11]

The second issue on appeal was whether there was a special and complex relationship between the Franciscan faculty and the college that would present a conflict of loyalties for the Franciscans. The NLRB argued that there was a group of overlapping relationships between the Franciscan faculty members, the college administration, and the board that would distinguish Franciscan interests from those of the lay faculty. The NLRB said of these relationships: some are adversary, some arise out of obedience, and some arise from identity of commitment.

The court found no adversary relationship between Franciscan and lay faculty, but rather concluded that both have an adversary relationship with the college. On the vow of obedience itself, the court said the record showed that it pertains only to religious matters and was irrelevant to the employee-employer relationship. The court rejected the argument based on identity of commitment between Franciscan faculty and college administration because the record contained no evidence of the nature of such commitments. In a footnote, the court added that the NLRB seemed to be calling its attention to a "general allegiance," aside from the vow of obedience, that Franciscans share because they are a close, fraternal group with a common religious commitment. Again, the court could find no evidence to show that anything in these relationships resulted in significant differences between lay and religious faculty concerning collective bargaining interests.

The court then decided that the NLRB abused its discretion in excluding the Franciscans from the bargaining unit and that its decision that the Franciscans lacked a community of interest with the lay faculty was arbitrary and unreasonable.

It is important to understand, as the court noted at both the outset and at the end of its opinion, that its decision was based purely on a consideration of its interpretation of the application of the NLRA and that, in its view, exclusion of the Franciscans was based on grounds that were neutral in terms of religion. This is important, because Saint Francis College had argued that the result of the NLRB decision was to violate the First Amendment regarding the Franciscans' religious freedom because it was based on the NLRB's interpretation of the operation of their religious vows.

Since the court decisions, the NLRB has decided two more cases. The first was *Mercy Hospital of Buffalo*.[12] In that case, the hospital bylaws provided that more than one half of the hospital's board of trustees must be members of the Sisters of Mercy. In addition, the hospital administrator was both a member of the Sisters of Mercy and a board member. Based on these facts, the NLRB refused to permit a sister to vote in a representation election, because as a member of the Sisters of Mercy, she was "related" to the employer hospital. The NLRB distinguished this from *Niagara University* by noting that the Vincentians did not hold legal title to the university property and that its members could not constitute more than one third of the board of trustees.

In a footnote, the NLRB in effect decided not to follow the Third Circuit Court of Appeals in *Saint Francis College* by stating:

In Saint Francis College the court alluded to the employer's contention that although a majority of the members of the board of trustees were Franciscans, the order did not own or administer the employer. To the extent that the court implicitly may have found that majority control of a board of trustees by a religious order does not constitute a basis for excluding members of that order from a bargaining unit, we respectfully disagree. In any event, as noted above, there exists here the additional factor that the hospital administrator is a member of the order.[13]

In 1981, the NLRB decided *Catholic Community Services*,[14] in which the petitioning labor organization contended that members of various religious institutes employed by Catholic Community Services should be excluded from the bargaining unit. The religious employees were subject to the same terms and conditions of employment as other employees, received the same rate of pay, performed the same job functions, and were subject to the same personnel policies. Some of the religious received part of their compensation in the form of living expenses, since they resided in the same building rented by the Catholic Community Services for a daycare center. The NLRB noted that although federal taxes are not withheld from the religious, this is because of the Internal Revenue Service (IRS) policies rather than any special employer treatment. In addition, one of the religious institutes whose member was an employee made voluntary contributions to the employer. Based on these facts, the NLRB held that no special relationship existed between Catholic Community Services and the religious employees; therefore, the religious shared a community of interest with the other employees and should be included in the bargaining unit.

Summary of the NLRA

In the following summary of the NLRA to date, it can be seen that the critical factors are:

1. The institution's corporate structure;[15]
2. The terms of employment; and
3. Whether the case was decided by the NLRB or one of the U.S. Courts of Appeal.

It makes no difference if the institution is a college, university, hospital, nursing home, or church social agency. The religious obligations of members of religious institutes may still be an important factor, especially before the NLRB. With the above in mind, I offer the following conclusions:

I. In cases decided by the NLRB and the courts, religious who have substantially different terms of employment or who receive a substantially different wage will be found not to have a community of interest with their coworkers and have been excluded from a bargaining unit.

   A. Hiring practices have not been the subject of discussion in these cases; however, since hiring practices (except the "hiring hall") are not the subject of collective bargaining, the fact that religious were hired by means of a different process than others would not exclude them from the bargaining unit. In the above cases, religious were hired in substantially the same manner as other employees.

   B. Religious will be excluded from the bargaining unit if they are paid at a different rate or have significantly different working conditions than other employees.

    C. Religious may refuse some fringe benefits and be included in the bargaining unit.

    D. The vow of poverty does not create a sufficient lack of interest in wages to exclude religious from the bargaining unit.

    E. The vow of obedience has not been a deciding factor in excluding religious from a bargaining unit; however, the NLRB's attempt to exclude religious as a result of a "special relationship" with an institution operated by a religious institutes appears to take account of the vow of obedience.

    F. Donation of services by religious would probably exclude them from a bargaining unit. The donation of a portion of a salary has not been allowed as a reason to exclude religious from a bargaining unit. The *Niagara* case distinguishes between voluntary and contractual salary donations.

    G. Religious may not be excluded from the bargaining unit if they do not receive their salary personally.

II. In cases decided by the NLRB where a majority of the board of trustees is required by the bylaws to be members of the sponsoring religious institute, the employee members of the religious institute will be excluded from the bargaining unit.

    A. In the case of *Saint Francis College* decided by the Third Circuit Court of Appeals, the fact that a majority of the board of trustees was, according to the bylaws, to be members of the sponsoring religious institute was not sufficient to prove a special relationship and cause the employee members of the institute to be excluded from the bargaining unit.

    B. Both *Seton Hill* and *Niagara* have focused on the issue of the importance of legal title to land and buildings, although its relevancy has never been explained. Nevertheless, it remains as a potential reason for excluding religious from a bargaining unit.

III. Religious can be included in the bargaining unit if the labor organization wishes to include them; however, in cases before the NLRB, it is still an open question where the religious institute has a majority on the board of trustees.

IV. So far, neither the NLRB nor the courts have reached any conclusions regarding the applicability of the First, Fifth, or Fourteenth Amendments or civil rights legislation in deciding whether religious should be excluded from a bargaining unit.

V. It has not yet been decided whether Catholic health care organizations are excluded from the NLRB's jurisdiction.[16]

The Decision To Join the Union

At the heart of the legal process is the question why labor organizations have, for the most part, objected to religious being included in the bargaining unit and why Catholic institutions have supported their inclusion. The answer seems to be that labor organizations expect the majority of religious to vote against them. The cases, of course, do not indicate if the labor organizations were aware of the manner in which religious would vote; however, it seems safe to assume that labor organizations did not argue to exclude employees whom they expected to vote for the union. If it is true that labor organizations expected religious employees to vote against them, regardless of how they reached this conclusion, it may be asked what reasons would motivate a religious to vote for or against a labor organization.

A religious would favor a labor organization for some of the same reasons as any other employee. Religious need to feel secure in their jobs, to have appropriate working conditions, to be protected by tenure or seniority, to receive appropriate wage and retirement benefits, and to be a part of a collective voice that speaks to the institution's administration.

Although there is no statistical data on the matter, the experience of talking to some religious shows that they may feel distant from administration or trustees on important employment concerns or even totally disagree with institutional policies. The fact that another member of the religious institute is sometimes the chief administrator or that the members of the institute sometimes are the members of the corporation or constitute a majority of the board of trustees does not mean agreement on institutional policies. Therefore, a labor organization may be an attractive vehicle for a religious employee to express concerns or to bargain for a desired policy.

The constitutions, directories, and personnel policies of religious institutes normally contain provisions covering the institute's apostolates and the assignment of members; however, they usually do not contain specific directives about voting in a representation election or membership in a labor organization. Membership in professional and employment organizations is usually encouraged by religious institutes for individual growth and development. Only those organizations that stand for positions contrary to Gospel or Church teaching would be incompatible with religious commitment.

Assuming a labor organization won a representation election and permitted religious to join, the individual religious would be free to make such a decision in the specific situation. The individual religious, however, should take into account Church teachings in making a decision. The recent document issued by the Sacred Congregation for Religious and Secular Institutes, *Religious Life and Human Promotion,* states:

> In principle there does not seem to be any intrinsic incompatibility between religious life and social involvement even at trade-union level. At times, according to different laws, involvement in trade union activity might be a part of participation in the world of labor; on the other hand, such involvement might be prompted by solidarity in the legitimate defense of human rights.[17]

This principle is prefaced by the caution that a religious involved in trade union activities should have a clear awareness of the pastoral objectives as well as the limitations and risks of exploitation that could result in religious' lives and activity. Although this commentary may be more directed to trade union activity in Eastern Europe or Latin America and although the political involvement that this document mentions may pose "difficult problems," it still offers principles applicable to religious in the United States. The document further notes that:

> Within a body as influential in society as the world of labor, religious are the bearers of human and Christian values which will oblige them to repudiate certain methods of trade-union action or of political maneuvering which do not respond to the exact demands of justice which alone are the reason for their involvement.[18]

It is clear from the Sacred Congregation's statement that religious have the responsibility to be informed on the policies and practices of a specific labor organization in order to reach a decision based on Christian values. In addition, individual religious have the personal responsibility to be informed on the Church's social teachings, and religious institutes have the obligation to see that their members are adequately educated in these social teachings. Thus, a religious may have concerns beyond those directly related to employment in an election or when deciding whether to join a labor organization. These concerns, however, would not be different from any committed Christian looking for the broader implications of the impact of a vote or membership in an organization.

The reasons why a religious would not favor a labor organization are again the same as other employees' reasons. Employment concerns such as salary, working conditions, tenure or seniority, and retirement benefits may meet expectations, and a labor organization may not be able to produce better results. Employee organizations other than those certified by the federal or state government may be, in the eyes of some, a better vehicle to produce desired results in employment conditions. Certain labor organizations may have a reputation of being ineffective or insensitive to employee interests, while being more concerned with extending their own base of power. In addition, charges of corruption or illegal activity in some labor organizations have made them unattractive bargaining agents.

As noted above, a religious who believes that "certain methods of trade-union action . . . do not respond to the exact demands of justice" will have cause not to favor a particular labor organization. As the Holy Father has recently taught, the strike is still recognized as legitimate if exercised in the proper situation.[19] A strike is an extreme means not to be abused, however. In addition, "when essential community services are in question they must in every case be ensured, if necessary by means of appropriate legislation."[20] Therefore, if a labor organization has a reputation for abusing the strike or for causing disruption of essential community services, a religious would have cause not to become a member.

It should be recognized that even though all religious are to be committed to social justice, individual religious have given a wide variety of responses. Thus, individual religious can be expected to be on opposite sides of an attempt to organize a specific institution depending on their understanding of the benefits and drawbacks that can be expected. A religious, however, could not in conscience vote against a labor organization if it would result in the deprivation of wages or working conditions necessary to coworkers' welfare.

Should a religious decide to join a labor organization, there are benefits that can accrue to the institution, the religious institute, and the labor organization. The public commitment of religious to the Gospel can make them a powerful witness in their undertakings, including membership in a labor organization.

An institution that is publicly committed to Christian values will find itself challenged in the best sense of the word when religious are members of labor organizations that support an institution's specific direction or policy. The religious institute that has members who are administrative employees and employees who belong to a labor organization will benefit from the lived experience of their members who are involved in two different areas of service. Labor organizations that have religious as members will be reminded by their participation to be faithful to the demands of justice to employees, employer, and the people served.

There are two matters in religious institutions different from most employment situations that deserve mention.

The first is the desire of Catholic institutions to employ qualified religious. There are two reasons why Catholic institutions want to hire religious. One is that the decreasing number of religious at institutions operated or sponsored by a religious institute makes the hiring of more religious an objective in order to increase the religious presence at the institution, since this presence and influence is one of the reasons why many people wish to be served at the religious institution.

The second reason is the specific religious services that can be performed by such personnel, such as spiritual counseling and direction or sacramental ministry for those ordained or installed in such ministries. This is so whether the religious is specifically hired for a ministerial position or because of vocation is available for such ministry even though hired for another position. This is not to devalue lay ministry, which is valuable in and of itself. An institution does not have a religious atmosphere or presence solely because religious are employed there. On the other hand, the specific charism of a religious institute can hardly be embodied if no religious are present.

The first area leads into the second, which is the practice of some religious donating a portion of their income to the institution at which they are employed, although the donation is a gift and not an obligation that varies depending on the income and expenses of the local religious community. Such a gift may be an added incentive to hire a religious.

The donation back to the institution has already been held not to be a reason for excluding religious from a bargaining unit. The desirability of hiring a religious comes from the nature of the institution itself, and since the terms of employment rather than hiring practices are the subject of collective bargaining, it would not seem to have much impact on the determination of a bargaining unit.

Another area of concern in representation elections has been the hurt and dissension caused between religious and lay employees over the issue of inclusion or exclusion. Many religious who felt a real spirit of fellowship with coworkers were hurt when they learned that a segment of coworkers wished to exclude them from the bargaining unit. It may be asked if this decision occurred before consulting religious about the advantages and disadvantages of a labor organization. If religious were not consulted, they were isolated early in the process and pushed toward an antilabor organization position. Since the usual procedure for objecting to the composition of the bargaining unit is for the employer to challenge it before the NLRB, religious were left to have their right to be included in the bargaining unit litigated in the hearings between the employer institution and the labor organization. Labor organizations may have lost the support of religious because they assumed they knew the position of individual religious on the labor organization and acted on that false assumption.

Finally, although a Catholic health care facility is usually a separate legal entity and, in the sense of the John Paul II in *Laborem Exercens,*[21] a direct employer, the religious institute and the Church itself are at least indirect employers who affect the outcome of labor negotiations and are called to take account of the message of the Pope in his encyclical. Institutions operated by religious should be especially sensitive to employee interests, since their relationship with diocesan bishops as described in Church documents covers some of the same matters that would be included in the collective bargaining process.[22] Granted that the parallel is not perfect, the clarity and satisfaction produced by discussion between the diocesan bishop and the head of a religious institute leading to an agreement on the nature of the work, the assignment of personnel, and financial arrangements should help religious institutes and their members be sensitive to employees' and coworkers' needs.

In summary, the NLRB and the courts have dealt with individual religious in terms of their common interests with other employees. Since in many cases religious will have sufficient common interests to be allowed to vote in a representation election and to join a labor organization, it is important that they be familiar with Church teachings and be able to apply them to their particular situation. Religious institutes should promote familiarity with Church teachings among their members; however, they should not compromise their freedom to apply the teachings in a given situation, even though individual religious may differ in their decision in the same situation.

Administrators of Catholic institutions who are members of the religious order should be careful to address the question of representation by a labor organization to their brothers and sisters in the same way that they would address other employees in order to respect their freedom.[23] There is more than the complex law of unfair labor practices involved in such a case; there is the important principle of respect for a brother or sister. In addition, labor organizations should approach religious in the same manner as other employees, not assuming that they know the attitude of religious on the subject of representation by their labor organization.

When a new situation arises, there is bound to be some difficulty in reaching a satisfactory solution. But if religious are treated fairly under the NLRA and then are able to apply Church teachings in making an unhurried and judicious decision, a large step will be taken toward resolution of the issue.

---

1. A representation case is first heard by one of the NLRB's regional offices. If the decision is not satisfactory, either party can petition for review by the NLRB. If an NLRB decision is not satisfactory, either party may petition one of the U.S. Courts of Appeal for review.
2. 193 NLRB no. 23, 1971.
3. 210 NLRB no. 155, 1973.
4. 202 NLRB no. 7, 1973.
5. 220 NLRB no. 139, 1975.
6. 223 NLRB no. 224, 1976.
7. 225 NLRB no. 104, 1976.
8. 558 F. 2d 1116 (2d Cir.), 1977.
9. 562 F. 2d 246 (3rd Cir.), 1977. A more detailed analysis of the *Niagara* and *Saint Francis College* cases can be found in J. Hite, "The Status of the Vows of Poverty and Obedience in the Civil Law," *Studia Canonica* 10 (1976) pp. 131-193; J. Hite, "Religious Vows and the NLRB," *Review for Religious* 37 (1978) pp. 920-934; T. Lowry, "Labor Law (NLRB v. Saint Francis College (1977))," *Villanova Law Review* 23 (1977-78) pp. 940-949; I. Margules, "The Bargaining Status of Religious Faculty at Church Affiliated Universities," *Catholic Lawyer* 23 (1977) pp. 33-40.
10. 549 F. 2d 873 (2nd Cir.), 1977.
11. The NLRB also argued that because the Franciscans did not spend money on themselves and because they professed a vow of poverty, they were less interested than the lay faculty in the amount that they earned. The court found that the evidence showed that the Franciscans did have a definite interest in a salary based on their professional status and that they had a further interest based on their obligation to care for the elderly, train the young, and support their missions. The record also showed that, in fact, the only faculty member who refused to sign a contract until the salary was increased was a Franciscan. The court said that it could find no rationale for the rule that employees who spend less on themselves, or have less need of money, lack a sufficient interest in their wages. In addition, the NLRB

itself admitted in the *Niagara* case that an attempt to inquire into the manner in which a person spends his income would be irrelevant, involving the NLRB in an area in which it has no competence to deal.

12. 250 NLRB no. 136, 1980.
13. A federal appellate court decision is precedent only within its own circuit; therefore, the NLRB is free to make its own decision until a decision by the Supreme Court or the federal court of appeals for the circuit.
14. 254 NLRB no. 90, 1981.
15. Corporate structure also raises a series of theological-canonical issues. See A. Maida, *Ownership, Control and Sponsorship of Catholic Institutions,* (Harrisburg: Pennsylvania Catholic Conference, 1975); J. Coridin and F. McManus, *The Present State of Roman Catholic Canon Law Regarding Colleges and Sponsoring Religious Bodies,* pp. 141-153; Moots and Gaffney, *Church and Campus,* (Notre Dame: University of Notre Dame Press, 1979); and M. Stamm, "Emerging Corporate Models of Governance in Contemporary American Catholic Higher Education," *Current Issues in Catholic Higher Education* 2 (1981) pp. 38-45.
16. In *Catholic Bishop of Chicago* v. *NLRB,* 440 U.S. 490, 1979, the Supreme Court held that Catholic elementary and secondary schools are not under the NLRB's jurisdiction. The issue was raised in the recent case of *Saint Anthony Hospital Center* v. *NLRB,* 92 LC, no. 12,934, 1981, but was not decided by the court because the question was not raised in the initial hearing. See also, *NLRB* v. *St. Louis Christian Home,* 92 LC, no. 13, 109, 1981, in which a center for abused and neglected children, affiliated with the Christian Church Disciples of Christ, which received 55% of its funding from government sources, was held to be subject to NLRB jurisdiction because it did not involve a religious enterprise comparable to a church-operated school and therefore was distinguishable from the decision in *NLRB* v. *Catholic Bishop of Chicago.*
17. *Religious Life and Human Promotion,* no. 10.
18. *Religious Life and Human Promotion,* no. 10c.
19. *Laborem Exercens,* no. 20.
20. *Laborem Exercens,* no. 20.
21. *Laborem Exercens,* no. 17.
22. *Ecclesiae Sanctae,* I. no. 30, par. 2; *Mutuae Relationes* no. 57.
23. This does not raise the NLRB argument of "special relationship" again, since the same situation would occur in any household in which one spouse or family member was an administrator and another an employee.

DISCUSSION QUESTIONS

1. Which governmental agencies and courts decide questions relating to unionization, such as union membership?

2. What relation do these agencies and courts have one to another?

3. What is a bargaining unit?

4. When there is a question of religious belonging to a bargaining unit, does it make a difference if the union wishes to include them or not?

5. When there is a question of religious belonging to a bargaining unit at an institution, does it make a difference if the legal title to the institution is in the religious community?

6. When there is a question of religious belonging to a bargaining unit at an institution, does it make a difference if the majority of members of the institution's governing body are members of the religious community?

7. When there is a question of religious belonging to a bargaining unit, does it make a difference how the religious were hired?

8. When there is a question of religious belonging to a bargaining unit at an institution, does it make a difference how the religious are paid?

9. When there is a question of religious belonging to a bargaining unit at an institution, does it make a difference if the religious receive different fringe benefits than lay employees?

10. What difference does a vow of poverty make in determining whether religious are proper members of a bargaining unit?

11. Does a vow of poverty create a lack of sufficient interest in wages among religious, so as to require their exclusion from the bargaining unit?

12. What difference does a vow of obedience make in determining whether religious are proper members of a bargaining unit?

13. Does a vow of obedience create a conflicting loyalty in religious who work at institutions operated by their religious community?

14. How have vows of poverty and obedience been misunderstood by governmental bodies making bargaining unit determinations?

15. How have members of religion been considered both employer and employee at institutions operated by their religious community?

16. What reasons have been given as to why religious would not be fully loyal to the concerns of other, nonreligious members of a bargaining unit?

17. Can the donation of services by religious cause their exclusion from a bargaining unit?

18. Can the donation of salaries paid to religious by an institution cause the exclusion of religious from the bargaining unit at that institution?

19. Does it make a difference whether this "donation" is spontaneous or contractual?

20. When there is a question of religious belonging to a bargaining unit, does it make a difference if the religious perform different work or work different hours than lay employees?

21. When there is a question of religious belonging to a bargaining unit, does it make a difference if the religious do not directly receive an individual salary for their work?

22. What factors result in a finding that religious have a special employment relationship different from that of lay employees?

23. Does the developing labor law recognize the right of religious to bargain collectively?

24. Can religious be said to have a greater identity of commitment with the administration of institutions operated by their religious community than they can with their fellow workers?

25. Is the First Amendment guarantee of religious freedom violated by an exclusion of religious from a bargaining unit?

26. How can the community of interest among workers which qualifies them for membership in the same bargaining unit be described; what areas does this community of interest include; what does it exclude?

27. Why do labor unions, for the most part, object to religious membership in the bargaining unit?

28. What does this movement to exclude religious say about organized labor's perception of the values of religious?

29. What reasons exist for a religious to favor a labor organization?

30. Does the identity of interest between religious workers and religious administrators, which has been used to exclude religious workers from bargaining units, really exist?

31. Is membership in a union compatible with religious commitment? (Would the answer change with one given union over another?)

32. Are there any reasons why a religious should become a member of a union?

33. What steps must a religious take prior to joining a union?

34. Are there any reasons why a religious should not join a particular labor union?

35. What benefits accrue to an institution wherein religious are members of the union?

36. What matters of common practice in religious institutes differ from most employment situations?

37. What effect does workers' desire to exclude religious from the bargaining unit have on religious?

CHAPTER 7

CRITERIA FOR UNION MEMBERSHIP: ARE THE VOWS RELEVANT?

Sr. Melanie DiPietro, SC, JD

Representation elections at service institutions sponsored by religious congregations affect individual religious in two ways. First, the exclusion of religious from the bargaining unit[1] because of the vows or because membership in a sponsoring congregation calls into question the appropriate relationship of the vows and congregational membership to the external legal and economic structures and relationships in which a religious is inextricably situated. Second, the representation question invites a deeper examination of the quality of the entire institutional system. Inherent in the labor-management relationship are questions of social justice. The participative process of a representation election, may be the catalyst to move the community to ask the more significant questions of social justice within the context of the Gospel and the comprehensive social teaching of the church: What ownership image controls the management and administration of the resources accumulated in the educational, health care, and charitable institutions sponsored by the Church—that of a proprietor or that of a steward? What is the operational significance of these ownership images in the management and budgeting processes? How equitably are the resources and assets of these institutions distributed? Is the "community" the service beneficiaries, the patient, or the student? Or is the "community" the beneficiaries and providers—professional, nonprofessional, skilled, and unskilled jointly? What assumptions and values control the status, dignity, and participation of each member of the "community" within the given institution?

Sr. Melanie is an associate with Mansmann, Cindrich, and Huber, Pittsburgh, PA.

What is the relationship between the comprehensive teaching of the Church and the actual operation and management of the institution? What are the practical ways and means by which each participant can exercise an influence on the resolution of some of these questions?

This essay is confined in scope and is divided into two major parts. The scope is limited to a responsive reflection of the issues raised by the determinations of the National Labor Relations Board (NLRB) involving the question of admitting religious to the bargaining unit. Part I considers an alternative interpretation of the vow within the narrow context of the NLRB's decisions in congregationally-sponsored corporations. This alternative proposes that the vow of poverty does not, as the NLRB suggests, negate one's interest in wages, but rather commits the religious to a concern for an equitable and just direction and allocation of the wealth and resources created by his or her work. The focus of Part I is on the functional importance of the vows in the contemporary work situation of religious and suggests that religious may have a very real interest in preserving their right to participate on either the management side or labor side of the issue, depending on their own factual position in the work environment. The purpose of Part I is to suggest a more meaningful significance of the vows than that which is presently suggested by the NLRB. Part II focuses on the legal question of the right of religious who are members of a congregation, to be in a collective bargaining unit in an institution sponsored by their congregations. Part II suggests that the NLRB's conclusions are not supported by adequate investigations of facts and that the criteria which the NLRB has used are not properly based in labor law.

PART I

Fr. Jordan Hite, TOR, in his introduction to "The Status of the Vows of Poverty and Obedience in the Civil Law," indicates that an examination of the civil cases seems to suggest that "religious face the loss of some right, and in a few cases are deprived of rights because of the legal effect given to the vows."[2] The current representation cases present a concrete situation that may support his conclusion. It is my belief that the potential loss of legal rights of American religious may result from the failure of religious themselves to analyze and articulate the functional significance of the vows in contemporary corporate and economic situations. This analysis must differentiate between the faith and spiritual dimension of the vows; the minimum legal obligation of the vows; the jurisdiction and limitation of the vows; and the personal and communal dimension of the vows.

Sometimes, in a context foreign to the religious dimension, the application of a vow involves its dissection or limited application. This is problematic because a vow has no meaning to the religious in isolated, dissected parts; it is an integrating force in his or her life. The focus of the representation hearing, however, is not from a common religious frame of reference or from a perspective of the pursuit of enlightenment concerning an integrated religious belief. Often, in practice, the legal proceeding becomes adversarial. Unlike a teaching process or scientific investigation, there is often no ascertainment of a common frame of reference, common definition of terms, or opportunity to differentiate parts of the whole or to carefully interrelate the significance of parts to each other or to the whole. Consequently, the religious may have to dissect the vow when examining it and relating it to a nonreligious or at least pluralistic situation.

For example, it may be true that if a religious is an integrated person, his or her religious beliefs influence the way he or she uses professional skills. It is not necessarily true, however, that his or her obligations of the vow in relation to the religious congregation controls or predetermines relationships or rights vis-á-vis an employer or supervisor in a separate legal entity, even when that person also belongs to the same religious congregation. Consequently, the question "Can you separate the vow from your professional life?"[3] will probably be answered with a quick, undifferentiated "no" by the religious. But whether that answer has any meaning or significance in determining a "community of interest" with other employees in "matters of wages, terms, and conditions of employment" within the purpose, meaning, and standards of the labor statutes is really not determined without more precise and mutually understandable inquiry. In the same fashion, simply ascertaining that a religious does not keep his or her salary does not provide a reasonable basis for the conclusion that he or she has no interest in a salary and, therefore, no interest in the guts of collective bargaining.[4]

The vow of poverty, contrary to negating one's interest in wages, imposes a concern with one's salary precisely because that wealth is dedicated to a mission and has two obligations attached to it, acquisition of necessities for the congregation's members and the promotion of the mission of the congregation in this time and place. The vow of poverty does not negate the right of the religious to earn a salary: it controls the use and direction of the wealth created by the religious. The teaching or basic law of the Church concerning the vow does not negate the creation of wealth by a religious or of his or her right to receive value for labor done. Rather, the vow directs the use of the wealth created by a religious.[5]

Although many models of poverty exist within the multiple congregational traditions of the Church, the Church, both in law and in tradition, has described some basic requirements of poverty that are relevant to the use of the wealth and assets religious create in the Church's name. Those characteristics are (1) following the example of Christ, (2) listening to the cry of the poor, (3) fraternal sharing, (4) giving external witness to personal and community poverty, and (5) bearing witness to the human meaning of work.[6]

The human meaning of work is extremely complex and differs according to historical-theological traditions.[7] On the most basic economic level, however, human work has value because it creates wealth. Ordinarily, that wealth is used to change the material quality of the worker's life through its expenditure or investment. For the religious, it is also true that work creates wealth. The vowed person voluntarily and perpetually agrees to have the congregation direct the wealth resulting from this labor to the congregational mission, not only as a witness of fraternal sharing in community and witness of personal and community poverty, but as a means by which collected wealth, through collective energy, can be used to teach, heal, and minister. Instead of using the wealth created by labor to increase one's dominion and control over wealth or to accumulate personal wealth, the religious irrevocably and perpetually dedicates it to improve the well-being of the whole society—especially the poor.

The history of congregations explicitly testifies to this. Religious earnings fed, clothed, and educated the needy and built the network of institutions that are now the subject of the unionization question. The present institutions are the wages of religious under a different form. It is ironic that now religious who face great needs in providing the perpetuation of their congregations and apostolates, precisely because they dedicated their wealth to the creation of what have become major industries, are portrayed as being bodiless and having no interest whatever in their salary.

This irony is worsened by the possibility that the corporate structures in which they operate separate them from any real influence or control over the quality of the work environment or the equitable distribution of the institution's resources. It is simply incorrect to say that the religious has no interest in a salary because of the vow of poverty. In addition to defeating the significance of the vow, in the direction and allocation of wealth, it characterizes the vowed person as childishly irresponsible and implies that the only value of labor is to create wealth for personal, competitive consumption and not for fraternal sharing.

It is the responsibility of the religious to articulate and apply the vows to contemporary situations. In doing so, the religious should be sensitive to the relationship of the focus of a spirituality or tradition to its historical context. In an earlier day, when the congregation was completely autonomous, and the religious functioned within closed systems, the spirituality and focus on personal detachment was adequate and was understandably inattentive to the consideration of the *processes* involved in the creation and distribution of the wealth individual religious earned. The dramatic change in congregational control necessitates a reconsideration of the processes both of earning wealth and distributing wealth within Church-related institutions and in the larger society.

Given the closed system that congregational life was, the spirituality and training of religious tended to stress the spirit or goal of personal detachment to free one for service and community life. The formation did not consider or integrate the "temporality" side of the individual's creation of wealth. Nor did it consider an economic or organizational analysis of the processes involved in creating resources, in delivering services, and in preserving an equitable distribution among the beneficiaries viewed holistically as the providers and recipients. This could be so precisely because religious existed in a closed system that functioned with an identifiable common task and a singular and concentrated authority. There was no separate corporation or "employer." The congregation had complete control over all the parts of the service system—the capital assets, the personnel, the policy making, the administration, even the determination of "the market." Given that historical situation, there was no compelling need to differentiate the parts of the whole or to examine the relationship or rights of individuals in the system. In that time, there in fact was only one entity fusing private life style and work. The worker was not separated from the end result of his or her labors. The product of an individual's poverty was clearly observable. Religious could see the school or health care facility being built and the needs of the people being addressed. There was no need to be attentive to the *process* that was involved in directing the wealth individual religious earned to the visible systems of schools, universities, and health care facilities that served human need and redirected the distribution of health and education resources from the privileged few to the masses. The process was simpler, more linear, and worked because the political and economic system in which it functioned was simpler. It was a volunteer system. If the goal was to change the quality of life for the poor by teaching, healing, and caring, obviously this goal was achieved.

The radical changes in corporate structure which separate ownership from sponsorship, the sharing and diffusing of corporate control, and the change from a voluntary charity to an ''industry'' alienate religious and separate them from the end result of their work. Not only are they separated from control over their work, but the possibility exists that the systems they created in the past will be used to affect results contrary to their original purpose or to the Church's teachings. The separate incorporation of schools and health care facilities necessitates an attention to the *processes* of the creation of wealth and the distribution of assets. The separate incorporation often transferred title to property, diffused authority and control, included participation of persons with varying theological and value perspectives, and created a reliance on monies and the creation of capital no longer completely or substantially generated by religious. Increasing alienation results from the development of regulatory and administrative law, from the development of public social welfare programs, and from the rise of professionalism and the evolution of the random delivery of charity to the ''service industry.''[8]

This milieu necessitates a more consciously integrative analysis, articulation, and application of religious life and the vow of poverty to the contemporary situation. The vow's contemporary relevance requires that vowed religious attend to the subtle processes controlling the creation and allocation of the wealth and resources he or she has earned. This analysis, articulation, and application of the vow must be done through collective deliberations that integrate the facts of contemporary economic and social institutions with the entirety of the Church's teachings.

The vow invites religious to evaluate the equitable allocation of economic resources. The conversion from a closed system to a pluralistic, diffused system requires religious, now employees of a separate corporation, to consider the ''system'' as it creates and distributes assets. It is this belief that leads me to suggest that the serious questions of social justice exposed by the union contests are: How should the institutional assets originally created by religious and evidenced by the network of schools, health care facilities, colleges, and social service agencies be managed? How does the religious or lay employee influence that management?

The school or health care facility often has a multimillion dollar plant and operating budget and employs highly trained professionals, technicians, skilled and unskilled labor. It has economic significance not only because of its individual power as an employer, or as a conduit for economic activity within a local community, or as a provider of beneficial services to the community, but also because it is part of an entire economic and social system. Catholic colleges, schools, or health care facilities represent a political constituency, and, either by active participation or by default, they have contributed to national policy in education, health, or social welfare. It is an open question whether health care, education, and welfare institutions and national policy center around patient, student, and individual needs or whether the service client is really the conduit through which selected participants, whether institutions themselves, administrators, physicians, professors, insurance carriers, lawyers, accountants, consultants, clerical workers, maintenance workers, and so on, benefit disproportionately from either the ostensible service clientele or in a relationship to each other. The system, especially the Church system, must be analyzed holistically and integrally in terms of the totality of the Church's teachings.

This analysis raises such questions as: Is it appropriate that a Catholic health care facility caters to the physicians' position as census builders to the possible detriment of the dignity and proper recognition of the indispensability of nurses, aides, housekeepers, and engineers? Should not Church teaching have some influence in the recognizing and balancing of interests and the authentic recognition of the dignity of each participant in providing health care? Is it appropriate that Catholic education spirals toward the upper-middle class? Is it appropriate for Church-related institutions to pay less than an acceptable wage as encouraged by Church teachings?[9] Is it appropriate that the operation of some educational facilities depend on such low wages that some workers are eligible for food stamps—and the question of wages gets debated in terms of dedication, usually the workers'?

The point of these questions is that the vow should provoke religious to ask "systemic" questions that expose the operation of "the system." In origin, these institutions may have delivered services to cope with human need. Currently, the organization of the program in which the services are delivered may be the potential cause of inequities. While the system may have once been focused on human need and human largess, charity today is a big, complicated business. It cannot be viewed in simplistic terms. How is the total community, especially the needy, served by these "Church institutions"? How are the resources distributed within the institution—among workers as well as to the client? Do these institutions cope with, or change, a larger socioeconomic system in which they exist? These questions are functions of the vow, especially of the vow of poverty. Without a sensitivity toward these "systemic" questions, religious cannot realistically influence the direction of the wealth they earn. These questions suggest a careful analysis of the whole system, the worker, the provider, and the beneficiary and an evaluation of the allocation of resources with due concern for each participant's rights and needs. They are significant questions because they deal with the true intent of the vow: the direction and use of wealth, and not the negation of any interest in wages.

Given the facts that religious no longer work in closed systems and that individual religious have become separated from control over the creation and direction of their wealth, it becomes imperative that religious be allowed an option for a presence on every level of social and economic activity in which they engage so that they may exercise their legitimate influence on the system. Earlier I described the closed system in which religious previously worked. This system allowed congregational control over both the determination of what work religious would perform and where the wealth created by that labor would go. In that system, religious may not have been involved in the decision-making process, but they had influence and a proximity to the authority in the congregation that, at least, did not alienate them from the results of their works. That simply is not true today.

The religious vowed to a congregation's mission and common life is not required, in many cases relevant to this discussion, to work for the congregation. There is both a real and logical distinction between a congregation's mission, its works, and its sponsored institutions. There oftentimes may be a difference of opinion within religious congregations on their institutions' nature and administration. The association to a religious congregation does not automatically mean a unanimity of vision or conviction on what and how something should be done.

An individual sister may find herself in a staff position in a health care facility or college where she is a minority. The institution is invariably a corporation separate from her congregation where there may be or may not be a religious administrator. Even if there is a religious administrator, the two may not have an influential relationship. The administrator, of necessity, is a person who moves toward the board and those persons or positions who help affect his or her administrative authority. The momentum of organizational life may probably have more in-

119

fluence on their work relationship than common membership in a congregation. The designs of a legal structure may not be the facts of real influence and management of the corporation. There is the real possibility, especially in such environments as health care facilities and colleges, that the religious faculty or nurse may have very serious differences with the administration. There is a very real possibility that the disillusionment of religious staff at health care facilities and colleges is related to their disapproval of and disagreement with the operation of the institution—with the terms and conditions of their work environment and with their helplessness. Numbers on a corporate board are no remedy. Since there is no jurisdiction in the congregation to control the separate corporation, there is no process in the congregation to examine questions that are internal to the separate corporation. The religious has no forum for influence in the separate corporation because she is only an employee who is a sister.

The real situation may be that access to membership in a bargaining unit is the only forum in which a religious faculty member or nurse would be able to exercise some influence over the wages, terms, or conditions under which she works. She cannot reverse the diffusion of power and control that has occurred through separate incorporation, geographical distance, and pluralism of values represented by management and workers in separate corporations. A willingness to give wages to a congregation and to share its common religious life should not force a religious into a powerlessness and disenfranchisement that is not imposed on any other class of persons. This is especially true when it occurs, not through a factual inquiry into the patterns of power and influential relationship as measured against labor law precedents, but merely through sharing an association with a religious congregation.

The vow may compel the religious to protect fiercely the influence he or she has over earned wealth and over the environment and system in which he or she earns it. The analysis of the vow should differentiate between motivation, personal use of wealth, and the real economic and political structures in which the religious exists. In the old closed system, there may have been a direct relationship between self-negation and the delivery of human service. In the contemporary situation, there may be no relationship between motivations, spirituality, and the actual quality of the work environment—Church related or not.

Contemporary society operates institutions and structures that, although ostensibily committed to ideals of equality, justice, and due process, do not have linear, direct, progressive movements. Although recognizing the persistent imperfection of human collectivities and although acknowledging that the "Kingdom of God" is not necessarily achievable in a concrete historical time, the believer, and particularly the apostolic religious, truly believing in an incarnational and redemptive theology, is compelled to participate in and influence human processes and structures to move them toward a closer reflection of the values resulting from these religious beliefs and political and social theory. The methodology of shaping structures, compromising interests, and creating a public policy will necessarily be imperfect, a process of success, failure, growth, and diminishment. For the religious, this involvement in the methods and processes of influencing social structures and policies necessitates a conscious and collective deliberation that integrates theology, ecclesiology, a comprehensive understanding of the Church's social teaching, and the charism of any given religious congregation. These concepts and values, whether they are political (e.g., respect for private property, rights of collective bargaining, nonviolent resolution of conflict) or religious (e.g., the view of the Church as a mediator and servant), take on human significance only because there is some relationship between concrete acts and these ideals.

As noted by political philosopher, John Dewey, in discussing definitions of "the public" or "the state,"

> "all deliberate choices proceed from somebody...Some John
> Doe and Richard Roe figure in every transaction...Some John
> Smith and his congeners decide whether or not to grow wheat
> and how much, where and how to invest money, what roads to
> build and travel, whether to wage war and if so how, what laws
> to pass and which to obey and disobey."[10]

The practical questions for religious are: How do they "figure in every transaction"? How do their values legitimately influence human transactions in the systems in which they operate, particularly in their work environment?

PART II

Basic to a functional answer to this question is a threshold decision concerning the available legal structures for involvement in a political or economic process. It is assumed for this chapter that the basic design of collective bargaining in the NLRA is acceptable.[11] Following that threshold question, the religious needs to determine whether there is some limitation in participation in the NLRA structure that is inherent in the vowed life. It appears that there is not.[12] If the religious answers these questions and reflects upon the situation with some of the con-

121

siderations suggested earlier, it may be that, given the present corporate structures and diffusion of power and control in the separate corporation which is his or her employer, he or she may have no other means to affect management decisions, the quality of the work environment, and the allocation of resources within that system than through membership in a union. It is for this reason that religious should articulate for themselves what they believe to be their interests and the significance of their vows in their social, political, and economic relationships.

The question of the inclusion or exclusion of religious from a bargaining unit of an employer that is, although separately incorporated, historically related to a sponsoring religious congregation of which the employee is a member is a complex legal question, involving questions of labor law and the First Amendment. There is no doubt that there is a basis in the NLRA's purpose and intent to justify an examination of what, if any, influence membership in a sponsoring congregation may have on a religious employee's "community of interest" with other employees in the bargaining unit. As in any other inquiry, however, the findings and conclusions in these cases should be based upon a case by case basis and upon a fully developed record.

The NLRB's continuing reliance on the vows and congregational membership per se as determinative criteria for the commonality or similarity of interest of religious with employes in a bargaining unit jeopardizes the proper exercise of its jurisdiction which is to implement the NLRA's policies.[13] Further, the NLRB risks the denial of the rights of individuals as granted by the NLRA on religious associational grounds rather than on finding of facts relevant to the law. The threatened consequence violates not only the NLRA's purpose and intent, but the First Amendment. The NLRB's reputation for credibility and neutrality are also seriously threatened.

Before developing the above position, it is necessary to clearly indicate that no doubt exists that, in some circumstances, religious may properly be excluded from the bargaining unit. My position is that such an exclusion should be based on a factual inquiry tailored to the total work environment and based on a credible fact-finding process rooted in the NLRA's purpose and precedents. Even though inquiry into the relationship of the religious to the sponsoring congregation is inevitable, that relationship alone and person's religious life style should not determine that person's collective bargaining rights.

Because the *Seton Hill* case[14] has become a precedential case in the determination of the rights of religious to be in a bargaining unit, it shall be used for illustrative purposes in this essay. The major weakness in the *Seton Hill* decision is the direction and depth of the inquiry. An important function of the NLRB is to enforce the policies of the NLRA. An essential right of the NLRA is granted *to employees* ''to self-organization, to form, join, or assist labor organizations and to bargain collectively through representatives of their own choosing...''[15] The individual's right is based on the ascertainment of ''employee status'' as set forth in the NLRA. The NLRA confers on all employees the right to freely choose their bargaining representative.

It is vitally important that the inquiry faces the quality of the employer-employee relationship and on the internal integrity of the bargaining unit. This is especially so when determining the rights of employees whose status or association was not explicitly dealt with in the statute and who are not part of the common experience in the employer-employee relationships that were considered in the design or implementation of the statutes. The inquiry should also be sensitive to the historical context so that the significance of a fact can be properly determined.

The NLRA gives the NLRB broad powers of investigation and broad discretion in determining the appropriateness of a bargaining unit. The breadth of this power does not, however, negate the necessity of examining facts in terms of their relevancy to the NLRA's purposes. The rights granted to employees can only be mitigated or denied if required by the statute, as when an employee's circumstances or interests substantively destroy or threaten to destroy any mutuality, similarity, or commonality of interest with other employees as determined by the NLRA's purposes and intent. The proper focus should be on evidence concerning mutuality and commonality of interest among employees and the probabilities for ''the fullest freedom to exercise employee rights'' and not on religious associations or life styles.

The misplaced focus on the vows and the congregational association as exemplified in the *Seton Hill* case did not produce evidence that was measurable by the NLRB within the NLRA's terms. Nor did it produce relevant and material evidence for determining employee rights. The testimony on the vows consistently established that their jurisdiction is limited to matters of religion internal to the congregation.[16] Despite uncontradicted testimony that the religious has an obligation to support members of the congregation,[17] the NLRB concluded that the vow means religious have no interest in wages. There is no evidence in the testimony or in the NLRB's opinion to show the logic of such inferences or conclusions based on the records. This is more easily illustrated by a comparing of the pattern of fact finding in other court and NLRB decisions dealing with the questionable relationship of some employees to their employers to the record in *Seton Hill*.

In reviewing cases suggesting a lack of "a community of interest" among employees because an employee may have a familial relationship to a corporate shareholder, officer, or manager, the NLRB and courts have considered such factors as the dominance of the relative on the level of directorship, office, administration, and supervision of the corporation and the living proximity and economic dependency between the employee and the employer relative. A familial or economic interest of the employee with the employer must be of the degree that "sufficiently distinguishes" that employee from other employers to warrant exclusion. The interest of the employee must be so sufficiently identified with management, either in fact or in appearance, that it destroys commonality of interest or seriously threatens other employees' free exercise of rights. One of the factors considered is the likelihood of the conveyance of information to the employer which would threaten the union's ability to function.[18]

The NLRB in similar fact-finding processes focused on whether the interests of the related employee were identifiable with those of management. In one case, the NLRB allowed the inclusion of an employer's mother-in-law when the evidence failed to show that her interests were allied with management.[19] In other cases where corporation employees were stockholders and directors, the employees were not excluded from the bargaining unit since they had no voice in determining company policy.[20] In other instances where the facts showed that stockholder employees could influence management policies and had divergent employee interests, the stockholders were excluded from the unit.[21] In another case, the employees were parents of the employer who differed from other employees in some of their working hours and in vacation allowance. The NLRB held that "such evidence of filial generosity was not intended to, nor did it in fact, alter the employer-employee relationship of the parties, nor did it change the conditions of employment of the parents." The NLRB held that the deviations shown in that case were not sufficient to negate the parents' community of interest with other employees.[22]

In these cases of familial and potential economic ties, the decision focused on the pattern of the familial or economic ownership and control over the actual operation of the business and its effects on the relationships and interests of the employees within the work environment. The religious does not have a close familial or economic relationship to the management of the corporation as in the above cases. Yet, the *Seton Hill* inquiry lacks the care and continuity that is shown in these familial or economic relationships that are practically and statutorily more suspect than the relationship of the religious to the college or health care corporation. The fixation on the vows and the lack of understanding of congregations' nature precluded an inquiry patterned along traditional lines as evidenced by these cases. If it follows its traditional inquiry patterns, the NLRB's holdings in the religious membership cases would be more credible, fair, and neutral, especially given the fact that nothing in the NLRA supports the exclusion of religious on associational grounds.

The presumption of the law is that employees have a protected right to collectively bargain. The NLRA's policies are best served by granting representation wherever possible.

> It is hereby declared to be the policy of the United States to eliminate the causes of certain substantial obstructions to the free flow of commerce and to mitigate and eliminate these obstructions when they have occurred by encouraging the practice and procedure of collective bargaining and by protecting the exercise by workers of full freedom of association, self-organization, and designation of representatives of their own choosing, for the purpose of negotiating the terms and conditions of their employment or other mutual aid or protection.[23]

Exclusion of employees is tolerable only when there is some fact situation or relationship to the employer that may substantially lessen the mutuality or similarity of interest in wages, hours, and working conditions, or that may appreciably and reasonably inhibit other members of the unit from "enjoying the fullest freedom in exercising the right's guaranteed by the Act."[24] Employee exclusion from a bargaining unit can only be based on a fact-finding process that clearly, incisively, and accurately focuses on the employer (management) employee relationship and, particularly, on patterns of control or influence between them that seriously negate the mutuality of interest between members of the bargaining unit which is necessary for meaningful collective bargaining.

Given the infinite variety of traditions of religious congregations, the fact that no two are alike, and the fact that there is no unanimity in the structure or the substance of the control or influential relationship patterns that exist between religious and their congregations and between the congregation and the employer corporation, no exclusion can be fairly made and have a reasonable legal basis except on a case-by-case factual analysis. The analysis must focus on the facts of the relationship among religious and lay employees and between the employees, religious and lay, and the employer and not on mythical interpretations or conclusions made by the NLRB on what a vow means to a particular person. Only a religious can explain how he or she regards the vow.

In the *Seton Hill* case, there is a noticeable absence of inquiry into the nature of the control or the influential relationship between the congregation and individual sisters, between the congregation and the corporation, and between the management of the corporation and the sister-employee. There is limited inquiry into whether management or supervisory control over the sister-employee is substantially related to or different because of her religious association. There is also no factual inquiry into whether the status of the religious was a real or reasonably feared inhibition on other employees. The record in the *Seton Hill* case is particularly interesting for the unexamined conclusions that seem to control the decision and for the absence of any inquiry focusing on management-employee relationships similar to the traditional inquiry referred to in the above illustrative cases.

The NLRB's decision begins with a random enumeration of statements, many of which provided little if any information on how a particular "fact" creates a control or influence that would seriously lessen the mutuality of interest among lay and religious faculty which is necessary for meaningful collective bargaining. The NLRB held that "although the work and working conditions of the two groups might be identical, their interests were divergent." The Board supported this conclusion by finding that "the relationship of the religious who is a faculty member to the College is more complex. She is an employee, but also is in a sense part of the employer since the Order owns and administers the College."[25]

There is a serious question in the record on how the "order own(s) and administers" the college. The record indicates that the congregation owned land and buildings which it leased to the college for $1.[26] No testimony on any of the terms of the lease indicates whether the congregation had any governing or controlling influence over the college corporation through the lease. Nor is there any testimony of how that lease relationship between two corporations—the congregation and the college—affected the community of interests among the religious and lay employees. The evidence in the record on the corporate structure and operation does not indicate any basis for piercing the corporate veil, i.e., for saying that the college corporation is identical to the congregation. The congregation may have "owned" the college before it was separately incorporated with a lay board of trustees in 1969; however, the separate corporation, both in structure and in operation, does not show such "ownership." The record indicates that 50 percent of the college corporation trustees are ex-officio Sisters of Charity. This is not, per se, a controlling power. It presumes many unproven assumptions, e.g., that all sisters vote identically at all times. Or, even if they did, that that has any relationship to either the religious faculty or to membership in the congregation. The record has no other information that would provide a reasonable basis, either in law or in fact, to show "ownership" or management by a corporation outside the college corporation.

There is no evidence that the congregation controls—in law or in practice—either the sister-trustee complement of the college board or the college board itself. There is no examination or comparison of the authority or position of the mother general in the congregation and her authority or position in the college corporation. In fact, the record shows that she has only one vote on the college board. There is no other specific testimony on the legal or practical relationship between the congregation and the college to "pierce the corporate veil" and support the finding of "ownership" or that the congregation was the "employer" of all those at the college. In addition to that vacuum, the record is absolutely void on the relationship either in law or in fact of sister-faculty-members to the congregation or to the college, which would support the board's conclusion that membership in the congregation makes sister-faculty-members employers at the college.

The conclusion that the Order administers the college likewise lacks reasonable support in the record. In fact, the testimony on administration of the college clearly shows the college's autonomy. The president testified that she had ultimate decision-making powers and that the president and college board had complete authority over all college practices. The mother general had the limited ability to refer a sister to the college only upon request by the college for a referral. The record indicated that the college freely selected sister personnel and that sisters had refused to apply to or accept positions at the college. The testimony further indicated that "it is not possible . . . for the mother general to decide who shall come to the college." In the testimony regarding the equality between religious and lay faculty on such areas as class assignment, committee structures, grievance procedures, and supervisors there was no evidence that the congregation had knowledge of or influenced those processes.[27]

Additionally, there was no evidence of the congregation's having any dominant control or influence on the board level either.

The record intimated a legitimate threshold question of the nature of the congregation's relationship to the college, but it never went into an examination of the pattern or quality of that relationship. The conclusion of the "order owning and administering the college" blatantly ignores the legal significance of separate corporations and lacks any supportive testimony on the organizational and operational actualities of the separate corporations. The existence of a lease, which terms were not examined, shows ownership of lands and buildings, not of a college. The college corporation's board, one-half of whose members are Sisters of Charity, administers the college. Although numbers on the board may appear significant, a number without a contextual examination of dominance and control, committee structures, and manner of selection, is inconclusive. Structure without substance and context creates only an associational relationship between two corporations, not with or among employees. It does not determine whether the association's nature and operation so influences the relationship that the standards of law are met to "pierce the corporate veil" and deny an associate of the congregation his or her presumed right as an employee of a separate, autonomous corporation to bargain collectively.

The *Seton Hill* case is very ambiguous in the identity of the parties, their legal relationships, and their practical relationships. The evidence is scant on a clarification of the parties and on details which would show actual patterns of control or influence either between the sister and the congregation; between the congregation and the college; or between the sister, through the congregation, and the college, which would change a sister's status from employee to employer.

The NLRB next stated in its decision, that "she has ties of allegiance to other members of the order and owes obedience to the mother general who is a member of the board of trustees. As a member of the bargaining unit, she would therefore be subject to a conflict of loyalties."[28] But there was no testimony on the nature of these "ties of allegiance to the other members of the order" or on how that allegiance is related to membership in the bargaining unit of the college, thereby producing the fatal conflict of loyalties. Despite the lack of testimony in the record on the relationship and communication of sister faculty to members of the order concerning college matters, one may argue that common experience allows the NLRB's assumption. In matters of the practical implementation of a goal and belief, however, common experience suggests that there is no such phenomena as the general, undiscriminating loyalty as the NLRB suggested. One need only notice that many religious orders are a result of schisms within a congregation where a common allegiance to a mission spawned diverse, often schismatic, views on the practical implementation of that mission. The record in *Seton Hill* indicates that sisters were known to reject positions at the college.[29] Although a sister witness thought that a sister would be hesitant to strike, she also indicated that it would not be impossible.[30]

A superficial notice of the news indicates that there is not only historical evidence of independent and energetic differences among religious, but that contemporary religious are more inclined to be independent thinkers and, if necessary, organizers. The point here is that the record does not support the leaps of logic which the NLRB makes to get to its conclusion. Individuals were disenfranchised on the basis of association and assumptions about the meaning of religious associations that were not grounded in a factual inquiry. The NLRB's conclusions are not factually or reasonably inferred from the record or from common experience. It is important to remember that no sister-faculty-member testified on what she believed her loyalties were or how she believed the vows influenced her relationship to the congregation in matters of her faculty status or what, if any, relationship her vows had to the college administration. The NLRB implies, but does not explain, that the conflict of loyalties in a bargaining unit is present because the sister-faculty "owes obedience to the mother general of the order who is a member of the trustees." That is perhaps the NLRB's more serious error on the loyalty issue, because it does not result from a vacuum in the testimony or from disregard for "common experience" but rather flatly ignores and contradicts the only testimony in the record on the issue.

Each sister who testified on the scope of the vows indicated that they pertain only to religious matters and are confined to life in the congregation.[31] The evidence in the record indicates that the mother general influences the internal decision within the congregation to the degree that she asked sisters to apply for positions when the college invited her to make a referral.[32] There is no further testimony on either the real, formal, or informal influence or control of the mother general on the college or on the individual sister. In fact, the testimony indicated that, at times, the college rejected prospective sister-faculty-members and sisters refused teaching positions at the college. There is no indication that, in expectation or in practice, the vow had any relevancy to a sister's faculty position, loyalty, or obligation to the employer-college. Substantial testimony indicated, to the contrary, a consistent denial of the vow's relevancy to internal college matters. The NLRB's conclusion is simply not reasonably based on the testimony.

The NLRB also concluded that the economic interests of the lay faculty and sisters did not coincide. The NLRB cites the vow of poverty as the basis for this finding. Again, the NLRB discounts the testimony concerning the religious' obligations to provide not only for her own needs but for the education and care of young and retired members of the congregation. It also ignored the testimony of the treasurer that sisters in other incorporated institutions had taken the initiative to question their salaries, believing that they were underpaid.[33] Considering the actual testimony within the context of the earlier discussion on the vows in Part I, one can see that the NLRB is dangerously beyond its competence when it renders conclusions concerning the meaning of the vows and association in a congregation.

While the NLRB's reference to fringe benefits is its most relevant consideration, the probative value of the facts is, again, not clear from the record. Of particular interest is the NLRB's conclusion that ''the fact that the college has unilaterally established separate programs of fringe benefits for lay faculty and sisters indicates recognition on its part that the two groups have different interests.''[34] The conclusion that this practice proves the college's recognition that the two groups have different interests is not substantiated in the record. There is no inquiry on the rationale or reason behind the practice. The facts lack a context, and therefore the significance the NLRB attached to them is questionable. The conclusion is questionable because it does not put the incident in its historical context either in relationship to the college administration or to the realities governing pensions or social security coverage of religious. If the lay board was created in 1969 and there was a change in administration, it is just as possible that the practice was a remnant of a past corporate structure and not a conscious recognition by the college corporation ''that the sisters lacked a community of interest'' with their colleagues. The NLRB speculation that the college management thought the two groups of faculty had different interests is not evidenced by the testimony nor does it lead logically to the conclusion that the sister faculty perceived their interests as different from their colleagues or the same as management. Again, the president testified there was never any perception of two faculty divisions, one lay and one religious. The traditional experience in the college was a unified perception and treatment of faculty.[35]

The point of this examination of the record is not necessarily to argue that the *Seton Hill* decision is in error. It is to argue, rather, that the existence of religious vows and congregational associations are not appropriate or useful criteria for determining employee rights. They should not be determinative to allow the disenfranchisement of religious unless they are tailored to examine the realities of the operating relationships more accurately and then measured against statutory standards. As the record stands, it reveals only assumptions about the association of a religious to the congregation and the congregation's association to the college. There is an assumption of a unity and equality in these relationships relied on by the NLRB not only to pierce the corporate veil between the congregation and the college but also to make one who is an associate in a religious congregation an "employee" in a separate, autonomous corporation.

There must be some clarity on the nature of the relationship of the individual religious to the congregation. Generally, the vows commit one to a life style, to an interdependency with the congregation, to a mission of the Church, and to a particular congregational mission. Clearly, the vows do not negate one's individual identity, judgment, and free will nor do they commit one to an abstract, consuming "allegiance" or "loyalty" to the congregation, much less to a separate corporation, no matter how closely it may be affiliated with the congregation. The religious is an autonomous individual, and there is no such general undiscriminating allegiance as assumed by the NLRB.

The source of confusion is the failure to differentiate among the corporation, the association, and the individual. An incorporated congregation may not be the same entity as the congregation itself. Very often membership in the congregational corporation is limited, e.g., to major superior and council, while membership in the congregation is broader. The power of individual members may include a right to vote only on the nomination of the major superior and council or, in few congregations, a right to elect these officers. An individual religious may have a right to elect a representative to the legislative body for the internal law of the congregation. Neither of these are necessarily rights in the congregational corporation. In very few, if any, instances does a member of a congregation, through membership per se, get a voting right or a consultative voice in the congregation corporation or in a separate corporation sponsored by the congregation. Very few constitutions of religious congregations would even require a major superior and council to inform or consult with members on issues relating to separately incorporated institutions. The record shows no attempt to examine this relationship nor does it indicate anything of the substantive relationship even between the sisters. There is no evidence that the sister-teachers knew or communicated with the sister-trustees or had any influence over the trustee selection. There was no evidence of any special communication of college administrative information among the sister-trustees, administrators, or faculty. There was no evidence of or testimony to indicate a loyalty to the college substantially different from that of the lay faculty. The point of this enumeration is to indicate that very little inquiry was made, at least in the record of *Seton Hill*, into the specific substantive nature of these relationships. Despite this, conclusions were made that a sister-teacher was ''in a sense part of the employer since the order owns and administers the college.''[36] Without specific inquiry along the lines suggested above, an employer status was ascribed through an unexamined association.

This fact is significant when one realizes that the NLRB, without any meaningful analysis, reached its conclusion in *Seton Hill* by relying on the petitioner's (union's) brief that, ''the sisters are not interested in wages'' . . . *They* return their wages to the college by a contractual agreement . . . The *sisters* own the college and would not strike . . . *They* serve on the college board. The Sisters of Charity as a group own and manage the college . . .[37] [emphasis added] Nowhere does the record differentiate or identify the ''they.''

The NLRB accepted conclusions on the unidentified ''they'' about individuals, their allegiances, beliefs, values, loyalties, and possible actions without one ''scintilla of evidence'' from the individuals involved or one clarification of who ''they'' were. There is no testimony that the religious faculty returned their wages to the college. The ''they'' was the congregation and there was no evidence that individual religious faculty members influenced or controlled that congregational determination or its contractual basis. Individual religious faculty were not parties to the contract. As far as the sisters' ownership of the college is concerned, legal title to the land was held by the incorporated congregation. Neither canon nor civil law would support the conclusion that the sisters or the religious faculty held title to the property or that a title owner of land owns a separately incorporated college operating on the land. That sisters would not strike is also not supported by substantial evidence. The testimony indicated a possible hesitancy to strike, but whether that hesitancy was substantially different from any employee's hesitancy or inherent in the association to the congregation or even a valid generally applicable characterization was not examined.

The weakness of the record and the NLRB's decision in the *Seton Hill* case lies in its lack of direction and depth. The direction of the inquiry should be on ascertaining facts on the patterns and substantive quality of the relationships that actually exist in the working environment which reflect on the commonality of interests among employees. The differences discovered in fact should then be put in a context which determines whether the differences are substantive, connected to the vows, rooted in the relationship to the congregation, and operative both in the religious and in the perception of fellow employees. A focus on such questions as the following may be more legitimately informative than the NLRB's present approach.

- Does the religious have any advisory position in the congregation that directly or indirectly relates to the college or health care facility?
- Does the religious have any formal or informal access to the information concerning policies adopted by the college board or health care facility board?
- Does the religious have any vote, control, or influence on which sisters are trustees?
- Does the social pattern in the congregation cause a religious to work closely or share common responsibilities and tasks with the management of the separate corporation?
- Does the religious have any regular formal or informal reporting or discussion with the major superior and council or other sister-trustees concerning policies, wages, terms, and conditions?
- Has the major superior, either through her congregational authority or corporate position and influence, given advice or direction on a sister-employee's status?
- Does the ex-officio status of religious on the board have any other influence over the identity or autonomy of other board members?
- Are the tenure requirements, disciplinary methods, wage scale determinations, or other management questions subject to or influenced by the congregation?

The point of this short illustration is to suggest that it is far more appropriate to investigate factual relationships to determine whether one's interests are those of an employee or management than to assume that "it must be there" because "they" all take vows and "they" are members of a religious association. Although the circuit courts and the NLRB in more recent cases have begun to move toward a more employment and organizationally oriented inquiry, it is still necessary to stress the need to operate from a labor, employer-employee paradigm and not a religious paradigm, especially on the part of the NLRB. Recently, in a hospital case, the NLRB denied a sister nurse membership in an employee unit because, in addition to 51% membership on the board, the order controlled the day-to-day operation of the hospital through the hospital administrator who was a member of the order.[38] Again, this appears to be a religious associational argument, and not a factually based labor law argument. An associational argument based on religious grounds, whether it is on the management level or the employee level, is still a violation of statutory and constitutional rights.

The above discussion illustrates the inappropriateness of a primary focus either on the vows or on congregational association. The NLRB's present focus and conclusions do not further the NLRA's policies because they do not favor the exercise of the rights to collectively bargain as is explicitly stated in the NLRA. Basic to the denial are the unexamined presumptions about religious life: the presumption that there is one sister's perception which is applicable to all "the sisters" and that religious associations and a religious life style per se are controlling. Religious associational relationships are not suspect relationships in the NLRA and are especially protected by the constitution. If they are to be used by the NLRB at all (and there are good arguments why they ought not to be), they certainly should not be so mis-used.

The NLRB's neutrality is suspect when one merely observes the fact that religious have only been excluded from the bargaining unit when the petitioner seeks their exclusion.[39] Otherwise they were admitted. The courts have not excluded them from the bargaining unit. Religious employees have no advocate at the NLRB level and must rely on an appeal procedure to get a review in the courts of the NLRB's decision. This is very costly, and there is no guarantee that an employer will pursue such an appeal on behalf of its religious employees. Given the statutory design of the NLRA, religious have no mechanism for protecting their rights. If for some reason the petitioning unions wants them excluded, they must rely on an employer to press their case. This is an obvious detriment to their rights since the employer may have no reason to advocate for them and because the employer cannot be a credible advocate for employee rights. The NLRB has the statutory obligation to protect collective bargaining rights and the power to conduct independent inquiries and to seek testimony from employees. In failing to do so, the

NLRB risks the violation of its own neutrality and statutory mandate and the violation of the statutory and constitutional rights of employees who are religious.

Conclusion

It is hoped that this essay has led the reader to only one conclusion: that in order to practically contribute to the effectuation of social justice in the labor-management arena and in the political and economic system generally, religious must analyze and articulate a contemporary and functional dimension of the vows and apostolic religious life. "A radical change of mentality and attitudes is needed to apply evangelical commitment to the concrete and often disturbing problems of human promotion."[41] Religious must protect themselves from an exclusion from the arenas where the concrete problems of human promotion are resolved. Their continued apostolic viability may necessitate participation in such forums as bargaining units.

The two parts of this essay may appear disjointed. The presentation, however, is deliberate to suggest to the reader the need to view an apparently single-dimension question from many perspectives. Religious must watch the legal forums, such as the NLRB. Lawyers, administrative agencies, and courts must be sensitized to the error in conclusions drawn on antiquated or erroneous religious paradigms and to the diligence necessary to apply common law and statutory concepts to a fact situation that is not within the common or traditional experience of the common law or statutes.

Finally, and most importantly, it is hoped that the ideas introduced will focus attention on the significant question of social justice emerging from the labor union movement—just how is the Church, in its institutions, defining "the community" and how equitably and justly, as measured by the Church's social teachings, are the resources of the congregationally sponsored institutions being distributed.

---

1. Jordon Hite, TOR "Members of Religious Communities and Unions" in *Issues in the Labor-Management Dialogue: Church Perspectives.* ed. Adam J. Maida, (St. Louis: The Catholic Health Association, 1982), pp. 91-111.
2. Jordan Hite, TOR, "The Status of the Vows of Poverty and Obedience in the Civil Law," *Studia Canonica* 10 (1976) p. 131.
3. *Seton Hill College,* 201 NLRB No. 155 p. 1027 (1973).
4. *Seton Hill,* p. 1027.

5. Consider Canon 95, *Schema of Canons on Institutes of Life Consecrated By Profession of The Evangelical Counsels*. (United States Catholic Conference, 1977) p. 85.
6. Pope Paul VI, *Evangelica Testificatio (The Evangelical Witness of the Religious Life), The Pope Speaks*, XVI (1971), pp. 108-128.
7. See John Paul II, "Work in the Subjective Sense," *Laborem Exercens (On Human Work)* (Boston: St. Paul Editions, Daughters of St. Paul, 1981) pp. 15-16; John C. Bennett, "Reinhold Niebuhr's Social Ethics, *"Reinhold Niebuhr, His Religious, Social and Political Thought,* ed. C. W. Kiegley and R. W. Bretall (New York: Macmillan Co., 1967).
8. See "The $9 Billion Charity Industry," *Forbes* 126 (February 5, 1979).
9. See Pope John XXIII, *Pacem in Terris (Peace on Earth)* (Washington, DC: National Catholic Welfare Conference, 1963) p. 7.
10. John Dewey, *The Public and Its Problems.* (Athens, OH: Swallow Press, 1954) p. 18.
11. The National Labor Relations Act is not structured for concepts of community or stewardship.
12. Cardinal Edward Peronio and Archbishop Augustin Mayer, "Religious Life and Human Promotion," *Origins,* vol. 10, no. 34, Feb. 5, 1981, pp. 529-541.
13. The NLRB in cases subsequent to the *Seton Hill* case is placing less emphasis on the vows. However, *Seton Hill* is still cited as precedent with or without discussion. Therefore, the NLRB is continuing to reinforce a religious paradigm instead of a labor paradigm.
14. In the *Seton Hill* case, the NLRB denied religious faculty, who were members of Seton Hill's sponsoring religious congregation, membership in the bargaining unit. The decision will be discussed later in this chapter.
15. 29 USCA 157.
16. Official Report on Proceedings Before the NLRB, Seton Hill and Seton Hill Professional Association, Pennsylvania State Education Association, 6-RC-6217 (Aug. 18, 1972) pp. 23, 115, 124, 125, 129.
17. *Ibid.,* pp. 121-123, 125, 137, 143.
18. For a discussion of these criteria, see *NLRB v. Caravelle Woods Products, Inc.* 504 F.2d 1181, 7th Cir. 1974.
19. *Olden Camera and Lens Company,* 108 NLRB 35, 37, 1954.
20. *Mutual Rough Hat Company,* 86 NLRB 440, 444, 1949.
21. *Brookings Plywood Corporation,* 98 NLRB 798, 1952.
22. *Buffalo Tool and Die Manufacturing Company,* 109 NLRB, 1343, 1344, 1345, 1954.
23. 29 U.S.C. §150—Preamble to NLRA.
24. *Caravelle,* p. 1187.
25. *Seton Hill,* p. 1027.
26. Official Report, *Seton Hill,* p. 140.
27. *Ibid.,* pp. 23, 24, 43, 45, 125, 129. See testimony of President Sr. Mary Schmidt.

28. *Seton Hill,* p. 1027.
29. Official Report, *Seton Hill,* p. 45.
30. *Ibid.,* pp. 142-143.
31. Official Report *Seton Hill,* pp. 23, 115, 124, 125, 129.
32. *Ibid.,* pp. 32, 43, 125, 129.
33. *Ibid.,* p. 134.
34. *Seton Hill,* p. 1027.
35. Official Report, *Seton Hill,* pp. 38, 41, 49, 51. See testimony of President Sr. Mary Schmidt.
36. *Seton Hill,* p. 1027.
37. *Seton Hill,* p. 1027.
38. *Mercy Hospital of Buffalo,* 250 NLRB 949, 1980.
39. Hite, ''Members of Religious Communities and Unions,'' pp. 91-111.
40. *Origins, supra* n. 12, p. 531.

DISCUSSION QUESTIONS

1. What interpretation has the developing labor law given to the vows of a religious in defining a religious' relationship to his or her order or religiously sponsored institution?

2. What has been the basis for the developing labor law's interpretation of the vows and of religious life?

3. Do the vows legitimately exclude religious from participating in the legal forum and processes where public policy is created and implemented?

4. Who is responsible for articulating the operational effect of religious' vows to the courts and administrative agencies?

5. Does the vow of poverty render the value and use of wealth nugatory?

6. How can union membership assist an individual religious to implement the meaning of the vows?

7. What factors must a contemporary analysis of the vows seek to integrate?

8. What basic requirements of poverty has the Church articulated?

9. What effect do the vows have on the wealth generated by the labor of the vowed person?

10. Is the vow of poverty more properly directed to the denial of wealth or to the use of wealth for the poor?

11. Given the proper context of the vow of poverty, what is the vowed person's proper interest in wages, job security, and other benefits?

12. What distortion of religious life and of the responsibilities of individual religious are caused by statements like "a religious has no interest in his or her salary"?

13. What type of deliberation is required of religious who wish to be involved in the methods and processes of influencing social structures and policies?

14. Is there some limitation to participation in the NLRA structure that is inherent in vowed life?

15. What factors govern the inclusion or exclusion of a religious from a bargaining unit where the employer is an institution sponsored by his or her religious community?

16. What unexamined conclusions have controlled the decisions of the NLRB regarding religious' membership in a bargaining unit?

17. On what "facts" does the NLRB rely to pierce the corporation veil of religiously sponsored corporations to find that such a corporation is equivalent to its sponsoring congregation, or is owned by the congregation?

18. How has the NLRB used the concept of conflict of loyalties to exclude religious from bargaining units at religiously sponsored institutions?

19. How has the NLRB misused the concept of the vow of obedience and the vow of poverty to exclude religious from bargaining units at religiously sponsored institutions?

20. What is the genuine scope of the vows of obedience and poverty?

CHAPTER 8

RELIGIOUS INSTITUTIONS AS MORAL AGENTS: TOWARD AN ETHICS OF ORGANIZATIONAL CHARACTER

James A. Donahue

What makes Catholic health care facilities distinctively Catholic? This issue has been discussed and analyzed intensively by many persons in Catholic health care over the past decade. Still, the question nags. Apart from some few concrete manifestations of Catholic presence (i.e., no abortion or sterilization services, "identifiable" religious personnel), most answers have pointed to such indicators of institutional Catholicity as "the type of care given," "concern for the dignity of the whole person," and "religious presence." These are no doubt true and important indicators, but they are vague and general. This limits their usefulness in contributing to the ongoing functional operation of a Catholic health care facility.

The issue of unionization in Catholic health care facilities brings the Catholic identity question squarely into focus once again. Both labor and management appeal to the notion of "Catholicity" as justification for their prounion and antiunion positions. Each sees Catholic identity as requiring different courses of institutional action. Labor is quick to support its prounion position by pointing to the historical affiliation of the Roman Catholic Church with the labor movement, citing particularly the social encyclical tradition beginning with Leo XIII's *Rerum Novarum*. Management, on the other hand, often justifies its resistance to unions by appealing to a fundamental conviction that if Catholic institutions live up to their beliefs and principles, there really should be no need for unions. Moreover, they claim the creation of community (presumably Catholic) is better served without third-party participants

---

Mr. Donahue is assistant professor of theological ethics, University of Santa Clara, Santa Clara, California.

in communication among members of the community. Each of these positions offers insight into a complex problem, and yet each offers only a limited perspective. The seeming contradictions of these outlooks pose a difficult dilemma for the Catholic Church in health care. This dilemma, although creating conflict and tension among health care and Church personnel, need not be irreconcilably divisive.

My purpose here is to develop a framework and process for analysis that both labor and management might use in resolving some of the essential conflicts surrounding the unionization issue in Catholic health care. The concept of organizational character, I believe, can serve as an integrating focus for institutional analysis and policy making in that it properly attends to both the ethical demands of religious organizations as well as to the concrete requirements of effective institutional administration.

In capsule, my argument is this: Catholic health care facilities possess distinctive identities, each having an organizational character that is fundamentally both religious and moral. This ''character'' provides the basis upon which an institution, as a moral agent, relies for its own moral self-identity. From this character an institution seeks ethical guidance and direction in the development of policies and programs. Integral to and distinctive of this character for Catholic health care facilities is the notion of ''Catholicity.'' It provides the focal point for any understanding of the ethics of these organizations. To resolve the unionization issue successfully, both labor and management must look once again to their understandings of the Catholic character which undergird their health care institutions. This quest takes the form of a search not only for the norms and principles that guide an institution's moral direction, but also for a process of moral discernment by which the entire institutional community can decide how to exercise its moral responsibilities in light of its Catholic character.

Character and Institutions

One of the distinguishing features of Catholic health care institutions is that they perenially ask: ''What does it mean to be a Catholic institution? In what ways are we different from the community hospital down the street?'' This is no trivial characteristic but goes to the heart of some of the substantive differences between Catholic and other health care facilities. Constant concern for finding adequate answers to an institution's self-identity creates an organizational climate or ethos that, over time, develops particular identifying characteristics—a configuration of values, concerns, and styles. These characteristics become institutionalized referents for policy decisions and serve as the basis for justifying the legitimacy of any course of organizational action. These often resist precise quantification but are nevertheless real and have a significant effect on how institutions do, and should, act. An institution's particular dispositions, outlooks, habitual ways of acting, convictions, beliefs, and intentions may be said to manifest its character.[1]

This concept of character has traditionally been referred to in theological and philosophical terms as an individual's orientation to the virtuous life. Yet the notion of character seems appropriate to collectivities as well, particularly institutions, in constructing some basis for understanding the ethical behavior of organizations. To speak of character is to make moral reference. When labor and management in Catholic health care use "Catholicity" as the basis for their judgments, they refer to some foundational notion of "Catholic" character. To judge the adequacy of these appeals, it is essential to understand how character does, and can, function in ethical, religious, and institutional terms.

The Ethics of Character[2]

What does it mean to say that a person has character? It indicates the existence of certain attributes or qualities of personality that particularize that person's moral identity. It implies certain modes of behavior that one is likely to engage in or kinds of actions that one can be expected to perform in a given situation. Virtue is the name given to these qualities of the agent that illuminate and characterize the moral excellences of a person's unique identity—his or her own disposition to the good.

When making moral judgments, it is necessary to look at more than simply one's individual actions and choices in isolation from one another. These particular acts must be situated in the larger framework of a person's overall moral orientation. The notion of character provides this larger understanding. Each individual embodies certain qualities— for example, a disposition to be loving, to be faithful to one's promises, to treat others justly. These virtues are ordered in a unique way within the self, and when seen as a whole in their relationship to one another, a particular and distinguishing moral identification emerges. This constellation of virtues in their particular configuration acts as a source of moral guidance. As such, it is a standard or focal point for making determinations about right and wrong. The question might be asked, therefore,

"Is action X morally right in light of the character of the person acting?"
Is it consistent with who the person is and what they say about what he or
she believes to be true about themselves? Is there continuity with past actions and direction toward stated goals? An ethics of character shifts the
moral focus from the act performed to the agent performing the act, from
a focus on doing to being. This shift is crucial for an adequate moral self-
understanding.

Character is not restricted only to the self and personal morality,
although most contemporary discussion manifests an excessive focus on
the individual. Groups possess character. So do institutions. The meaning of the latter will be essential for adjudicating labor and management
issues in Catholic health care. Is there some way of understanding
"Catholic" character that will offer institutions guidance in resolving
conflicts over unionization? Before such a theory of *institutional* moral
character can be put in place, it is essential to first consider in a more
detailed manner what constitutes moral character in general. This is best
done by analyzing some of its essential component parts. These include:

1. The concept of character as unifying the moral self;
2. The meaning and role of convictions in morality;
3. The use of narrative, story, and images in ethics;
4. The role of vision and choice in morality; and
5. The process of moral discernment.

Character and the Moral Self

Character is central to the task of ethics in that it is the distinguishing
feature of a unique moral self. In that it "designates the distinctiveness
and individuality of the self," it is the basic aspect of one's life and serves
as the primary focus from which one makes moral determinations.[3]
Character directs and orients the self and serves to unify the many and
varied pulls and conflicts that one experiences morally. By the continual
cultivation and peformance of virtuous actions, one develops a pro-
pensity to act in certain ways and also a set of convictions and values that
constitute one's own moral self-identification. These virtues are both the
source and result of moral actions. They are shaped and reshaped
through continuous transformation. Character unites the past, present,
and future of a person's moral life and also unifies the doing and being
aspects of the moral personality. What one does morally is given moral
value by its meaning in the overall world view of the person who acts. In
the words of theologian James McClendon:

To have character is to enter at a new level the realm of morality, the level at which one's person with its continuities, its interconnectedness, its integrity, is intimately involved in one's deeds. By being the persons we are, we are able to do what we do, and conversely, by these very deeds we form and reform our characters.[4]

Character formation does not occur in isolation. A moral self is shaped by the community and society of which it is a part. It will be important, therefore, to develop a keen sense of critical judgment about the content and influence a community has in the development of one's moral outlook.

Convictions

Understanding character involves some basic insight on how convictions are related to moral actions. McClendon defines a conviction as "a persistent belief such that if X (person or community) has a conviction, it will not be easily relinquished without making X a significantly different person than before."[5] Our identity is tied to our convictions, usually those beliefs that are articulated as defining who and what we are. It is necessary to correlate these convictions with one's actions to determine if, in fact, we are truthful to what we believe about ourselves. For example, to be a Christian is to identify oneself as having fundamental convictions about life that are focused on the reality of Jesus Christ as Lord. To determine whether one is a good Christian requires some correlation between the content of one's beliefs and the meanings and performance of one's moral actions. A Christian is part of a convictional community. The nature of this community is constituted in the beliefs, descriptions, and statements by Christians about who they say they are. *Christian* is a description of a particular kind of character. It suggests certain perspectives, dispositions, and intentions that have taken shape historically and are central to one's self-identity. The moral task involves determining how convictions shape our moral selves and how our actions shape and create convictions. In this interactive process, moral identity develops. Moral analysis must attempt to explicate the form and content of this process.

Narrative and Story: The Role of Images in Morality

The use of story has become increasingly popular of late in theological circles.[6] There are several reasons for this. Finding prevailing theological paradigms lacking in power and ability to address contemporary religious experience, many theologians have sought more adequate constructs by going back historically into the experience of religious communities to recapture those events that gave shape and form to present theological propositions. Story represents the quest for new understandings and new paradigms that will emerge from reinterpreted history.

Character involves having certain identifiable norms and principles that express fundamental beliefs about what is considered right action—to be loving, to keep promises, to obey the commands of Jesus, and so on. These standards have meaning only as they are perceived as deriving from a more foundational self-identity that is the result of a particular series of historical developments of a self (and a community) over time. The stories of our own growth and history provide the ''meaning-world'' that gives coherence and intelligibility to our norms and principles. Telling our story, articulating the images and metaphors that guide our self-understanding, and understanding others' stories, are essential for moral judgments about specific behaviors and actions. Just as our character is the result of our histories, our future growth depends on our ability to develop stories that have coherence and continuity in light of our fundamental convictions about human life in a changing world. As Christians, these stories are shaped by our perceptions of Jesus Christ, belief in whom is the integrating center of our religious and moral self-identity.

A focus on story represents an attempt to unify the relationship of principles and process in moral reflection. Most moral analysis in Roman Catholic theology has been of a casuistic nature—applying moral principles to particular cases in a deductive fashion. This has led to a high degree of certitude traditionally in moral theology. Since Vatican II a change in moral reflection has occurred. It is marked by a shift from a deductive to inductive methodology, a change from a rigidly fixed view of truth as absolute to one that sees truth as perspectival, a movement from a static to dynamic understanding of nature and reality.[7] Ethics has begun to focus on the process of moral discernment and the dynamics of moral development and growth. Principles, in this approach, need to be constantly interpreted and reinterpreted in light of experience and history. The ethical task is to constantly correlate these principles with their underlying stories and the evolving process of human life to judge the most adequate responses to moral situations. Character, convictions, and narrative provide the normative framework for this.

Vision in the Moral Life

The stories that shape one's character consist not only of the historical recounting of experienced events but also include the myths, the images, the symbols, and the rituals that capture the imaginative expression of our deepest longings and perceived meanings. All these have an irreducibly aesthetic dimension. They represent a way of apprehending the world, a mode of viewing reality, which affects those responses and actions we deem appropriate expressions of our authentic selves. As Notre Dame theologian, Stanley Hauerwas, says, "The moral life is more than thinking clearly and making rational choices. It is a way of seeing the world."[8] Acting rightly depends on seeing the world clearly so that we are not deluded either by our own personal proneness to self-deception (egoism) or to ideological bias (either cultural or political). The goal is not to eliminate these distortions (which would be virtually impossible), but rather to act rightly despite them, constantly aware of their presence and attempting to transcend and overcome them in pursuit of that which is good and truthful.

One way of attending to these issues is to become conscious of those compelling objects, persons, ideals, and images that have evocative power in calling forth specific kinds of actions and behaviors in us and by being critically aware of the descriptions of reality that we identify as representing that which we believe in, or wish to become, or consider most historically accurate and worthy of emulation. The "good" that we seek is represented in the particular objects of our attention. The implications for the moral life that follow from this insight are innumerable. Moral judgment involves focusing one's attention on those (good) objects that most accurately represent that vision of life deemed worthwhile, truthful, and authentic. Christians make the claim that Jesus Christ is this proper object of attention. The more difficult task, then, becomes the determination of which representations, stories, and images most adequately express the reality of this man Jesus. This is at the heart of the theological endeavor. At the same time it is the most central issue for Christians' moral lives. We search for those objects of attention that will pull us out of our self-deceptions and allow us to see the world and others as it and they really are. Developing character entails the continual sharpening of our moral vision.

Moral Discernment

An emphasis on character manifests a distinct "turning to the subject" in moral reflection. Narrative, vision, and conviction all point in some way to the centrality of the moral agent and one's "meaning-world" in coming to determinations of what constitutes right action. James Gustafson has suggested that ethics requires some notion of discernment as an appropriate focal motif for understanding morally "what God is enabling and requiring us to do."[9] Being discerning implies the ability to see or perceive something with a critical eye; to discriminate the important from the unimportant; to be sensitive to nuances and see relationships between things and suggest inferences that can be drawn from some body of information. Philip Keane defines discernment as follows:

> A process of decision making in which the person or community faces several alternatives or choices and determines which of these choices is God's will more through a reflection on the stirrings or movements or responses which the person or the community subjectively experience vis á vis the possible alternatives than through an analysis of the objective factors which might help to indicate which of the alternatives is the best choice.[10]

The implication of this approach for the moral life means cultivating those qualities that would make one more likely and able to perceive the requirements of right behavior (the will of God) in any particular situation. This shifts the moral focus from single acts and decisions to those beliefs, intentions, dispositions, perspectives, rules, and values that form the underlying and identifying features of a person's being. Discernment entails the development of these qualities and characteristics that make one able and likely to perceive what one should do, how one should respond in a moral situation. There are distinct similarities here with the way one speaks of having virtues. To be discerning one has to possess certain characteristics (virtues) that are developed only through extensive moral reflection and continual learning. These qualities are "learned skills" acquired through repetition, trial, and habituation.

As a process of moral reflection, discernment is not restricted to individuals acting alone. It is a feature of groups and organizations "that seek guidance for their actions as they make choices, decisions and commitments in everyday life."[11] I turn now to a fuller treatment of the notion of discernment and "character" with regard to institutions, particularly Catholic health care facilities.

Character and Institutional Analysis

Character has received some attention from organizational theorists and sociologists, although the moral aspects involved in the concept have been scarcely delineated in that literature.[12] And yet it seems clear that there is a moral stake in understanding organizational behavior. My effort here is to describe the elements of a theory of organizational character to determine how such an understanding can enable decision makers in organizations to find moral guidance for policy making and to realize the moral implications of certain policy alternatives. It is my hope that such an outlook will shed some light on the complex issue of unionization in Catholic health care facilities.

Any organization, regardless of its type, size, or purpose, possesses a history. Over time an organization commits itself to particular ways of acting through its decisions, its investments of resources, and its continual responses to both external and internal situations. Taken together with an original founding purpose, an articulation of an organization's mission and role, and a set of guiding principles, these historical choices shape a distinctive character that becomes an integrating feature of the organization's self-identity. This character provides the locus, or center, from which actions and behaviors receive their coherence, purpose, and direction.

These historical choices are commitments about values that "fix the assumptions of policy makers as to the nature of the organization's enterprise—its distinctive aims, methods and roles in the community."[13] As organizations change, they develop a network of convictions that define and describe the institution. These convictions, in turn, provide the basis for future organizational growth; any proposed policy, or fundamental change of direction, must be assessed in light of this convictional network. If a policy is consistent with these convictions, it will usually have little difficulty acquiring the assent of those in the organization. If not, it will seldom have the legitimacy that authentic organizational policy requires.

For Catholic health care facilities the substance of these convictions, values, and character-defining commitments is somewhat problematic. As with individuals, convictions in organizations are not always unequivocally clear and consistent. Often they defy explicit formulation. In a formal sense, they may be definable—"I am committed to Gospel values"; "we are committed to caring for the poor"; and "we believe in the dignity of the whole person." But these rarely are specific enough to facilitate a choice between conflicting policy alternatives, both of which may purport to represent the same value or conviction. Being "Catholic" is the closest one can come to arriving at a general identifying and distinguishing characteristic for Catholic health care facilities. What do Catholic convictions mean in health care facilities?

There is no single Catholic conviction to which one can point as the constitutive feature of Catholic identity. Certainly identification with the magesterium as a source of authority is a feature distinctive to the Catholic community. But it is not the only distinguishing aspect, and even it is given to multiple and conflicting meanings and interpretations. Richard McBrien, in his landmark work, *Catholicism,* warns against too absolute and reductionistic an identification of the Petrine office as the primary characteristic of Catholic identity. And as Avery Dulles in his *Models of the Church* has shown, there is a variety of models by which one can understand the Church. For Catholic health care facilities the implication of this is that the official teachings and pronouncements of the Church are an important, *although not the only,* source of moral guidance and authority in policy formulation.

Determining the content of Catholic convictions in an institution is made even more difficult by the fact that it is not merely the collection of all the beliefs of the individuals in the organization. Rather, institutional convictions are given content by the way individual's stated beliefs are translated into organizational action by leadership through specific policy choices over time. What an organization believes is specified through the types of actions it performs. For example, what it means to believe in Jesus Christ, is given concrete form only by engaging in actions in which the organization intends to manifest this Christian identity.

Catholic institutions engage in activities intended to express their Catholic convictions and character; in the case of unionization, positions can either favor or oppose unions. Whatever position an individual in an organization proposes, it is necessary to show how that course of action is the intended manifestation of that person's convictions about what he or she believes to be true about the Catholic identity of the institution. The responsibility of the institution as a whole is to provide the conditions under which a deliberation upon these positions can occur. The institution must create a context in which the intentionality of the Catholicity can be actualized, where the character can take shape. It must set in motion those processes that allow an open and participatory deliberation involving the actors in an organization to come to some specific determination of what Catholic convictions mean collectively in a particular situation. Institutional convictions, in this view, are the result of a process of communal discernment by all the constituents in an organization. Catholic facilities, therefore, have an obligation to permit and encourage open, active discussion about what is the most adequate communal expression of the institution's Catholic convictions about labor unions. This expression will emerge from the understandings of the individual members of an institution about the meaning of that institution's Catholicity and will take concrete form through institutional policy.

There is an inherent pluralism of convictions within every Catholic institution. In health care facilities, for example, nurses, patients, nonprofessional staff, physicians, and administrators all have unique, and frequently differing, perspectives on the health care enterprise and what constitutes the "common good." Organizational character must be comprehensive enough to include these pluralities. An institution must provide some means by which its character can be articulated and shaped by the various sectors that comprise the organization. In this view, one of the fundamental requirements of organizational ethics would be the search for a shared mission and common purpose that provides coherence and direction to the institution and which can be used as criteria for resolving conflicts. The more concrete this common purpose, the stronger will be the institution's ability to act and respond to specific problems.

There is even a more fundamental moral task here than merely justifying one's convictions about unions. Where one stands vis à vis unions is indicative of a more fundamental attitude about the world, the nature of the self, and the God in whom one believes, trusts, and remains loyal. If Catholic health care institutions are to fully embrace their religious self-identity, the nature of the discussion concerning unions must take place at the level of these underlying values and beliefs. The union discussion between labor and management is fundamentally a religious and theological dialogue with particularly moral manifestations. Questions of the right of workers to better salaries, to more involvement in the delivery of medical services, and to professional entitlement express at least implicitly basic convictional stances about the nature of reality, the self, and God.

For a health care institution to be Catholic entails attending to the implicit religious framework and convictional world that underlies people's concerns. In terms of institutional character this means pushing the discussion to the level where these basic issues are consciously addressed. It will entail attention to the narratives and stories articulated by the various participants in the conflict, some sense of the values that are represented by different positions, an investigation of the "common good'' or ''master images'' that serve as integrating and cohesive features of the discussion, an exploration of the loyalties and commitments of the parties, and an articulation of the character that informs particular choices. At this level the institution's religious character is given the prominence it deserves.

The concept of organizational character is important for making moral determinations about the unionization issue in Catholic health care facilities. The specific requirements and imperatives of character for each institution will vary, but there are some general norms that emerge from the foregoing analysis that provide a guiding framework for institutional policy decisions. These cannot be precisely formulated as action guides. Instead, they are best expressed as a series of questions that must be considered and answered satisfactorily in the consideration of any course of organizational action. How a particular institution responds to these questions will, in large part, determine the parameters within which moral self-identity will be both created and discovered. A delineation of these normative questions can best be developed under the constitutive categories of an ethics of character.

Character
Organizational character attempts to reunify particular institutional decisions with the organization's overarching moral self-identity. For this reason it is vital that the style and process of organizational decision making adequately connect the organizational act and the institutional agent. Is the framework for decision making attentive to the unity of the part and the whole, the specific and the general? Are questions of coherence and consistency given priority over issues of expediency and unexamined spontaneity? Do the ''collective character'' of the organizations' constituents and the ''common good'' have a centrality in the adjudication of conflicting claims? Have attempts been made to articulate the Catholicity of the organization with any degree of specificity and content so that it is more than just a collection of general beliefs and values with no real substantive impact on organizational behavior? Have the implicit values of the organization, both formal and informal, been explicated and made manifest so that decisions are made with a heightened moral awareness? Character is a unifying category that provides a means for bringing these diverse considerations together in common focus.

In regard to the unionization issue, the above questions assume even more specificity. Is the prounion option more integral to the institution's character configuration? This can only be determined as the involved parties engage in discussion and negotiation about the value dimensions that characterize moral identity. This would imply that the union discussion must occur at the level of convictions and beliefs that provide the underlying justifications for particular positions if moral authenticity is to be attained. It implies, too, that moral questions of the common good, value, and right action are integral to considerations of strategy and politics. Only in this intermeshing will some comprehensive ethical solution emerge.

Convictions

Being moral in an ethics of character means expressing in our actions what we say we are. We attempt to manifest in our actions our deepest convictions about our vision of the good life. Organizationally, being moral means attempting to create the kinds of institutions that we say we believe in based on some belief about the purpose of human life. Policy decisions must emerge from the deeper convictions of the organization. These are found most clearly in such formulations as statements of mission and role, articulation of both short and long range goals, the stated priorities of leadership, budget and resource allocation, and other similar indicators.

Character ethics makes certain requirements of organizational decisions—namely, that they be consistent with the convictions that give meaning and coherence to the institution. Are particular policy choices, either prounion or antiunion, adequate to the convictions of the Catholic health care facility? Does one course of action better manifest an organization's integrity vis à vis its convictions? Is *this particular union* the best way to bring convictions and actions together organizationally? Would another alternative, another union, be more conducive to institutional integrity? Does this administration or this union embody the values that constitute the convictions of the organization as a whole? If not, what policy choices would best manifest these?

All the above concerns assume a form of decision making that is essentially processive. Policy making in an ethics of organizational character is marked by the dynamic interaction of the constituents of the organization itself in an *ongoing process* of policy formulation. It is a participatory model in which the moral self-identity of an institution is continually being defined and actualized by those who are in the organization. This, of course, occurs in the context of the developed history and identity of the institution. Organizational leadership will play a predominant role in this process and has particular responsibilities for initiating and facilitating it. Much has been written about participatory decision making and the difficulties such a model presents for effective and efficient administration. Still, it seems clear that some variation of a participatory decision process is essential for an adequate and comprehensive embodiment of organizational character to emerge. More attention must be given to this issue in the future.

Stories, Narratives, and Images

Stories provide the context, history, and experiences that give shape to character. They also give the framework within which moral decisions can be judged right or wrong. The narratives of organizations function in much the same way as personal stories. They describe how and why beliefs and outlooks have developed to where they are now. The contemporary unionization issue is situated amidst a much larger history in Catholic health care, and it is to that larger story that our present attention must be drawn.

It is clear from even a cursory analysis of Roman Catholic social history that the story of the institutional Church, as shown in Church teaching and dogma, has a prounion identification. Historically, the Church, particularly in the United States, has been a strong advocate for the rights of all workers to unionize.* The roots of this tradition were born in historical times in which the conditions of the workers were severely oppressive in almost all sectors of the industrial population. The bias in favor of unions, although clearly present in the discussion of the issue, must be assessed in light of the contemporary situation in order to ascertain the movement and development of the Church's story in its present-day form.

What position on unions best captures the essence of the continuing story of the Church in the health care ministry? Does historical commitment by the Church to a prounion stance necessitate the continuation of such a posture? How do present social and political circumstances alter the development of the ongoing narrative and make new and different response necessary? What is the compelling truth of the story of the Church in health care that calls forth our responses to meet the demands of our character and convictions? Does this compelling truth lead to a posture in support of or opposed to unionization *at this time in these par-*

---

*This has been re-affirmed in the most recent encyclical of John Paul II, *On Human Work,* issued on Sept. 15, 1981.

ticular circumstances? How do multiple stories combine to create a collective corporate story in a pluralistic setting? These are the hard questions that decision makers must face boldly and honestly if they are not to evade the difficult challenges of their corporate responsibility in health care.

Stories are told through images, metaphors, and myths as well as through the recounting of events. The power of the images we use to shape our moral lives is enormous. Consequently, they deserve critical scrutiny and analysis in ethical reflection. Health care institutions must give careful attention to the predominant images that give direction and vision to a facility's ongoing operation and from which constituents draw their norms and parameters of expected and required behaviors. Images create a symbolic world of interaction that sets the moral basis of what is considered right and appropriate in ordinary behavior.

What images of health, of Church, and of organizations permeate Catholic health care facilities? Are they institutions of health or sickness? Is the apostolate there one of healing and service for others? Is it an extension of a technical, scientific, rational, and impersonal world view? How are these multiple images, each real and perhaps even necessary, integrated within an institutional ethos? What images of organization and authority does the Church manifest institutionally? Do these reveal a hierarchical, democratic, autocratic, or participatory leadership style? These are again the difficult and yet crucial questions that an ethics of organizational character raises for health care facilities.

It is of central importance that both management and labor understand the stories and images that inform and shape the other. Although it is not necessary that these be the same for each, there must be some basis of commonality and shared vision expressed in these images that both institution and union agree upon. Unions will vary in their stories and images as will health care institutions. In discussion, participants need to look closely at the similarities and dissimilarities of these. Does enough commonality in purpose and intent exist to make a constructive relationship possible? This will only be discovered in the ongoing process of discussion. Questions of style are also important in these considerations. Is the primary *modus operandi* for facility or union of a combative, negotiating, or reconciling nature? Is decision by consensus, fiat, or majority vote? Which of these approaches can be welded into viable working relationships in pursuit of agreed-upon goals? Are goals in fact agreed upon, at least generally? Are there certain fundamental differences in outlooks and purposes? These issues are best understood in the language of story, images, and symbols. An understanding of them requires the cultivation of an institutional imagination. This is best achieved in the arena of the policy process.

Vision

The adequacy of an image is judged by its ability to enable us to perceive reality as it actually is. Images can convey the significance of someone or something to us, however, only if we are open to seeing the power and possibilities the images contain. This requires the development of our own skills of perception, our own capacities for seeing critically and clearly the world which is before us. When our vision fails us, our images become reduced; they lack comprehensiveness. They represent only a partial, and sometimes distorted, view of the truth.

In an institutional setting clear vision is cultivated by the quality of the decision-making process and the fostering of critical outlooks directed both internally and externally. The ability to be self-critical and open oneself to challenges by others is the only way in which we can be pulled away from our own proclivity for self-deception.[14] Institutions, to achieve this, must engage fully with those both inside and outside the organization, those both likeminded and critical, in order to discover how the institution's decisions can give substance to its organizational character and enable its direction to take shape.

In terms of the unionization issue, vision is sharpened by analyzing and reflecting on just how unions have functioned in the past in health care. What changes and benefits have resulted because of unions in the past? Have they been conducive to furthering the Church's health care ministry? Have they helped to bring about quality and efficient service to those most in need? Have they sufficiently protected the rights of the workers whom they represent?

The institution's perspective is clarified by reflecting on its own organizational history and discovering the patterns that have characterized its behavior. Has it conducted itself fairly and honestly in the past in its relationships with its employees? What events have precipitated union activity in a particular situation? Has the leadership and decision process been conducive to good worker-employer relationships? If not, why? Reflecting on these questions will enable an organization to see more clearly its present situation as well as alternative courses of action in the future.

Discernment

Particularly important for religious institutions is their seeking to understand how God is acting and being revealed in the processes of everyday organizational activity. In that the primary impulse for mission in health care lies in the nature of the religious convictions that inform an organization's purpose, the need for constant discernment of God's actions in the organization's life is of paramount importance. To distinguish the movement of the ''spirits'' in the process of communal (corporate) life is the central moral task of a religious institution and one of its characterizing and distinguishing features.

Corporate discernment for Catholic health care institutions requires that a community ''establish *at least to a degree* a common basis of subjectivity, a common area of understanding of God against which various courses of action can be tested.''[15] For organizations this will be a difficult task, particularly in the pluralistic settings in which the U.S. health care system is located. Discernment, then, is primarily a discussion about means and not ends. When various sectors of an organization engage in debate and discussion about an issue, there must be some agreed-upon beliefs, convictions, and values for successful discernment to occur. Without this, discernment breaks down into hopelessly conflicting disagreement with little basis for moving the process to some successful resolution or decision point.

Discernment of the unionization issue raises the following basic institutional questions: Does a commonality about desired ends between unions and the institution exist to make discernment possible? In what ways has God's presence been manifest in previous organizational decisions? What pattern of spiritual direction has emerged over time in this organization's history and how can this pattern be used to make current policy decisions? What have been the times and circumstances when God's presence or absence has been most acutely felt by the corporate body? How can present actions (either prounion or antiunion) be justified in light of this institutional spiritual path? What have been the situations where the organization has experienced the clearest embodiment of its own character, its own deepest convictions? Admittedly, the language of discernment does not translate easily into an institutional framework. Problems of the relationship between an individual's discernment and corporate decision making is an exceedingly complex issue. The price of not attempting to work out the comparisons, however, is great. In not undertaking the challenge, Catholic institutions risk losing not only significant possibilities for moral self-understanding, but they also fail in defining themselves clearly and forcefully in the public arena. The unionization issue is a most appropriate beginning point for undertaking these challenges.

Conclusion

There is no easy or single solution to the unionization issue in Catholic health care. To force a solution or to artificially reduce the complexity of the issues at hand would be a violation of the problem itself as well as of the persons involved. It is important for the participants in the debate to realize that in speaking of Catholicity, in speaking of unions, in speaking of health care institutions, one speaks of what one philosopher has termed "multiple realities."[16] There is no one agreed-upon monolithic meaning for these realities. By expanding the notion of moral character to apply to institutions as well as to individuals, I have suggested that a focus might be found for addressing the unionization issue, particularly its moral and theological aspects. The concept of character is useful not only for a theological and ethical self-understanding, but also in policy formulation by decision makers within the organizational context. I believe that by focusing on character, a common frame of reference and a process for organizational moral analysis can emerge. By using this, both labor and management might find sources of agreement or perhaps at least a method for constructively addressing their disagreements. Only testing and engagement will reveal how well this will be accomplished.

---

1. For a more precise delineation of each of these characteristics see, James Gustafson, *Can Ethics Be Christian?* (Chicago: University of Chicago Press, 1975), pp. 38-47.
2. The understanding of character developed here draws from the insights of a number of contemporary writings in theological ethics but is derived largely from the work of Dr. Stanley Hauerwas, professor of theology at the University of Notre Dame (IN). See particularly his *Character and the Christian Life: A Study in Theological Ethics* (San Antonio: Trinity University Press, 1975); *Vision and Virtue* (Notre Dame: Fides Publications, 1974); *Truthfulness and Tragedy* (Notre Dame: University of Notre Dame Press, 1977); and *A Community of Character* (Notre Dame: University of Notre Dame Press, 1981). For other works on the ethics of character see James Gustafson, *Christ and the Moral Life* (New York: Harper & Row, 1968) and *Can Ethics Be Christian?* (Chicago: University of Chicago Press, 1975); David Harned, *Faith and Virtue* (Philadelphia: Pilgrim Press, 1973); and *Images for Self*

Recognition (New York: The Seabury Press, 1977); Donald Evans, *Struggle and Fulfillment* (Cleveland: William Collins Publishers, 1979); and Enda McDonagh, *Gift and Call* (Bristol: Gill and Macmillan, 1975).

3. Hauerwas, *Vision and Virtue,* p. 52.
4. James McClendon, *Biography as Theology: How Life Stories Can Remake Today's Theology* (Nashville: Abingdon Press, 1974), p. 30.
5. James McClendon, *Understanding Religious Convictions* (Notre Dame: University of Notre Dame Press, 1975), p. 7.
6. Some works that have been particularly responsible for this trend include John Dominic Crossan, *The Dark Interval* (Niles: Argus Communications, 1975); Michael Novak, *Ascent of the Mountain, Flight of the Dove* (New York: Harper & Row, 1971); Peter Slater, *The Dynamics of Religion* (New York: Harper & Row, 1978); and Thomas Groome, *Christian Religious Education* (New York: Harper & Row, 1981).
7. For a more extended treatment of these issues see Charles Curran, *Themes in Fundamental Moral Theology* (Notre Dame: University of Notre Dame Press, 1977), particularly pp. 27-80.
8. Hauerwas, *Vision and Virtue,* p. 36.
9. See his "Moral Discernment in the Christian Life," in *Theology and Christian Ethics* (Philadelphia: Pilgrim Press, 1974).
10. Philip Keane, "Discernment of Spirits: A Theological Reflection," in *American Ecclesiastical Review,* Vol. 168, p. 43, 1974.
11. H. Richard Niebuhr, *The Responsible Self* (New York: Harper & Row, 1963), p. 48.
12. The concept of organizational character was first developed by Philip Selznick in *Leadership in Administration* (New York: Harper & Row, 1956) and *TVA and the Grass Roots* (Berkeley: University of California Press, 1949). It was later used by others in sociological literature; see particularly Burton Clark, *The Open Door College* (New York: McGraw-Hill, 1960) and John Finley Scott, *Internalization of Norms: A Sociological Theory of Moral Commitment* (Englewood Cliffs: Prentice-Hall, 1971).
13. Selznick, *Leadership in Administration,* p. 55.
14. For an extended treatment of the role of self-deception in the moral life, see Hauerwas, "Autobiography and Self Deception," in *Truthfulness and Tragedy.* pp. 82-98.
15. Philip Keane, "Discernment of Spirits," p. 59.
16. Alfred Schutz, "On Multiple Realities," from *Collected Papers,* Vol. 1 (Hague: Nijhoff Publishers).

DISCUSSION QUESTIONS

1. What effect does the "unionization" question have on the "Catholic identity" question for health care facilities?

2. How is the self-identity of an institution formed?

3. What does it mean to say that a person or institution has character? What are its components?

4. How is a person's and institution's moral identity formed?

5. How will an understanding of organizational character enable individuals within the organization to find moral guidance for the organization's actions?

6. What are the constitutive elements of Catholic identity?

7. How are institutional convictions different from the collective beliefs of individuals who make up the institution?

8. In moral terms, what relationship does belief have to action?

9. Discuss previous institutional actions which demonstrated institutional beliefs.

10. Discuss the processes in which Catholic institutions can engage for the formation and discernment of institutional character.

11. What relationship does institutional character have to the plurality of beliefs of the individuals who compose the institution?

12. What theological issues are basic in the union discussion between labor and management in the Catholic health care facility?

13. What is the basis of organizational policy decisions and where is this basis articulated?

14. What is the relationship between organizational conviction and particular policy choices?

15. What does the concept of organizational character assume about decision making within a health care facility?

16. What effect does the history of the traditional Catholic response to industrial unionization and the history of the Church in the health care ministry have on the institutional character of a Catholic health care facility today?

17. What steps must institutions take to insure that their institutional vision is open to self-criticism and the challenges of others?

18. What does organizational discernment require of Catholic health care facilities?

19. What basic institutional questions are raised by the institution's discernment of the union issue?

CHAPTER **9**

LABOR UNIONS
AND
TWO CONCEPTS
OF
SOCIAL JUSTICE

Leonard J. Weber, PhD

There are a variety of perspectives from which to view the question of the appropriate place for labor unions in Catholic health care institutions. For those who are committed to the pursuit of moral excellence, the labor union issue will be adequately resolved only when it is resolved *justly.* Justice is a fundamental concept of social ethics, and it is to a consideration of justice that we need to turn in understanding our moral obligations as members of human society.

Recognizing the importance of acting justly does not make the unionization question easier to resolve. It is very difficult to apply the principles of justice to the complexities involved in the unionization issue. There is another difficulty as well. For most persons, what justice demands—even in principle—is not clear. We have been influenced by a variety of understandings of justice, and these understandings are not always compatible with one another. The result is, frequently, some confusion about the meaning of justice.

American Catholics are likely to have been influenced by two major interpretations of our social obligations. One influence on us has been the dominant social philosophy and social values of the American culture. Our economic and political systems have been shaped by these values, and these values are still appealed to as justification of decisions and policies. The other major influence on the beliefs of American Catholics in regard to social ethics is the teaching of the Catholic Church on social justice, especially the development of the Catholic social prin-

---

Dr. Weber is associate professor of philosophy and religion, Mercy College of Detroit, Detroit, MI.

ciples that has taken place in the last 100 years. Although the extent to which the principles that have been explicated in Catholic teachings on social justice have become part of the identity of local churches varies greatly, many American Catholics have been influenced by this tradition to some extent.

In order to speak clearly to the issue of labor unions in Catholic health care institutions from the perspective of social justice, it is important to understand what concept of social justice is being used. This essay is an attempt to identify some of the key beliefs in each of the two traditions that have been identified and to indicate ways in which the two understandings of social justice differ. Persons committed to the moral life do not always agree with one another on what is required in certain concrete instances. When that is the case—as in the unionization issue—it may be helpful to step back from the issue for a time and reflect again on the moral beliefs and social philosophy that have affected one's stance. Clarification of how one determines the demands of justice may help to clarify how one approaches the union issue.

Dominant American Social Values

Certain characteristics of the dominant American value system can be identified. Among them are individual freedom, the right to private property, humanitarianism, practicality, self-interest, equality, and rationality.[1] Most Americans, throughout history, have been deeply committed to these values.

Americans have typically emphasized the value of the individual person and championed the rights of the individual both against despotism and against the belief that community welfare comes first. Society is made up of individuals; values like the common good have to be subordinated to the value of individual rights. Individual freedom is often equated with economic freedom or with "free enterprise."

The economic dimension of individual freedom includes an emphasis on property rights and ownership rights. What one has is frequently seen as his or hers to do with as one sees fit. One of government's functions is to protect property rights and to refrain from interfering with them. In a system that understands individual freedom as economic opportunity, success is often measured in terms of material wealth, income, and consumption levels.

The materialism of American culture does not represent the whole of the culture, however. There is, as well, a strong humanitarian emphasis. Individual dignity and freedom is not simply reduced to economic rights. Human rights are to be respected, and basic human needs are to be met. The humanitarianism is exemplified by the outrage that many Americans feel when they hear of violations of human freedoms and rights and by the well-known American response of help to victims of disasters.

Americans, by and large, pride themselves on being a practical people. The focus is on finding practical solutions to tasks that are presented; there is often a reluctance to ask questions about the ultimate value of what is being done. Practicality means that the emphasis is often on short-range problems and issues.

Self-interest should not be understood as the same thing as selfishness. Selfishness usually means that there is little or no regard for the needs or welfare of others. Self-interest, at least as it is valued in America, often goes hand-in-hand with a serious concern for others. It is the belief in America that the whole of society will benefit if each individual pursues his or her own self-interest. It is the belief that the system functions best (and, thus, others benefit) if we act primarily for ourselves rather than for others. Self-interest is therefore the most appropriate motive for behavior, especially economic behavior.

Equality, like freedom is a value that is of fundamental importance to most Americans. But freedom and equality may sometimes be in apparent conflict: where everyone pursues her or his self-interest freely, the result is not likely to be equality. The conflict has basically been resolved in our culture by understanding equality to mean equality of opportunity rather than equality of result. Most Americans are committed to ensuring everyone an equal chance, but equality does not mean that free competition after material accumulation should be restricted.

The type of rationality that is highly valued in American culture is not the same as Aristotle's in his famous definition of humans as rational animals. The capitalistic understanding of rationality seems to have been most prized in America. Planning and calculating in the pursuit of one's goals is what is meant by rational behavior. Thus, it goes along with the emphasis on practicality and acquires an important dimension when coupled with self-interest. Rational, dedicated pursuit of one's self-interest is a widespread American value, particularly in the business sector of society.

Although some of these values pull us in somewhat different directions, there is a certain sense in which most of them form a coherent package of beliefs. As a society and a culture we have been very much influenced by the philosophical tradition known as Liberalism. Liberalism focuses on political and economic freedom and has John Locke and Adam Smith as two of its most important spokespersons. (Classical Liberalism should not be confused with the popular use of "liberal" to designate one opposed to "conservative"; in fact, most contemporary American "conservatives" are closer than "liberals" to the beliefs of Classical Liberalism.) Liberalism has dominated American culture for most of our history. Locke has been particularly important. In the words of Louis Hartz: "Locke dominates American political thought as no other thinker anywhere dominates the political thought of a nation. He is a massive national cliche."[2]

The starting point of Locke's philosophy is his belief that human beings are, by nature, free, equal, and independent. Society is the result of a social contract in which individuals give up some of their independence in order to acquire protection of their rights. One of Locke's major contributions to political theory (and one of the reasons he originally became so popular in America) is his justification of revolution. Government power, he argued, is limited to the task of protecting individual rights, and where governments attempt to exercise absolute power over the lives, liberty, and property of the people, they forfeit their power. In those situations, the people have a right to resume their original liberty. This doctrine of Locke is embodied in the American Declaration of Independence and indicates Liberalism's full commitment to the principle of popular sovereignty.

Just as important to Liberalism as the concept of the minimal state is Locke's theory of property. Property is an essential individual right, and the individual has a right to as much private property as she or he can acquire through labor. The rational person, in the Liberal tradition, is the person who seeks as much private property as possible. The pursuit of maximum private profit (this is one of the contributions of Adam Smith to the Liberal doctrine) benefits the whole of society because it leads to more productive industry and cheaper products. Property is a fundamental right in the Liberal tradition, and the pursuit of private property is beneficial to society.

Liberalism has been the dominant social philosophy in the United States in the last two centuries, and the emphasis on individual rights is at the heart of American values. Some of the basic concepts of Liberalism have undergone some change, of course. When the United States became a nation of large organizations, free enterprise came to mean "private enterprise"—which means anything that is not government.

The free initiative of General Motors or Exxon is to be protected as much as the free initiative of the neighborhood grocer. The heritage of Liberalism remains very much alive, despite significant changes.

Both the "conservatives" and the "liberals" of twentieth-century political and economic debates are inheritors of the Liberal tradition, although they strongly disagree on the role of government in protecting individual liberty and rights. The New Deal, which many "conservatives" identify as the beginning of programs that undermine individual freedom, has been defended by "liberals" as a necessary means of protecting individual rights. (In the words of Franklin Roosevelt: "We have come to a clear realization of the fact that true individual freedom cannot exist without economic security and independence."[3]) Although the "conservatives" stress the need for restricting government power and defend a free private enterprise system and the "liberals" stress the need to protect the welfare of the disadvantaged in society, the two are often only different applications of the same Liberal emphasis on the individual and his or her rights.

The fact that American social thought has been dominated by a concern for the individual has, of course, greatly affected American understandings of social justice. Social justice has come to be defined almost exclusively in terms of distribution. The question of how best to distribute the benefits and burdens of society among individuals has been the almost exclusive focus of the discussions of social justice.

The concept of distributive justice focuses on what is owed to the individual by society. A commitment to justice with this understanding of the meaning of justice has led to some powerful efforts at social reform. An emphasis on just distribution protects individual rights; it attacks discrimination; it protests double standards. This understanding of social justice has provided the basis for some important commentaries on civil freedoms, on racism and sexism, on violence, and on poverty. Rights, fairness, and equality are basic concepts in the American meaning of justice as distributive justice.

Not everyone has agreed, of course, on what constitutes fair distribution. Principles of just distribution that have received a great deal of support in American thought include the following:[4]

- To each according to merit or desert;
- To each according to contribution in satisfying whatever is freely desired by others in the open marketplace of supply and demand; and;
- Similar treatment for similar cases.

Debates about the meaning of social justice in American thought are usually debates about which principle of just distribution (one of the above three or another) is most adequate. Different principles represent a different understanding of the types of claims that individuals can make upon society, and they represent, therefore, somewhat different understandings of individual rights. But perhaps more important than the differences is the fact that most parties in the debates seem to assume that issues of social justice have to do with what individuals deserve to have as individuals.

The Liberal emphasis on individualism has contributed to the identification of social justice as distributive justice. The dominant American social value system inclines us to think in these terms, in terms of the rights of individuals, when we think of justice. Some of the implications of this approach for the unionization issue will be considered after a review of the Catholic social justice tradition.

Social Justice in the Roman Catholic Tradition

In traditional Catholic ethics, justice takes three forms: commutative justice, distributive justice, and legal or general justice. The three differ in terms of the relationships involved. Commutative justice refers to what individuals owe to one another. Distributive justice involves the obligations of society to its members. General justice refers to the individual's obligations to the social whole or the common good. All three forms refer to some kind of indebtedness, but that indebtedness is different in each case. What is ordinarily understood by social justice includes the second and third types.

This traditional distinction indicates that in the Catholic tradition, obligations are seen as multifaceted. One dimension of justice should not be ignored while another is focused on. When we think of justice as fairness, attention is drawn to our responsibilities in commutative justice and in distributive justice, but general justice tends to be ignored. We recognize the injustice in breaking a contract (commutative justice) or in a system that denies equal opportunities to women or minorities (distributive justice) but, where the obligation of general justice is ignored, we do not acknowledge that justice demands that we individuals sacrifice, at times, for the sake of the common good.

The modern Catholic emphasis on social justice issues dates back about 100 years; it is usually regarded as beginning with *Rerum Novarum,* the encyclical letter of Pope Leo XIII in 1891. In modern Catholic social thought, social justice is understood primarily in terms of two basic beliefs: first, that the dignity of each individual must be preserved and individual needs must be met; second, that justice means promoting the common good of humankind. Because of the insistence upon the dignity of the individual, the Catholic tradition is opposed to any political system or practice that completely subordinates the individual to the good of the larger group. Because of the emphasis on the common good, it opposes a system of individualism or one based almost exclusively on individual self-interest.

These two fundamental principles of social philosophy are based upon a particular understanding of human beings. Each individual is inherently good and sacred and should, therefore, never be treated as an object or as a means to some other good. On the other hand, the human being is a social being. She or he lives in society and has responsibilities to others. The belief in the inherent dignity and in the social nature of human persons is at the heart of the modern Catholic social value system.

There is, at times, some tension between these two fundamental principles. The first emphasizes the individual, while the second emphasizes the larger human community. At times, one may be stressed more than the other.[5] But both are to be affirmed and neither should be denied. The two principles are, in fact, complementary. Individual rights exist, but rights have a social character. The common good must be served, but the common good is "that order of society in which every member enjoys the possibility of realizing his true self by participating in the effects of the cooperation of all."[6]

The obligation to work for the common good is the obligation to work for an entire social order that is good. The good that must be done is not the good of an individual (as in the Liberal tradition) but the good of all, the good of persons in community. The concept of the common good means that there is a certain identity between the good of the individual and the good of the whole human race. The individual finds his or her own good in common with others.

It is not contrary to human nature for individuals to subordinate their own self-seeking to the pursuit of the common good. Self-seeking and lack of concern for others are realities, but the potential for cooperation is also a reality. This is the meaning of the traditional Catholic doctrine of original sin. This doctrine, even though it insists on the reality of human sin, differs fundamentally from the view, often found in Christianity, that human nature has been thoroughly corrupted. Andrew Greeley sums up the traditional position and its importance for social ethics:

Humankind is not fundamentally destructive, selfish, individualistic. There is a selfish, aggressive, destructive aspect to our nature; but there is also a generous, trusting, and cooperative aspect to it, and Catholicism is more aware of and has far more confidence in that aspect of the human personality than does Protestantism. Though under no illusion about the present condition of human nature, Catholicism ... makes the fundamental assumption that you create social order by an appeal to humankind's cooperative disposition and not by force or by Hobbesian constraints.[7]

The recognition of an obligation, in justice, to work for the common good means that, in the Catholic tradition, there is more to the meaning of social justice than fair distribution of the burdens and benefits of society. It is this common-good emphasis that puts Catholic social ethics at odds with the social ethics of an individualist philosophy. The individualist tradition believes that the best for all is served through each individual pursuing his or her own self-interest. The common-good tradition argues that the individual is best served by working for a system in which the good of all is central. This, it is argued, is not a denial of the individual for the sake of the whole community (an emphasis on individual dignity accompanies the common-good emphasis) but a realization that what harms the whole harms the individual who is a member of the whole.

Respect for the dignity of the individual requires a commitment to both political and civil liberties ("human rights") and to meeting social and economic needs. Respect for human dignity requires a social structure in which individual rights such as the right to political participation, the right to religious freedom, and the right to organize are recognized. Respect for human dignity also requires a system in which benefits are distributed in a way that meets the needs of everyone for adequate food, adequate shelter, and adequate health care. As David Hollenbach puts it: "Distributive justice will be realized when social patterns are so organized that they meet the minimum needs of all persons and permit an equal opportunity to participate in the public activities which meet these needs."[8]

Both the denial of liberty and the (effective) denial of basic necessities are social injustices. It is often difficult, however, to keep these two in proper balance. Catholic social ethics is critical both of those systems that so stress the economic freedom of individuals that the needs of the disadvantaged are not systematically met and of those systems that stress the priority of economic needs to such an extent that individual freedoms are denied. Both economic structures that produce poverty and political structures that deny civil freedoms are unjust.

Catholic discussion of the right to private property is an example of the attempt to reconcile individual freedom and the common good. For most of the last century, the Church strongly defended the right to private property and was very critical of forms of social organization in which this right was not respected. The defense of the right to own property was made in the context of some twentieth-century denials of personal freedom and thus was closely tied to a defense of individual dignity. In the encyclical *Mater et Magistra,* Pope John XXIII concluded the defense this way: ''Hence one may justifiably conclude that the exercise of freedom finds both a guarantee and an incentive in the right of ownership.''[9]

On the other hand, the defense of the right to private property has never been separated from the insistence that the resources of the world belong to all and that private property has undeniable social aspects. In recent years, the emphasis in much of Catholic social ethics has been placed on meeting the needs of the poor. In terms of private property, this concern has led to stressing the limits of the right of property ownership. As Pope Paul VI articulated in *Populorum Progressio,* the social nature of property at times justifies the taking of property from individuals or corporations:

> Private property does not constitute for anyone an absolute and unconditioned right. No one is justified in keeping for his exclusive use what he does not need, when others lack necessities ... If certain landed estates impede the general prosperity because they are extensive, unused or poorly used, or because they bring hardship to peoples or are detrimental to the interests of the country, the common good sometimes demands their expropriation.[10]

What Pope Paul is stating is a recent version of the traditional teaching of the Catholic Church that property and wealth exist for use by all. Pope John Paul II, in his encyclical on human work, made the same point very forcefully: ''The right to private property is subordinated to the right to common use, to the fact that goods are meant for everyone.''[11]

The question of private property exemplifies the main thrust of the modern Catholic understanding of social justice. Basic needs of persons must be met and personal liberties must be protected for human dignity to be respected. The right to property is a right because property is frequently necessary to satisfy needs and protect freedom. But the right to property is not an unqualified right. It does not entitle anyone to have more than necessary when the basic needs of others are not being met. The common good, the protection of the dignity of all, takes precedence over individual desires or convenience and even, at times, over what individuals can claim to have earned for themselves. The Catholic tradition leads to the conclusion, it would seem, that the distribution should be, first of all, according to need.

Labor Unions and Social Justice

Many times in the history of American Catholicism the question of whether a good Catholic can be a good American has been raised. At times it was raised by non-Catholic Americans who thought that Catholics represented values that were at odds with basic American values. At other times the question was raised by Catholics who thought the same sort of conflict existed. For most persons—Catholics and others—the answer has been that there is no inherent conflict between true commitment to Catholicism and true commitment to basic American beliefs and values.

The two social philosophies that have been discussed above are, indeed, very different in the basic starting points and in many of the beliefs that accompany them. Most American Catholics do not seem to be fully aware of the fact. There may be several reasons for this. In the first place, there are not too many pure examples of either approach; the sharp contrast between the two is not always indicated by the real people we know. In addition, the two positions, despite their important differences, are sometimes in agreement. The emphasis on individual dignity and on basic human rights is so important in each (especially by contrast with traditions that do not value human rights so highly) that they seem, without careful examination, to be similar belief systems. Perhaps most important, American Catholics themselves have been influenced by the Liberal tradition extensively; some of the most outspoken proponents of contemporary American individualism are Catholics.

It is not my purpose here to suggest that good Catholics cannot be good Americans, but it is important to recognize that classical Liberalism is a fundamentally different social vision from the one found in twentieth-century Catholic social ethics. They represent very different understandings of the role and responsibility of the individual in society. The two can be expected to lead, therefore, to different concerns on the proper role of labor unions in business and industry and in non-profit institutions.

In American history, labor unions had an extremely difficult time gaining acceptance. Nineteenth-century capitalists vigorously fought workers' associations. According to the logic of laissez faire capitalism, there was no place for unions. They were seen as interfering with the operation of supply and demand. Gradually, however, support for labor unions grew. Increasingly, citizens became convinced that low wages and unsafe working conditions justified the organization of workers into labor unions.

The unions that emerged in this country were, for the most part, unions dedicated to gaining what they could for the workers. They were usually not committed to fundamentally changing the system to produce a more just society (socialism did not have the appeal to the working class in this country as it did in some parts of industrialized Europe); they were, rather, dedicated to getting a larger piece of the market pie for the workers. Although there is some community emphasis in the very nature of a union, the American union movement did not fundamentally challenge a system based on individual self-interest. Labor unions came to be justified as a legitimate tool to protect the self-interest of workers against the self-interest of the employers.

Throughout the development of the labor movement in this country, the debate about unions has been conducted mostly in terms of Liberal values and concerns—the rights of employers, productivity, the rights of workers, and fair wages. "Conservatives" have emphasized the rights of employers; "liberals" have emphasized the rights of employees.

Catholic social ethics has been applied to the union issue since the beginning of its modern development, and Catholic leaders and social ethicists have generally been quite supportive of labor unions in the United States. The primary emphasis has been, for most of the century, on the right of workers to organize in unions. The defense of the right to unionize has been based on the conviction that the right to join with others is a natural right and that it may be necessary at times to form a labor union in order to secure a just wage and adequate working conditions. Both the freedom to form organizations and the need for fair wages and safe working conditions mean that the right to unionize must be stressed; human dignity demands it.

In recent decades, another dimension of the right to unionize has emerged in Catholic thought. Fundamental human dignity, it is argued, is the need of individual workers to participate actively in the management of enterprises in which they are employed. In the words of the bishops of Vatican II: "In economic enterprises it is persons who work together, that is, free and independent human beings created to the image of God. Therefore, the active participation of everyone in the running of an enterprise should be promoted."[12]

The context in which Pope Leo XIII first gave papal support for the union movement was a context in which workers were seen as being exploited by employers and at the mercy of a system of greed and competition. But it would be a mistake to think that the Catholic defense of labor unions holds only in that sort of situation. Unions are justified, as Catholic social ethics understands human dignity, not only to correct an injustice but also as an expression of a natural need of persons for participation and self-determination. Unions have a positive as well as a corrective function.

Catholic support for unions has been strong, but it has not meant that unions should be supported in everything that they do. Where labor unions fail, and to the extent that they fail, to work for social justice, they are not worthy of support. Strikes are justified only when they are a last resort and for a just cause. Unions themselves must be democratic and nondiscriminatory. Labor unions, like other segments of society, must always seek to meet the demands of justice.

Just as Catholic social ethics, in its understanding of social justice, goes beyond Liberalism's emphasis on individuals and distribution, so, in the discussion of labor unions, Catholic social ethics focuses on more concerns than the dominant American interpretations of freedom, productivity, and the economic rights of management and workers. If the attempt is made to draw out some of the implications of Catholic social ethics in regard to the contemporary issue of the role of labor unions in Catholic health care institutions, some of the following observations might result:

• Sometimes one hears hospital management being told that those institutions that get unions deserve them, that unions represent a failure of management. Someone who has been influenced by the whole of Catholic social thought would, it seems, seriously object to this sort of commentary. In the first place, such an observation suggests that unions have no positive function, that, in fact, they exist only to counteract injustices or correct mistakes. The fundamental need to participate in the running of institutions in which one is involved is being ignored. Unions may not always be the best way to participate but they are, at this time and place, a normal means to achieve that goal. Second, seeing unions as the result of failure on the part of management tends to put management in the position of having to oppose a unionizing movement as a way of proving that management has not, in this case, been a failure. It puts management much too much on the defensive. It makes constructive response much more difficult.

• One dimension of the union question that is of concern to many persons influenced by Catholic ethics is the adversary relationship between workers and management that unions sometimes seem to foster. This is a serious issue. In Catholic ethics, cooperation rather than conflict is viewed as the best way to achieve good results. Both employers and employees must deal with the adversary relationship issue. (It is important to recognize, though, that adversary relationships often exist between management and workers where there are no labor unions.)

• One of the objections sometimes raised to a labor union is that it will bring outsiders into the institution, that the bargaining agent is a sort of "third party" that interferes with the communication and relationship that exists between management and workers and that that party does not really understand or care about what is happening within a particular institution. This is a legitimate concern; it is one of the responsibilities of union leadership to truly represent the workers. Yet there is another dimension to this issue. Social justice requires working for the common good as well as working to ensure that one's own needs are met. For some Catholic ethicists, this obligation to work for the common good has been interpreted to mean an obligation on the part of workers to join with others (outside one's own place of employment) to work for justice in society. The institution, too, has an obligation to society generally as well as to those it serves immediately. An institution does not exist in a vacuum; whenever possible, its role should be seen in terms of the larger society. The concern about the "third party" bargaining agent may be a legitimate concern, but the need of both employees and employers to be part of the work for justice in the larger society is also a legitimate concern.

• Paternalism has become an issue in the unionization question in Catholic institutions. Catholic institutions, because of the Church's hierarchical organization and its tradition of emphasizing authority, have sometimes been quite paternalistic. Employers have sometimes seemed to think that they knew better than workers what was for the good of workers. Although this trait may be found in Catholic institutions, it cannot be defended on the basis of Catholic social ethics. The emphasis on human rights and on worker participation in decision making leaves no room for paternalism. Management may not think that a particular union is good for the institution or for the workers but what is best for the workers is clearly for the workers to decide. The manner in which management's position is presented thus becomes critically important when the unionization issue is put in ethical perspective.

The issues raised in the above four areas are in need, of course, of much more extensive consideration. They have simply been introduced here to indicate that social justice considerations, in the Catholic tradition, sometimes lead far beyond the framework in which they are addressed in the dominant American value system. The concept of justice that one adopts fundamentally affects her or his response to the unionization issue.

---

1. This list is based on Gerald Cavanagh, *American Business Values in Transition* (Englewood Cliffs, NJ: Prentice-Hall, Inc., 1976), pp. 19-24.
2. Louis Hartz, *The Liberal Tradition in America* (New York: Harcourt, Brace and World, 1955), p. 40.
3. Quoted by Ralph Gabriel, *The Course of American Democratic Thought* (New York: The Ronald Press, 1956), p. 432.
4. Gene Outka, "Social Justice and Equal Access to Health Care," *The Journal of Religious Ethics,* 2 (Spring, 1974), pp. 11-32. These are three of the five principles Outka considers.
5. John Pawlikowski, "Human Rights in the Roman Catholic Tradition," *Selected Papers* (Dallas: The American Society of Christian Ethics, 1979), pp. 145-166.
6. J. Messner, *Social Ethics: Natural Law in the Modern World* (St. Louis: B. Herder Book Co., 1949), p. 124.
7. Andrew Greeley, *No Bigger Than Necessary* (New York: New American Library, 1977), pp. 89-90.
8. David Hollenbach, *Claims in Conflict: Retrieving and Renewing the Catholic Human Rights Tradition* (New York: Paulist Press, 1979), p. 151.
9. Pope John XXIII, *Mater et Magistra* (Washington: United States Catholic Conference), #109.
10. Pope Paul VI, *Populorum Progressio* (Washington: United States Catholic Conference), #23-24.
11. Pope John Paul II, *Laborem Exercens,* #14 (Printed in *Origins: NC Documentary Service,* September 24, 1981).
12. Vatican Council II, *Pastoral Constitution on the Church in the Modern World,* #68.

DISCUSSION QUESTIONS

1. What are the characteristics of the dominant American value system?

2. What are the economic dimensions of the dominant American value system?

3. How has the dominant American value system affected our understanding of social justice?

4. What is the "liberal tradition" in the American scheme of social and economic values?

5. What major interpretations of our social obligations have influenced American Catholics?

6. What is the concept of distributive justice?

7. What principles govern a fair distribution of the goods of society?

8. How does the Catholic notion of social justice differ from the dominant American value system?

9. What are the traditional Catholic ways of characterizing the concept of justice?

10. What basic beliefs make up the Catholic notion of social justice?

11. How are Catholic social ethics at odds with the "individualist" philosophy?

12. What is the tension between personal liberty and the economic needs of society as a whole? How can it be resolved?

13. How does the Catholic notion of private property attempt to reconcile notions of individual freedom and the common good?

14. Do Catholic social ethics place any limit on rights of private property?

15. Is there a conflict between twentieth-century Catholic social ethics and classical American liberalism, or do the two coincide?

16. How does laissez faire capitalism perceive unions?

17. Are American labor unions tools of social change or agents for the economic success of their members?

18. Historically, how have Catholic ethicists looked upon unions?

19. What needs of the workers do Catholic social ethics emphasize?

20. Do Catholic social ethics support the right of workers to form a union where no economic injustice exists?

21. How valid are the following observations?
    a) Unions indicate a failure of management.
    b) Unions necessarily foster an adversary relationship between workers and management.
    c) Labor unions introduce a third party element in employer-employee dealings.

22. Is there a positive requirement in Catholic social ethics that workers join unions wherever possible?

23. How is paternalism an issue in the unionization of Catholic health care facilities?

24. What is the appropriate place for labor unions in Catholic health care institutions?

25. What does justice demand in deciding the unionization questions for Catholic health care institutions?

CHAPTER 10

THE CATHOLIC HEALTH CARE FACILITY: ROOTS IN THE GOSPEL AND IN THE NATION

Rev. Thomas Harvey, STL, MSW

From a theological point of view, the Catholic Church can be traced to the mission and the ministry of Jesus Christ. Indeed, in its official writings, the Church has described itself as the very Body of Christ. This incarnational self-consciousness demands that the Church be the continuing sacrament of God's immeasurable love for the human family.

Yet from a very human and practical point of view, the Church is a product of history. The Church, from its first institutional stirrings in Jerusalem, has enjoyed and suffered an almost symbiotic relationship to society and culture. One can see this in virtually every century. This relationship surfaced in the importance given to martyrdom in the first centuries as the Church endured the persecution of the pre-Constantinian Roman Empire. During the fifth, sixth, and seventh centuries, authority schisms divided the Eastern and Western Churches. These divisions were highly influenced by the secular, that is, by the political struggles and rivalries of the Byzantine and Roman seats of imperial government.

Even the shift in the Church's moral vision, introduced by the 1891 labor encyclical of Pope Leo XIII, cannot be divorced from the nineteenth-century social scene in Western society. This shift moved from an almost exclusive accent on preparing the individual for eternal life to a growing consciousness for responsibility in establishing God's reign on earth. Such a major transition reflected the irreversible impact

---

Fr. Harvey is chairman of the Committee on Pluralism, National Conference of Catholic Charities, Pittsburgh, PA, and pastor of St. Kilian Church, Mars, PA.

of the Industrial and French Revolutions—the former created leisure and longevity as well as the social evils so graphically described in that period's poetry and prose, the latter sowed the seeds of self-determination in the political arrangements of modern nations. Both revolutions placed a greater emphasis on life on this earth.

The Church, then, unites a demanding ideal with the constraints of a real history deeply rooted in society and culture. This creates an extraordinary dilemma for the universal Church and all its subunits: how can the Church and its institutions both undergo change and maintain their identity?

This tension exists on many levels. The very universality of the Church reveals one dimension of the problem because of the plurality of world cultures, but every Church institution and organized apostolate experiences this stress most intensely. These are the very instruments that the Church uses to mediate its idealism to individual nations and cultures.

This chapter intends to explore the situation of the Catholic health care facility as it has changed and maintained its Catholic identity in the American pluralistic society. My attempt will be to isolate some of the prevailing influences that have shaped modern Catholic institutions and thus will offer a context within which labor and management issues can reasonably be addressed. The question is precisely this: Are issues such as the organization of labor within service institutions approached more as a derivative of the Church's ideal or of the specific institution's assimilation into the larger secular society's organization, structures, and value base?

The Development of Policy by Consensus: The American Political Experiment

From the writings of Alexis de Tocqueville,[1] the nineteenth century French commentator on the American political genius, to those of John Simon,[2] current Augustus Lines Professor of Law at Yale University, the voluntary association of people to accomplish the common good has been extravagantly praised as unique to the American political experiment. Although the United States shares with many nations its basic democratic and free enterprise underpinnings, there is nonetheless a unique feature of the American social and political fabric—namely, the independent or nonprofit sector. This constitutes that part of organized society that is neither a government bureaucracy nor a profit-motivated corporation. This independent sector, although not easily defined

177

because of its amorphous and complex composition, includes special schools and colleges, hospitals, museums, child care institutions, and even symphonies. It is supported by private and public philanthropy and often mixes volunteer and paid personnel. These organizations generally have missions that would be undertaken by business or government in most nations.

In addition to the variety of institutions, the infusion of government funds into this sector by way of purchase of service, block grants, or third party payments has further extended the identity problem for many parts of this nonprofit world. The Catholic health care facility is part of this independent sector of society, and, in fact, it stands at the most vulnerable end of the continuum of institutions within this sector.

The Catholic facility as both a religious and a health care reality has a double identity within this sector of human service. As a Church reality, it is vulnerable as to its religious nature. Having developed with sectarian funds and a unique concept of minimally salaried religious personnel bound by a common and vowed commitment to serve the needs of specific constituencies, there was little question of these facilities' sectarian identity. But with a modern labor force that typically reflects the general religious pluralism of American society and funding mechanisms such as Hill-Burton for capital expansion and private and public insurance programs such as Blue Cross or Medicaid for operational costs, *the religious identity of the institution calls for constant scrutiny and restatement.*

Even if it were not a religious institution, however, the private, nonprofit facility has other identity pressures. In 1979, when John Simon announced a $1,000,000 research project of nonprofit institutions, he singled out the private health care facility as an especially ambiguous reality within the nonprofit or independent sector. He alluded to the claims of some economists who view the facility as having little life of its own as a voluntary association. They see it more as "a physicians' cooperative—a consortium of a lot of profit-maximizing surgeons, radiologists, anesthesiologists and so on."[3] Even if such a description is not warranted, its very suggestion by a leading researcher and legal mind shows the need for Catholic health care facilities to be very clear in placing their labor-management issues in the American situation rather than in the Gospel imperative. This will permit the real and pressing conflicts to be reviewed as practical challenges of all institutions functioning within American society. If this does not happen, the language of the Church's idealism will have little ability to resolve vital conflicts. In fact, the introduction of Church motivational language, separated from the political situation of the Catholic facility, will have the appearance of a corporate denial mechanism. This may well expose the Church facility to unnecessary criticism in its religious nature and deny it options that may best serve the needs of all.

A second important facet of a pluralistic society must be examined as well, namely, the actual process by which public policy is formulated. In the best of all possible worlds, a nation dedicated to the promotion of the common good and general welfare would have a rational process for creating public policies. Because Americans are so very proud of their stable history, they sometimes feel that at least at the national level, there is such a rational process. In fact, there is not.

Let me define the terms. A rational process of decision making would begin with a *needs assessment.* Having determined the needs, a study of the *available resources* would follow. Then it would be possible to consider a whole range of *policy and program options* that could alleviate such an identified need. Each could then be measured by how it would *resolve* the problem. An *evaluation process* would guarantee the effectiveness of the chosen plan of action. *Reconsideration* would then be possible.

Policies enacted by the Congress of the United States use no such process, however. The political scientist, David Truman, in his text *The Governmental Process* uses a series of case studies to dramatize how political, rather than rational, is policy development in the United States.[4] Decisions are made by the consensus that emerges from the rivalry of interest groups. These in turn reflect the pluralistic nature of American society.

Pluralism implies not only a tolerance for a multiplicity of philosophies and institutions, but values these differences as an ultimate source of strength for the nation as a whole: *E pluribus unum*—from the many, one. This adage written on our coinage poses the constant tension out of which our heritage emerges: a unity that does not stifle or impede diversity. Many of our national characteristics can thus be traced to this pluralism: freedom, tolerance, respect for the individual, *and our commitment to a public policy formed by consensus through political, rather than rational, process.*

The American political process then is a two-edged sword. It has deep roots in the national value base. At the same time, it mobilizes vested interest into a political decision-making process that can preclude a rational approach to the resolution of problems or to the alleviation of identified areas of human need. An example will serve to illustrate the point:

When unemployment runs high, legislation will create labor intense programs, such as the Comprehensive Educational Training Act, which permit the unemployed to work in the nonprofit sector but receive salaries from public money. This often increases the service capacity of such an agency or institution. As unemployment pressures recede, however, such programs are dismantled, even though they are fundamental to services dedicated to human need.

In order to appreciate the political process that has had such a profound effect on the Catholic health care facilities since World War II, let me review its history.

Perhaps an essential modern problem for the private, sectarian provider of health care services can be traced to a lack of a public policy in American history. In fact, the development of a public policy for a national approach to health care came a full century after a public policy for education. Both social needs are important—why was education addressed so much earlier in the nation's public policy? Why did education become a free service mandated for all and health care tied to fee for service and third party payments?

A brief review of these two developments in social policy may well serve to alert health care administrators and professionals of the need to appreciate how national policy influences private institutions even to the point of changing their corporate nature. The alternative involves the exposure of constantly being shaped and controlled by political process, rather than by the internal religious spirit that led to the founding of a health care facility. This religious spirit is often presumed to be the source of its identity, but is it?

The Development of a Public Policy on Education

The United States, even in its infancy, quickly developed a commercial and industrial base that rivaled that of England, France, or the German states. Nonetheless, this created a double pressure for a vital educational system. On the one hand, there was the obvious American problem of multiple languages due to the massive immigrations, especially in the nineteenth century; on the other, a rapidly expanding industrial society needed a literate work force. These two dimensions of early American life quickly brought the issue of a national, educational policy to the fore. In fact, stirrings for a free educational system date back even to the colonial period.

One documented attempt at free education involved a generous landowner in Elizabeth County, VA, who donated 200 acres and eight cows as an endowment for a free school in 1635.[5] In 1648, Massachusetts had its first free school in Dedham, "The Town School and Watch House."[6] After the founding of the Republic, federal land ordinances were passed in 1785 and 1787. These gave the early public financial support needed in the development of an education system. In general, the policy of that age was to provide free education for poor children and charge all others tuition.[7] In 1790, Pennsylvania adopted a new constitution that "directed the Legislature to provide, by appropriate legislation, for the free education of the poor."[8] An active attempt in Pennsylvania and in other states followed to grant the poor access to education. Some today attribute less than altruistic motives to the leaders of that movement. Common school reformers, as they were called, realized that schools could be used for social control and manipulation only if the vast majority of poor children, who were usually judged most in need of such control, were enrolled.[9]

Whatever their reasons, philanthropists of that period either financed schools directly or endowed positions for scholars in the regular schools to bring the poor children into the mainstream of education. This, of course, meant that the poor had to so declare themselves. This was demeaning. It created a stigma. Many refused any such charity scheme. At the other extreme of the social structure, rich parents did not like the idea of paying to send their children to a school that welcomed poor children free. They preferred more exclusive schooling for their money. With the withdrawal of the well-to-do, the regular schools were populated almost entirely by poor children. Free schools, supported by taxation and state grants, solved these problems. The free school mechanism was thus one of the first successful efforts to redistribute wealth to the poor by public policy.[10]

During the first half of the nineteenth century, the free school movement had some of the leading voices of the day: Horace Mann and James G. Carter in Massachusetts, Henry Barnard in Connecticut, Calvin Stowe in Ohio, Caleb Mills in Indiana, and many others. The movement was not local nor isolated; it was a mainstream effort. Adherents wrote pamphlets, articles, and reports. In general, their arguments were as follows: (1) tuition was an unfair burden for the poor; and (2) class distinctions would always disrupt the educational system until "free school" meant a tax-supported system for all."

In addition to the Whig Party, composed mostly of conservatives, middle class, and Protestant clergymen,[12] the newly formed labor unions called for universal and free education.[13] Thus, the advocates for free education represented a strange coalition of diverse interest groups.

Cities began to abolish tuition rates. New York City ended these rates in 1832; Buffalo followed in 1838, and Rochester, in 1848.[14] By the middle of the nineteenth century, most states accepted the idea of a free public school. State legislatures passed laws for local school districts to tax themselves for such schools; many states went so far as to offer state funds, as an incentive to local school districts to tax themselves.[15]

It is not my intention to imply that the creation of the public school system solved all the problems involved in providing for a universally literate citizenry. Catholics and other minorities founded their own school systems to avoid social controls. Many other children with special needs have attained their rights to an education only in recent years.[16] And the connection of public school and local tax base has played a significant role in perpetuating de facto segregation in society.

This historical overview, however, suggests that a particular set of circumstances led to a national public policy that guaranteed education as a right of citizenship, not wealth. As such, education enjoyed the security of tax support. It further suggests that the lack of extremes in the wages paid to education professionals in the field may be tied to this public policy, which virtually eliminated fees for service. The diversity of wages paid to the various professionals in the health care field stands in marked contrast to this. In fact, the institutional health care system in the United States has a radically different history.

The Development of a Public Policy on Health Care

The history of health care facilities in what is now the continental United States dates to the seventeenth century. In this period, Spanish conquistadores created institutions similar to those existing in Europe. These were generally under the auspices of the Church. The first successful attempt to establish a general hospital in the English colonies occurred in 1751 with the opening of the Pennsylvania Hospital in Philadelphia. The second oldest general hospital, the New York Hospital, was opened in 1791. Such early hospitals involved voluntary efforts by private citizens and were usually financed by subscription and bequests, not fees for service.[17]

Many of the early hospitals were especially designed to care for the poor and insane. In fact, often the word *asylum* was a more common term of description than *hospital* during the early 1800s. Such hospitals, which were often even associated with poorhouses, mainly served the impoverished. In turn, these relied mostly on either private or public charity for support. Catholic facilities, along with their counterparts in other religious traditions, developed in a creative fashion according to identified needs, with the commitment of religious personnel and virtually independent of any public monies or public policies. Wealthy citizens were generally treated under the private care of their physicians.

At the present time, both private and public facilities are operationally financed largely by payments for services. In today's world, however, such payments are heavily underwritten by Blue Cross or other health insurance. In addition, the government-supported programs of Medicare and Medicaid were introduced in the mid-1960s to offer an additional source of payments for such institutional medical services.[18]

The cost of health care in the United States has been rising steadily since 1945. Since the nature of health care involves a labor-intense service as well as the need for new and highly sophisticated technologies, it is not remarkable that these two components account for most of the cost increases.

Private insurance plans and the public programs of Medicare and Medicaid have not been without benefit to people previously unable to afford health care. Nonetheless, they have not proved themselves as an optimum system to ensure equal access to health care services. Even with such funding resources available to them, the elderly have been paying for health services at almost record levels. Guidelines such as a *prevailing and customary fee* can be interpreted as vague. In addition, there is an absence of a free market in hospital care, as opposed to the rest of the health care field. As a result, hospital charges are not overly susceptible to control.

When Medicaid was added to the Social Security Act in 1965, as Title XIX, its stated purpose was to ensure the availability and frequency of comprehensive health care to the nation's poor and near-poor in a reasonable time. Thus, through the mechanism of a federal subsidy, individual states were encouraged to provide care not only for the categorically needy, but also to medically indigent children and adults. In fact, even after Medicaid, nearly 50 percent of the elderly's health care expenditures must be covered by other private or public programs or remain the individual's personal responsibility.[19]

Serious analysts of the Medicare and Medicaid programs say that, like so many private insurance plans, they serve more to protect those who provide the service than those who need the care. For too many people, these programs have not improved either the quality or the quantity of medical services. On the other hand, they have guaranteed that the physician, the clinic, or the hospital would be paid for those services that often in the past were donated.[20]

Even the casual student of social policy can note that in the organization of the large private medical insurance plans of Blue Cross and Blue Shield, there is an especially guaranteed financial security given to surgeons. The division of the program into Blue Cross for general medical services and Blue Shield for surgical costs creates a privileged support base for one category of highly skilled labor in the health care field. This type of generally accepted funding affects the sectarian as well as the nonsectarian health care facility. It is part of the broad environment in which the Catholic facility must function. This particular aspect of the modern health care facility's financial reality stands as an invitation for less privileged workers to use organization, collective bargaining, or binding arbitration to attain a decent wage.

There are obvious parallels between the two social welfare systems, education and health care, in the United States. The differences, however, are relevant to this discussion.

Both the public policy for education and institutional health care have sought to be inclusive. Both have continued to adapt to new needs and new pressures. Both have involved a private and a public sector. Both have demanded high levels of professional training. Both have contributed dynamically to the quality of life in the United States. Yet most important, both have evolved through political and not rational processes.

Yet they have differed. Not only did a public policy of health care develop a full century after that of education, but the eventual policy was that one rejected in the early stages of educational policy—namely, the use of insurance or subsidy mechanisms to maintain the fee-for-service by ensuring payment for even the indigent. In education, fee-for-service was rejected for a tax-supported system. Ironically, even the suggestion of a publically supported national health insurance plan raises anxieties about socialism in medicine as if this were some compromise of the American experiment. Yet a totally free public school system with 150 years of history raises no such public outcry about socialism.

Supreme Court rulings have severely limited the use of public monies in private, sectarian, educational facilities. In health care facilities, these limitations have not been so extensive. Thus, there is much more contact between the Catholic health care facility and the public sector's funding and regulatory policies. This contact creates, as a natural consequence, a tension to diminish the unique nature of the private institution in comparison to its public counterpart. Both share a commonality in their financial underpinnings, however.

This blurring of the sectarian health care facility's unique nature and purpose because of the present public policy and financial arrangements is not tangential to the issue of the organization of labor in the Catholic facility. The Catholic facility is a voluntary association. It is Church when it reveals an awareness of the mission that Jesus Christ conveyed to his community of believers—namely, a mission of proclaiming hope-filled good news and reconciliation, a mission with the nobility of selfless love, and a mission with an urgency for justice in both personal life and institutional structures. When the Catholic institution has a willingness to interpret this mission in terms of the common good, it is indeed a Church reality. This mission willingly includes the involvement of nonmembers whether patients or workers. Thus, the Church-related facility is not merely a quasi-public agency perpetuating its existence with insurance and government monies. Although on the level of technologies there may seem no significant difference to other service providers in the health care field, at the ultimate level of its reason for existence there is. The facility that views itself to have a mission that arises from the imperative of the Gospel must find creative and hope-filled ways of mediating the extreme wealth made possible for one class of skilled labor and the virtual poverty standards imposed on another class of unskilled workers at the same institution. Other facilities without such a sense of the Gospel do not have the same burden of problem resolution in such matters.

If the Catholic facility's mission in practice, however, emerges primarily from the wider environment of private and public policies, then it should not only tolerate, but encourage, the establishment of all those mechanisms that are generally accepted by the larger, American society for the safe resolution of conflict, for the distribution of wealth, and the building of a public consensus that ensures good health care and adequate wages for all involved in the delivery of health care. A review of the dynamic impact of a national policy of health care on sectarian hospitals reveals the urgency for management professionals in Catholic facilities to interpret the basis of their religious identity in ongoing programs and policies. This is important not only in affecting the quality of life for patients in a Catholic facility, but also for affecting its workers and a society that is enhanced by every creative expression of diversity.

How the Catholic facility resolves the dilemma of how to change and maintain its religious identity in a pluralistic nation will be a valuable asset to all sectarian institutions in this society. If the dilemma is not resolved from within by noble programs, society will gradually blur the distinction between the public and private facility. And well it should. How the Catholic facility maintains or fails to maintain a Gospel imperative in its very organization within a society whose social policy is determined by political process will not be easy. If expediency and institutional self-interest for survival prevail, then the Catholic institution may become the catalyst for the whole Church within American society to confront its religious integrity and identity. If the Gospel is to be lived and proclaimed, it must have institutional expression. If present religious institutions have become assimilated into the prevailing culture, then new religious realities must be created.

1. Alexis de Tocqueville, *Democracy in America,* ed. Phillips Bradley (New York: Alfred A. Knopf, 1945).
2. John Simon, *Research on Philanthropy* (An Independent Sector Report: Washington, DC, 1979).
3. Simon, p. 1.
4. David B. Truman, *The Governmental Process* (New York: Alfred A. Knopf, 1971).
5. Frederick Eby and Charles F. Arrowood, *The Development of Modern Education* (Englewood Cliffs: Prentice Hall, 1934), p. 165.
6. Eby and Arrowood, p. 170.
7. John E. Sturm and John A. Palmer, *Democratic Legacy in Transition: Perspectives in American Education* (New York: Van Nostrand Reinhold, 1971), p. 30.
8. Eby and Arrowood, p. 549.
9. Robert L. Church and Michael W. Sedlak, *Education in the United States: An Interpretive History* (New York: The Free Press, 1976), p. 61.
10. Church and Sedlak, p. 60.
11. Sturm and Palmer, p. 30.
12. Church and Sedlak, p. 61.
13. Sturm and Palmer, p. 30.
14. Church and Sedlak, p. 61.
15. Sturm and Palmer, p. 30.
16. 24 Pennsylvania Statute, 13-1371 et seq.
17. George Rosen, *Encyclopedia Americana,* vol. 14 (Metuchen: Grolier, 1981).
18. Philip Bonnet, *Encyclopedia Americana,* vol. 14 (Metuchen: Grolier, 1981), p. 439.
19. Agnes W. Brewster; *Medicine in a Changing Society,* ed. Lawrence Corey, MD, Steven E. Saltman, MD, and Michael F. Epstein, MD (St. Louis: C. V. Mosby, 1972) pp. 168, 170, and 172.

20. Stephen Lewin, ed., *The National Health* (New York: The H. W. Wilson Company, 1971).

DISCUSSION QUESTIONS

1. What effect did the French and Industrial Revolutions have on the Church's moral vision?

2. To what unique sector of American social and political life do Catholic health care facilities belong?

3. What has been the effect of the infusion of government funds into the nonprofit sector in general?

4. How is the religious identity of Catholic health care institutions affected by the modern labor force and modern health care funding mechanisms?

5. How does the American context differ from the Gospel context in the conceptualization of labor-management issues for Catholic facilities?

6. What possible negative effect could result from conceptualizing labor-management issues solely in the Gospel context?

7. How is public policy formulated in modern American society?

8. What is the difference between the political formulation of public policy and the rational formulation of public policy?

9. What effect has the political process of policy formulation had on Catholic health care facilities?

10. Why has the formation of a national policy on health care lagged so far behind the formation of a national policy on education?

11. What set of circumstances led to the formulation of a national public policy which guaranteed education as a right of citizenship?

12. What effect has governmental provision of free education had on the salaries of professionals in education?

13. How do the health care wages and salaries contrast to those paid in education?

14. What is the result of the absence of a free market on health care costs?

15. Have government funded health care payments benefited the providers of health services, the sick and aged, and physicians?

16. What effect does the system of physician reimbursement have on Catholic facilities?

17. How has the development of a national health care policy differed from the development of a national education policy?

18. What effect does increased contact between Catholic health care facilities and the funding and regulatory policies of the public sector have on these facilities?

19. How can the Catholic institution today avoid being a quasi-public agency perpetuating its existence with insurance and government monies?

20. What burden does the Gospel imperative place on Catholic facilities with regard to the inequality of wage distribution at these facilities?

21. On what basis can the Catholic institution accept societal mechanisms for conflict resolution, wealth distribution, and the building of a public consensus regarding the provision of good, adequately remunerated health care?

22. How can an institutional expression of the Gospel preserve the religious identity of the Catholic health care facility?

CHAPTER 11

THE CALL FOR A PROPHETIC CATHOLIC HEALTH CARE SYSTEM

Joe Holland

The question of unions in Catholic health care facilities cannot be approached narrowly. If it is approached only as a *management* issue with guidance taken from conventional secular wisdom, the result will be great damage to the Catholic health care ministry's evangelizing thrust and its creative possibilities as a prophetic alternative. Rather, the question must be approached broadly. This certainly means dealing with the Church's social teaching on labor, but it means more. It requires placing the question within an analysis of the contemporary social crisis and the related crisis of the health care system, and within correlative reflection on the changing form of the Church's strategy for evangelization and on the relation of Catholic health ministry to it. These two frames—analysis of the social context and of the new directions in evangelization— provide the background against which this crucial moral and organizational issue must be set.

Pursuing the question of unions in Catholic facilities against this background will fundamentally challenge the operating styles of both management and unions within the Catholic health care system and suggest that both Catholic management and unions need to cooperate to create a prophetic Catholic health system that is based on an alternative health system model and responds to the evangelical commitment for the preferential option for the poor.

I should also say in advance that creation of such a prophetic Catholic health care system would move the debate beyond the liberal-conservative alternatives of central government planning versus free enterprise medicine. Both polarities are pushing the Catholic health care system

---

Mr. Holland is an associate of the Center of Concern, Washington, DC.

away from its prophetic call. Rather than being organized either on the politically bureaucratic governmental model or on the economically ruthless free enterprise model, the Catholic health system is prophetically called to reroot itself in community.

But before exploring that, let us review the new social context and the shifting strategy for evangelization, within which the contemporary question of management-labor relations in Catholic health care institutions surfaces.

The New Social and Ecclesial Context

The overall social context within which the modern health care system arises and contemporary management-labor conflicts emerge is industrial society in general and, for America, industrial capitalism. Indeed, many religious congregations presently ministering in health care were born out of the Industrial Revolution. Before the Industrial Revolution, modern social apostolates such as ministries in health, education, and other charitable works were limited phenomena for church and society.

Thus, the social dislocation of the Industrial Revolution led to the birth of many new religious congregations. Heroic women and men (more often women) were moved by great compassion at the sight of a disrupted peasantry cast from their rural roots into the heartless world of the new urban industrial centers. They looked around, saw the suffering of the unemployed, orphaned, homeless, and ill, and acted in spontaneous and direct ministries. They cared for the orphans, sheltered the homeless, nursed the sick, and taught the illiterate. But they did not act solely as individuals; in the midst of their ministries, they called others to join them. Thus were born the modern activist religious congregations, dedicated to social service for the poor.

Many of the European hierarchy were disturbed by these new religious movements, as they were by the modern world in general. They tried to defend the Church against the modern world and to prevent the emergence of these new orders. It was a conflict paralleling the ancient one between Peter and Paul: Should the church preach to the Gentiles or remain only with the Jews? Should the Church reach out to the modern world or retreat into a ghetto? While many of the bishops were building the walls of a Catholic ghetto, the new religious were already reaching out to the victims of the modern world.

In the United States, new religious orders either came from abroad or were born here after the great industrial expansion after 1840. Industrial immigrants poured in by the millions to work the mines, mills, and factories. They came to a society with few nurses, physicians, or hospitals. They were poor, underpaid, and often abandoned in illness or injury both by employers and by government. Into this context came the new religious, again mainly women, as their only solace. Thus, in early industrial society the face of Jesus often appeared to the sick poor in the image of the sisters.

These new religious congregations thus began their work in the disruptive and harsh context of early industrial capitalism. Their ministries were spontaneous, direct, and rooted in communities of ordinary people. Often these ministers were not well educated, but their zeal more than made up for any educational shortcomings. The great Catholic social institutions that exist today (hospitals, schools, and orphanages) are a continuing testimony to ordinary people's power to change the world.

This early period of industrial capitalism, concentrated in the nineteenth century, has been called the *laissez faire** period. The most outrageous example of laissez faire was the Irish famine of the midnineteenth century, where the British government held that it had no public responsibility to help the starving Irish peasantry when their potato crop failed. While potatoes (the crop of the poor) failed, other crops owned by great plantations and destined for export flourished. As a result, the problem was left to be "solved" by free market forces, with the resulting death or emigration of half of the population.

In the twentieth century, however, a new period of industrial capitalism took shape, namely the *social welfare* period. During this time, government intervened dramatically into the economy, especially on the poor's behalf. Institutionalization of Catholic social service ministries also occurred. On the one hand, this led to public social welfare institutions that competed with Catholic ones. On the other hand, it led to the incorporation of Catholic social welfare ministries into the heart of a revised Church strategy for evangelization.

Thus, while during the nineteenth century the official evangelization strategy rejected the modern world, during the twentieth century the Church competed with the secular modern world precisely on the terrain of social welfare institutions.

These Catholic social welfare institutions, which never before existed on such a scale, can be described as *parallel structures,* that is, as parallel-

---

*Laissez faire, a French term, refers to a political philosophy of no government intervention in the economy.

ing the main forms of socialization within industrial society. As parallel structures, they served two key functions (in addition to their immediate task): (1) to compete with their secular parallels for the loyalty of the Catholic people and so to provide defensive social environments where Catholic social principles could be protected while integrating the Catholic community into the modern world; and (2) to provide bases of influence for the Church in the wider society. This reorganization of the Church's strategy for evangelization around parallel structures marked a basic strategic shift.

During the laissez faire period, the Church's dominant and official strategy could be described as *traditionalist*. It rejected the modern world and tried to organize its resources to protect tradition against the modern world. To enter the modern world would threaten tradition, no matter how many persons would be helped. But during the social welfare period, thanks in part to the work of these pioneering religious, the Church adopted a strategy of cautious integration into the modern world. This can be described as a *liberal strategy,* not in the sense of liberalizing the Church internally, but of accommodating the Church to the liberal environment. The new Catholic social services, emerging as major institutional networks, provided the foundation and leading edge of that new strategy.

But it was not only the Church that changed; society had changed too. Industrial capitalism grew more benevolent, with increasing public and private concern for health, education, and welfare. Eventually, a federal cabinet-level department focused on these themes emerged. But even more important, the harsh and exploitative period of industrial capitalism had passed for many. Children and grandchildren of nineteenth century industrial immigrants were now more prosperous—receiving good salaries, working in better conditions, buying houses and cars, and sending their children to college. In sum, the American Catholic immigrant Church produced a substantial middle class, and with that change the institutional social service ministries took a more middle-class character.

The health care institutions accepted modern organizational techniques and objectives. Both acute and long-term care facilities developed larger complexes, more advanced technology, greater medical specialization, and contemporary management styles taken from major business schools. Eventually they hired large lay staffs in management, medicine, nursing, and supportive services. In fact, the Catholic health ministry became one of the largest social service employers in the country.

In this context, as health care costs rose, the costs were covered for the more affluent by private insurance programs and for the poor by government welfare programs. Thus, even though the Catholic health care system had begun in a context in which the sick were often abandoned both by employers and by government and left to voluntary charity, the tables were turned. Big business (insurance) and big government (welfare) today pay the bills, and the Church institutions act as channels for service.

Eventually, however, a series of interrelated crises emerged that marked the end of the benevolent social welfare period and is producing a shift in the Church's evangelization strategy as well. These shifts, too complex to analyze here, are leading to a general social crisis and a particular crisis in the health care system, plus a call for a more prophetic Catholic strategy for evangelization and hence for a more prophetic Catholic health care system.

In the new period of social history, sometimes referred to as *national security,* there may be long term economic hardship for the majority of the American people. On the one hand, business will no longer provide the reward for labor as it did in the social welfare period. Rather, living standards are already moving from prosperity to a new austerity. For the majority of Americans, this already means the receding of the "American dream." The majority may no longer be able to afford a house, a car, or a college education for their children.

At the same time, there are new attacks on the one instrument that can defend the rights of the working majority of the country, namely, unions. These attacks come from the media, from government, and from management. Some in the media portray unions as racist, corrupt, and too powerful, but they may be one of the better integrated institutions of the country, less corrupt than business, and often weak. Government, increasingly shaped by the New Right and neoconservative offensives, is attempting to undercut much of the pro-labor legislation constructed since the New Deal of Franklin Roosevelt. Finally, management, which a decade or two ago often accepted unions in principle, has now developed a new antiunion and even military style of management (e.g., "chief executive officer") that stresses management's prerogatives. Salaries continue to decline under inflation, and in many cases workers must work longer hours, at faster rates, or on several jobs just to break even.

Government is now backing away from its social welfare role, stressing instead deregulation of the economy and attempting to curtail social spending while expanding military spending. Over the coming years we will probably see reduction or termination of programs like Social Security, Unemployment Compensation, Aid to Families with Dependent Children, Medicare, and Medicaid.

There is not space here to explain the structural roots of the new situation; suffice it to say that because capital is now international and technology so capital intensive, *all* nations are forced to radically redesign their internal social systems in order to provide competitive investment environments in the world market system. This leads to pressures to (1) lower wages (often by breaking or forbidding unions); (2) lower taxes (by dropping social spending); (3) increase militarization (to guarantee access to strategic resources like oil, provide secure shipping and marketing abroad, and protect foreign investments); and (4) impose political stability (by suppressing dissent, either by direct force or by political manipulation).

Looking at the Church globally in this new context, one sees a new *prophetic strategy* for evangelization taking shape. In the laissez faire context, the Church was split between an officially traditionalist strategy and the new direct social ministries of new religious orders. In the social welfare context, the Church adopted a liberal strategy centered on parallel structures (e.g., hospitals and schools) as defensive and integrating instruments. Now in the new national security context the Church is beginning to redesign its ministries around the prophetic task of defending the poor.

But lest the prophetic strategy seem only negative, it carries implicitly the positive task of constructing new alternatives in health care, education, and the like, to serve and defend the poor's basic needs and fundamental rights.

In this new strategy, the Church is led to a prophetic encounter with the wider society—not simply to adapt itself to the modern world, but to transform it. The leading theme in this context becomes "Faith and Justice." The preaching of the Gospel is intimately bound up with defense of the poor. In this new strategy, the key task is to form basic Christian communities, especially among the poor, since they provide the seeds of a new society and a renewed Church. But the Church often pays a great price for this prophetic role, as did Jesus. A new wave of persecution is spreading across the Church in some areas of the world, as Christians are once again condemned for being subversive and are imprisoned, tortured, exiled, and even martyred.

What is the relevance of this discussion for the Catholic health care system or for the management-labor relationship within it? This brings us to our second major heading: the implications of the new social context and evangelizing strategy for the Catholic health care system. See Figure 1 below.

FIGURE 1: Summary of the Shifting Contexts of Health Ministry

SOCIAL CONTEXT	ECCLESIAL CONTEXT	FORM OF MINISTRY
Laissez Faire Stage—19th Century	Traditionalist Catholic Strategy—Pre Modern Institutions	Pre Institutional Health Ministry— Direct & Spontaneous
Social Welfare Stage—Early & Mid 20th Century	Liberal Catholic Strategy—Modern Institutions as Parallel Structures	Parallel Institutional Health Ministry— Modeled on Dominant System
National Security Stage—Late 20th Century	Prophetic Catholic Strategy—Alternative Structures	Alternative Institutional Health Ministry—Based on Option for the Poor

Implications for the Catholic Health Care System

It is no longer sufficient to maintain a parallel Catholic structure operating on the same managerial, or even medical model as the wider secular health care system. Why? Because the convergence of crises is pressing the health care system away from serving the poor, and even the majority of citizens, toward an increasingly expensive, technocratic, and in some ways ineffective health care system.

The new austerity may mean that the majority of Americans will be reluctant to use health care, except in very serious cases, simply because they cannot afford it. Insurance becomes ever more expensive for the middle class, paralleling the rise in health care costs, and leaves much uncovered. Welfare is being dismantled, and in turn will leave the poor unprotected. The only ones with adequate support for health services will be the affluent minority. This may seem an exaggerated prognosis, but it is the direction in which the American heath care system is pointed.

Thus, the Catholic health care system, if it continues on its present trajectory, could wind up the very opposite of what it was intended to be—not an evangelical mission serving those abandoned by society, but a nonevangelical institution reflecting secular logic, rejecting the abandoned, and serving the affluent.

I should quickly add that I do not believe that this will happen. I believe that those who preside over the Catholic health care system have the faith and commitment to search for more creative alternatives.

The search for alternatives will mean moving beyond reliance either on central state planning and subsidies or on free enterprise market mechanisms. One will withdraw support from the poor; the other will exclude the poor outright; and both will reinforce the dominant technocratic style. Rather, the key resources will come from *ordinary people in rooted community, searching for alternatives in health care to meet their basic needs.*

In general, such an alternative health system will shift the operating assumptions of the present system. The present health care system can be described as increasingly reactive, specialized, technocratic, and exclusionary. An alternative system would in turn be more preventive, wholistic, participatory, and encompassing.

To think such alternative thoughts becomes an imperative as the Church reorganizes its strategy for evangelization around the preferential option for the poor. But with such thoughts, *the Catholic health care system's key task is to focus not on management, but rather on creativity.* The task is not simply to manage what is, but to create what is not yet. If this creative task seems beyond our ability, we have only to recall the creative faith of the simple women and men who built the Catholic health care system; they were anything but realists.

In seeking to be faithful to their foundational charisms, the contemporary task is neither to repeat what they did (spontaneous, direct, noninstitutional ministry) nor to perpetuate what their successors built (a parallel Catholic institutional health care system), but rather to redesign the Catholic health care system, with its institutional strength, into a prophetic and alternative system organized around the preferential option for the poor.

This means that we need to begin to speak of *prophetic institutions.* Normally, we think of prophets as persons who reject institutions. Many of the more prophetic persons in religious congregations with a health care ministry have perhaps rejected the institutional forms of ministry and returned to the direct service more typical of their founders or foundresses. But although such individual witness is often heroic, is it sufficient or even desirable to abandon the institutional apparatus that in the long run may be of much greater service to the poor than countless individual ministries? For example, it is a wonderful thing for individual health ministers to work directly with the poor. But how much greater would it be if committed individuals could turn the whole direction of the Catholic health care system.

It is perhaps also easier for prophetic religious individuals not to address the complex problems right in their own backyard. Thus, we see in religious congregations today great concern for the poor in Latin America or Appalachia, but not always for poor employees in the institutions of their own congregations. Similarly, there is growing concern for the rights of women in the Church, but is there also attention to the rights of registered and licensed practical nurses, ward secretaries, and other staff in Catholic hospitals. There is danger here of the same dualism that has always infected the Church in its social mission—concern for those outside, but not for those inside. See Figure 2 below.

FIGURE 2: Contrast of Health Ministries' Underlying Models

PERSPECTIVE	DOMINANT MODEL	ALTERNATIVE MODEL
Temporal Axis:	Reactive	Preventive
Spacial Axis:	Specialized	Wholistic
Governance:	Technocratic	Participatory
Constituency:	Rich Favored	Option for Poor
Key Virtue:	Management	Creativity

The Question of Unions

Are unions an obstacle or a resource for Catholic health care ministry? Let me pose two distinct ways of addressing this question. On the one hand, *if the issue of unions is addressed from a framework that assumes that the present health care system is good, then unions will appear as a threat to its security.* On the other hand, *if the issue of unions is addressed from a framework that assumes that an alternative health care system is needed, then unions could become a resource.* These two ways of addressing the question need more discussion.

In the first case, we can assume that the Catholic health care system is on the right track in simply copying the technological and financial models of the wider society. But the health care system is experiencing serious strain. Costs of providing care are rising astronomically, while personal income is still limited. Further, a particular hospital has probably expanded over past years, making it a much larger enterprise than the early pioneers ever envisaged. Because of the complexity and financial expansion of health care and because of the shortage of sisters, governance of the health care institution is increasingly entrusted to secular or lay specialists.

The path of medicine and health in general is shaped by physicians, trained for long years at the cost of hundreds of thousands of dollars. These specialists in turn have grown into a class apart, living in a medical subculture and isolated further by the fact that their class is one of the wealthiest in the country.

Financial decisions in turn are shaped by high level business people who sit on boards of directors and are generally extremely wealthy persons (usually men). Of course they are not on boards because they are greedy—just the opposite. They are there to help the sisters, and they give abundantly of their time and expertise with no reward except the personal satisfaction of knowing they have contributed to a good cause.

Next, management is entrusted to lay people, sometimes Catholic, sometimes not. These people are trained in modern methods of secular management, perhaps at general business schools, but more often at specialized schools adapting general business training to health care institutions. These people normally have not been given any special training in the tradition of Catholic social thought or in the long history of the religious congregation's encounter with the modern world. It is assumed that their secular technical skills alone equip them for the task of management.

Finally, when difficult problems arise, outside guidance is widely available from law firms or management consulting groups, who have developed particular expertise in these difficult areas.

In sum, there has been a fundamental reversal in the nature of the leadership presiding over the Catholic health system. What was begun (for the most part) mainly by poor, religious, Catholic women in direct ministry to the poor is now mainly presided over by rich, secularly competent men trying to protect the economic security of the health care institution.

These technical experts are not bad people. Most often, I suspect their motives and dedication are superior to the general population's. But they take their orientation from the conventional secular wisdom of cost-accounting techniques. As such, they steer the health care system in a particular direction—*modeled on the modern business corporation.*

Then, along comes a union! Perhaps the employees have some legitimate grievances that have not been attended to. Perhaps the union organizer is only fishing. In any case, the union is there and the alarm sounds.

The sponsoring sisters immediately become frightened. They have no experience in this area and so turn to the "experts." The board

198

members, mainly business people, see unions as an enemy that cuts into profit margins. The physicians, one of the last examples of the successful independent entrepreneur, have little use for social solidarity and also see unions as the enemy—corrupt, money hungry, too powerful, and disruptive of the health care workplace. The managers, trained in new antiunion management styles, feel their authority is being undermined and also see the union as the enemy. They all seek help from law firms or management consultants.

In some cases, the union's presence may be unwarranted, and it is easily defeated. In other cases, it may be more ambiguous, and a struggle ensues. In still other cases, the employees may really want a union, and a bitter polarization occurs. As a result, the institution is marked with deep scars that may last for decades.

Whatever the case, the point is that the judgment is presided over by the upper classes of society—board members, managers, physicians, lawyers, and consultants. The Church is increasingly seeing the world through the experience of the poor, while the hospital is making decisions from a different perspective.

The same thing happened in Europe in the nineteenth century, when unions first arose. The Church viewed the question originally through the eyes of the rich—not then through rich technical specialists, but the rich landed aristocracy. To them, unions were a rebellion against the divine order of rich and poor and therefore the enemy. Most of the leaders of the European Church accepted this frame of reference, and ordinary people—working people—came to see the Church as their enemy. As a result, in those areas where the European labor movement took strength, it was forced to fight the Church, and many workers gave up being Catholic. The loss of the industrial working class to the European Church was the greatest pastoral tragedy of the nineteenth century. Why did it happen? Because the Church read the situation through the eyes of the rich and not the poor.

The same thing is happening again today, only the rich are no longer those who control the land (the landed aristocracy). Rather, today they control technical expertise and define the shape of our social system and its subsystems. Once again, we are seeing a new labor movement being born, not in the industrial sector, but in the service sector; not in Europe, but in America. As the labor movement arises, gathering constituencies from acute and long-term care facilities' workers, it shows itself to be a complex movement. Some organizers are ethical, others are not. Sometimes employees want the union, sometimes they do not. The union's actual behavior is not the deepest question. The deepest question is, rather, how the management of the Catholic health care system views the union, and frequently it views it as the enemy. Thus, it repeats the pattern of the nineteenth century European Church and jeopardizes the very loyalty of workers to the American Church, which was once our special hallmark and the foundation for a successful model of evangelization.

In this process, several rationalizations arise to justify the view of the union as the enemy of the Catholic health care mission.

First, it is sometimes argued that the Catholic institution, because it is religious, is different from the rest of the work world. It is claimed to be modeled on the Christian family, whereas the rest of the society is not. But any honest examination from a sociological viewpoint could disclose that in fact a Catholic hospital is usually very much the same as the secular hospital, except that it has a different sponsoring group, some religious services are provided, and certain medical practices are judged immoral. But the structure and style of management, that is, the nature of the employer-employee relationship, is no different. Indeed, antiunion Catholic management and antiunion secular management cooperate.

Hence, this argument becomes a smokescreen for authoritarian relationships between management and labor. It is particularly ironic, since religious congregations have been busy ever since Vatican II throwing off authoritarian models of governance from their own internal congregational life. But they have continued to impose them on their own employees.

A second argument often proposed is that the union is an outside third party that destroys the intimacy of the employer-employee relationship by driving a wedge between the two. But this argument overlooks the fact that the relationship is already encumbered on the employer side by multiple third parties who have already destroyed the direct and intimate character of this relationship. They are management itself (as distinct from ownership or sponsorship), boards of directors (who probably never meet most of the employees yet set policy for them); management schools that set the style of dealing with employees; and law firms and specialized consultants that are hired (often at great expense) to shape management strategy vis a vis employees. Thus, on one side are the sponsors, the board, the management, the university management schools, management associations, the law firms, and the consulting firms—a complex array of third parties. On the other side are the employees who stand alone. Should they desire a union, it would be nothing more than providing themselves with some of the same resources already assembled on the employer side—legal support, educational resources, and organizational strength.

A third argument, framed in response to the undeniable fact that Catholic social teaching has been basically prounion since the late nineteenth century, argues that although unions were once good and necessary, they have outlived their usefulness. Today, it is argued, they are too corrupt and too strong or else no longer necessary because of the new "participatory" management styles (e.g., open-door policies).

The first response to this argument could easily be that how strange no one told Pope John Paul II of this change, since defending the rights of employees to organize, free of harassment, has been one of his main social themes. His encyclical on the rights of labor *Laborem Exercens* refers to unions as an *"indispensable element* of social life.'' Obviously, no one told the Polish workers about this either, although communist governments make the same claim as some of Catholic management against independent unions, namely, that they disrupt the society or institution and that participation is already guaranteed.

Again the question surfaces, who is to be the judge of that question—the rich or the poor, the employers or the employees, the authorities or the ordinary people?

In fact, just the opposite could be argued, namely, that unions may be more necessary than ever and also may be weaker then ever. Precisely because American society is entering into a deep social crisis, there is the danger of trying to solve the problems of the health care institutions at the expense of the employees and the poor. But just the reverse is called for—not to exclude people from participation in decisions in order to solve problems, but to broaden the participation of ordinary people in basic decision-making processes precisely to guarantee that the solutions will be creative and human.

Thus, in this first way of solving the question of unions, the negative direction of the health care system and the authoritarian social control over it is reinforced. The institution begins to read the society and its health problems through the eyes of the rich rather than the poor. Unions are seen as enemies of management or as obstacles to *defending the institutional security of the present form of health care system*. The consequences of this response, besides deepening the crisis of the health system, contribute to a breakdown of evangelization by the American Catholic Church, since it threatens to repeat the de-Christianization of labor as happened in nineteenth-century Europe.

The second way of responding to the question of unions would require that it be tied to the possibility of an alternative health care system, in which case the union becomes a resource, not an obstacle. In this case, one could imagine a Catholic hospital faced with deepening fiscal crisis and perhaps even with closing. But management does not face this question alone. Rather, it faces the questions with its employees. Perhaps some union representatives are already on the board of directors of the hospital, or perhaps they simply have good working relationships with management, developed out of a cooperative and open bargaining spirit.

Labor and management then together would face the question of the hospital's future. Then both agree they want the hospital to survive and even to improve its service to the community in general and the poor in particular. New forms of cooperative management are developed, which can dramatically increase productivity. New forms of health technology are developed, which enable low-income people to get better access to health care services at lower costs. For example, an extensive program of paraprofessionals is developed, as well as new forms of outreach like home delivery midwife programs. The hospital reorients its philosophy around a wellness concept in health and develops community education programs in nutrition and prevention. New cooperative forms of payment are explored, like the health maintenance organization (HMO) concept. In addition, the union, with its extensive educational and lobbying apparatus, is able to develop new cost-cutting policies and to gain community and governmental support for them. Under union suggestion, day-care services are provided for employees, and new health outreaches into the community, through decentralized clinics, spring up.

The hospital workers, who belong to the union, are also members of the community of poor people serviced by the hospital and so are delighted that health care facilities will remain in their area. The hospital, and the sisters who sponsor it, come to be known as friends of the poor. Through their witness, the Gospel takes deeper roots in the community of the poor. See Figure 3 on page 203.

Suggestions for the Future

I would like to offer some practical transitional guidelines:

- *Begin a "precrisis" dialogue with labor.* There is need for a national

FIGURE 3: Contrast of Attitudes Toward Unions

UNION AS ENEMY	UNION AS RESOURCE
Guidance from elites: doctors, business people, lawyers, management consultants, management schools, management associations.	Guidance from communities of ordinary people, especially the poor, in shaping the health care system in service of basic needs for all.
Institution seen as modeled on Christian family with no need for unions, and presence of union organizing a sign of management's failure.	Institution seen as complex structure with need for union as mediating body required for successful management and an aid to good manager.
Union as third party destroying the intimacy of the employer-employee relationship.	Unions as employee's counter balance to multiple third parties on management side.
Fear of employees and concern for institutional security as motivational foundation.	Imagination of possibilities and concern for new alternatives as motivational foundation.

forum of dialogue between the sponsors and managers of Catholic health care and the leaders of unions active in this area. The focus of this dialogue needs to move beyond the "prerogatives of management." It also needs to move beyond a narrow self-understanding of the role of unions, which would see them only in an adversary relationship with management (letting management worry about how to make ends meet and about the nature of the health care system, and having the union only concerned with employee wages and benefits). Rather, the focus of the dialogue should be management's and labor's common concern for a creative, sustainable, and just health care system. If such a dialogue were to develop, I believe unions would appear much more an ally than an enemy.

• *Boards of directors should be microcosms of community.* If the health care system is to move in a prophetic direction, the nature of the boards of directors needs to shift. They should no longer be made up only of "technical experts" from business and medicine, but should reflect the wider community and include representatives from the labor movement in the area, perhaps even some elected employee representatives, as well as major health consumer interests (the elderly, the handicapped, and the poor). The poor in particular should have a privileged place on boards, as is required, for example, for grantees from the Campaign for

Human Development of the U.S. Catholic Church. It will, of course, be argued that the issues that boards address are too complex for "ordinary people," but just the opposite is true. What is at stake is shaping the fundamental values of the health care system—something too important to leave to experts.

• *Lay management needs the support of sustained Christian formation.* Although in recent years religious congregations have benefited from extensive education about the Church's growing commitment to the poor, lay managers are often hired only for their technical competence. The sponsors need to develop for these lay managers extensive training programs in the Church's new social orientation and in the background of Catholic social thought. In addition, where new management is being selected, Gospel values of commitment to the poor and a self-understanding of democratic management as a form of Christian ministry should be criteria for selection.

• *The management model should be increasingly cooperative.* Presently management models are taken from secular business schools, but Catholic health care institutions are much more than secular businesses. It would be well, therefore, to explore the alternative management model carried by the cooperative movement, to which the Church has been deeply committed in the past.

• *Beware of lawyers and the legal trap.* Lawyers should be used within limits. The United States is now the most lawyer-encumbered nation in the world, with the courts becoming the place where social questions are resolved. Unfortunately, this undermines the social fabric and is extremely expensive. The legal profession has a vested interest in adversary relationships, whether they be management lawyers or labor lawyers. Instead, we need to find new, less legalistic, and more cooperative ways to resolve conflicts. Especially, we need to beware of letting lawyers unduly expand their competence from technical experts in legal matters to master strategists setting the whole course for how to deal with unions. Lawyers should be prepared to explain what legal consequences a given course of action entails, but the sponsors must set the course, and preferably they will set a creative one.

• *Define the health mission around the preferential option for the poor.* Since Vatican II, the 1971 Synod of Bishops, Medellin and Puebla, there has been growing orientation of the Catholic Church's pastoral thrust to the poor. So should it be in the Catholic health ministry. It needs to be the defining principle around which ministry is eventually organized. This is a very different principle, by the way, than is normally mediated by management schools or legal advice. It requires long strategic planning and gradual shifting of the institution's directions. The important opening at this point is to find the few, small, but seminal steps that begin to lay the groundwork.

In conclusion, the coming decade of Catholic health care will be one of searching and reappraisal. It will probably also be marked by increasing conflicts over the underlying social and religious values. But I have little doubt that out of this conflict will come a new and deepening commitment to an evangelical and prophetic health care system, organized around the preferential option for the poor. As this happens, I also believe that unions (made up mostly of poor health workers) will be considered an enemy no longer, but a friend.

DISCUSSION QUESTIONS

1. Describe the social evangelical context in which the modern health care system developed and now exists.

2. What effect did the social dislocation of the industrial revolution have on religious congregations and ministry?

3. Is the laissez faire doctrine in industrial society compatible with Christianity?

4. Are Catholic social service institutions compatible with the modern industrial society?

5. Describe the effects of "benevolent capitalism" and an increasing public and private concern for social services on Catholic health care institutions.

6. What effect does a "national security" environment have on the Church and its ministry?

7. What trends constitute the "national security" environment?

8. How does the Church respond to this new environment?

9. What relevance will the Church's reaction have for Catholic health care institutions?

10. Are alternative systems available to Catholic health care institutions beyond reliance on state planning and subsidiaries or reliance on the free enterprise market?

11. How does exclusive reliance on business and professional experts affect the values that lie at the basis of the present American health care system?

12. How can the Catholic health care system be redesigned into a prophetic system?

13. Are health care workers' unions an obstacle to or a resource for Catholic health care ministry?

14. Compare and contrast the current response to unions in Catholic facilities with the response in Europe in the 19th century.

15. Is the assumption that unions are essential to Church mission and Christian community goals valid?

16. What are the consequences of this assumption for the Catholic health care system?

17. What arguments exist to justify viewing unions as necessary to the Catholic health care mission?

18. What are the consequences of viewing unions as an essential part of the Catholic health care mission?

19. What steps can be taken to achieve the integration of unions into the Catholic health care mission?

20. How are unions viewed in Pope John Paul II's encyclical, *Laborem Exercens?*

CHAPTER 12

CATHOLICITY
AND CREATIVITY
IN THE
COLLECTIVE
BARGAINING PROCESS

Rev. William J. Byron, SJ, PhD

Catholic health care facilities, like Catholic colleges, have distinctive characteristics that set them apart from their secular counterparts. It is not my intention here to explore the differences or probe the identity issue. What makes the institutions "characteristically Catholic" is of less concern to me than the question of what the Catholic character of an institution has to say about collective bargaining in that institution.

Bargaining in a Catholic Context
Collective bargaining deals with job security, salaries, and working conditions. I would assume that a Catholic institution would be careful to provide working conditions consistent with the dignity of the persons employed there. If not, the institution is not "characteristically Catholic" and thus outside the scope of this essay. I would also assume that Catholic institutions would not take lightly workers' concern for job security. That issue rises in importance as job opportunities decline. But even if an institution does respect the job-security concerns of employees and does provide them with both voice and choice in matters affecting their work environment, there will always be the distribution issue, the complicated question of remuneration. Wages are part of a larger picture. They relate, in the private sector at least, to price, to the charges borne by the recipient of the institution's services. In health care facilities and schools ("nonprofit" institutions), wages do not compete with profits. They do, however, represent a competing claim, on the expenditure side of the budget, with management salaries, necessary operating-fund surpluses, plant fund needs, overhead costs, reserves for contingencies,

---

Fr. Byron is president of the University of Scranton, Scranton, PA.

"venture funds" for the development of new services, and discounts or waivers of fees for the poor and others unable to pay for services the institution provides. The list of competing claims could be easily extended. Judgments about their relative importance will understandably differ. These differences set the stage for a collective bargain, a resolution of the competing claims.

Paternalism, not unknown in the history of the very best Catholic institutions, resents and rejects intrusions in the process of deciding what is "best for all concerned." Collective bargaining, backed by law, forces such intrusion. It takes a while for paternalistic (or maternalistic) managements to get comfortable with the presence of others in the decision-making process. Opening up the process voluntarily is an obvious way of avoiding the imposition of collective bargaining.

Whatever the forum for discussion, the focus of decision making will center on remuneration. The issue will naturally enlarge itself to include the "fringes," benefit considerations that move beyond mere *vivere* to *bene vivere*. But, in my view, the heart of the remuneration issue and thus the core of the bargaining debate relates to gain sharing. If the debate is to be honest and productive, the gain must be clearly defined. For the gain to be defined, management must have measures that are agreeable to, and can be audited by, the other party to the decision.

Despite their sometimes bombastic language, frail people sit on both sides of any bargaining table. The process would work beautifully if only the participants would not posture and pretend. All too often what Kermit Gordon once called "forthright evasion" lines up against bellicose bluffing. The words least likely to be belived are, "this is our top offer" and "this is our rock bottom demand." Thus, a cloud of distrust and ambiguity descends. Out of the confusion rise honest management fears about ability to pay while holding charges to a reasonable level, and honest labor concerns about keeping up with rising prices and making enough to get ahead. Encircling these concerns are honest fears about the interruption of necessary, even vital services in the event of strike. Such fears, in a Catholic institution, are, one must presume, prompted by professional integrity on both sides of the argument.

Survival of the institution is another deep concern. The presumption, often unfair, is that management takes a longer view than the more immediate paycheck perspective of the workers. The judgment made by one side against the other in this regard is usually faulty; the perspective on neither side is as long and altruistic as the proponents pretend. Moreover, there is nothing in Catholic doctrine that grants any Catholic hospital or school existence until the end of time. There is, of course, a time-honored Catholic social principle that attaches a simple conclusion to the argument of inability to pay a living wage: dissolve the enterprise.

Catholicity clearly requires of its adherents in the world of work an openness to collective bargaining. Creativity, enlarged by supernatural grace, can make the Catholic enterprise function in a way that collective bargaining (with its added financial costs, litigiousness, potential for distrust, and penchant for acrimony) can be rendered unnecessary. Or, if needed to bridge communication gaps and meet unattended problems, collective bargaining in a Catholic context can itself exhibit Catholic characteristics. Aside from charity, patience, justice, honesty, courage, and compassion on both sides, collective bargaining in a Catholic context should be characterized by creativity.

There is no such thing as Catholic collective bargaining. The process is a human construct, a social institution. When Catholics engage in the process, their Catholic principles and character can make the process work in new ways. Only creativity can make this happen. In the context of collective bargaining, creativity means generating new options all the time.

It must be said that not every good, service, or way of doing things in the world of work is always good for the use of everyone. To put it another way and simply, collective bargaining can be abused. It can provoke participants (all of them, as noted earlier, "frail" and in need of healing grace) to behavior less than virtuous. Not all negotiators are selected on the strength of their moral character or the depth of their faith. Nor is intelligence always a prime criterion. Sadly, force is sometimes an acceptable substitute for thought in the collective bargaining process. Collective bargaining is a device of human construction. It is open to abuse.

Collective Communication

One must acknowledge, however, that collective bargaining is a useful structure for communication. In the process, things get talked about—sometimes endlessly. I was impressed by British novelist Pamela Hansford Johnson when she explained that "something to talk about" can help keep a marriage together, as was the case in her marriage of many decades to C. P. Snow. Honest talk in a bargaining context can keep an institution together. But honest talk and fair dealing are possibilities, of course, in many workplace arrangements other than collective bargaining.

It is often remarked that the most effective union organizer is an unresponsive, heedless, doctrinaire manager. Case histories of unionization in Catholic institutions will not infrequently substantiate that assertion. If the "Son of Man came not to be served but to serve and to give his life as a ransom for many" (Matt. 20:28), one might expect institutions that embody Christian principles to be sufficiently sensitive to employees to listen to them. They, of course, should be sufficiently responsible to communicate in unexaggerated and unprovoking terms. But frail, fallible, and limited people line up on both sides of the communications gap. Often before they know it, they are saved from their own excesses by the mechanism of collective bargaining. Once the mechanism is in place, parties to a potential bargain relate to one another differently. This is not necessarily bad. What previously may have been random, even arbitrary decision making on remuneration issues is now formalized. Processes and procedures are rationalized. Accountability is focused.

As employee security increases, management freedom decreases. The relationship is not necessarily causal. A fully free and fully responsible (there's the rub!) management can use spontaneity, generosity, and surprise to advance the enterprise and benefit the employees. But a free and irresponsible, or at least insensitive, management can fail its employees and leave them with little choice but to organize.

Insiders and Outsiders

Once organized, workers can choose some of their own to represent them or opt for outside negotiators. From management's viewpoint, both choices have advantages and disadvantages. If the union negotiators are insiders, fulltime employees, one might presume easier communication, greater familiarity with the enterprise (particularly with patients, students, or other "clients" the institution serves), and deeper loyalty to the institution. Catholic management would consider all this important. It would hope for a commitment on the negotiators' part to the institution's religious mission, an understanding of its purpose, and a disinterested desire for its survival. But inside negotiators are, at least in the early years of unionization, inexperienced negotiators. They sometimes misapply the "big industrial union" model to themselves. They begin clumsily and end excessively dependent on outside legal counsel. Parallel problems appear on the side of management.

When an outside (national or international) union represents employees of a Catholic institution, administrators in that enterprise have, in addition to their discomfort over the ''intrusion,'' the genuine fear that the institution's Catholic purposes will be misunderstood or ignored. There are further fears that the institution's ''clients'' (patients and students) will be at best unknown and at worst disregarded and that the institution's survival will not count for much on a long list of outside negotiators' concerns. All these fears represent possibilities that need not be realized. Each one of these fears, moreover, is a measure of the responsibility management has to attend to the problems that prompt workers to organize in the first place.

Creative Sharing

I have mentioned creativity more than once in this essay. In those pursuits most obviously creative—acting, writing, composing, painting, sculpting—the medium provides an opportunity to start all over again. A new play, poem, or performance is a new creation.

Contracts expire, and the opportunity is there to start all over again. Collective bargaining represents a new beginning. The material to be shaped into a creative agreement is limited in that one important respect—it is material. It is subject to constraints. There is just so much to go around. The question is how much, and this brings the discussion back to the notion of gain sharing.

As men and women work for pay in a shared enterprise, they derive satisfaction from the achievement of measurable results. They also receive pay for their labor, for the time and skill they devote to the enterprise. If they work well together, they can realize economies; they can produce more for less. Gains of measurable dollar value, thus produced, should be shared. In a market economy, the expectation of sharing in the gain keeps all participants in the enterprise going. (I am prescinding now from the higher motives that normally draw people into service in Catholic institutions.)

Because the gain is by no means ensured before the fact, management is unwilling to commit itself in advance to wage payments that would presume the gain.

Labor, for its part, is unwilling to concede, long before the fact, that no gain will be there to be shared. Labor is thus reluctant to settle for a wage that, over the life of the contract, may prove to be significantly less than the wage an as-yet-unrealized gain will enable the enterprise to pay. So before the fact, labor holds out for more and management holds back.

If a nonprofit institution has a good management information system grounded on a reliable data base, a form of gain sharing can be worked out that will ease anxieties on both sides of the bargaining table, hasten arrival at agreement, and provide a guarantee of increased remuneration if the year ahead proves to be a good one. How is all this to be achieved before the fact?

Budgets, which are planning documents prepared before the fact, embody assumptions. In a hospital, for example, a large segment of the projected revenue is calculated on the estimated number of "patient days" for the next fiscal year, multiplied by anticipated patient payments. In a college, budgeted revenues will assume a certain number of "paid credits" or a "full-time equivalent" student count for the period in question, multiplied by a set preannounced price (tuition) that will not change over that same period.

Hospital employees may say the patient-day estimate is too low. College faculty may argue that enrollment projections are too conservative and that the revenue picture will be brighter than the budgeted number of paid credits would indicate. Rather than arguing over the estimates and pushing the institution into a high-risk position of antecedent commitment to a compensation bill it may not be able to meet (not to mention pushing the price to a level beyond the reach of its clients), why not agree that if patient days or paid credits (or whatever previously agreed upon, measurable, suitable number has been used in the revenue assumption) exceeds the estimated level, the consequent revenue gain will be shared with the workers on the basis of a formula that reflects labor costs as a percentage of costs incurred in providing the service?

Would the gain be shared as a bonus or fitted somehow retroactively into the wage structure? Let the bargainers decide. What if there is no gain? Then the revenue assumptions will have been proved correct and fiscal damage will have been avoided. What if there is not only no gain but a loss, a revenue shortfall? The remuneration agreed upon in the contract will not change. What is proposed here is gain sharing with employees, not risk sharing. The workers will not pay for management's estimating errors. Worker willingness to accept a gain-sharing arrangement would, one might hope, contribute to a better revenue-estimating environment by properly pressuring managerial competence.

Management's rights are not infringed by an audit of the appropriate records that reveal quite precisely the number of patient days or paid credits. The complete financial audit of the most recent fiscal year need not be disclosed. The point of an audit associated with gain sharing is to enable adjustments in pay to be made at the end of a fiscal year but before the "books close" on that year.

Although it would be most unwise to pit student versus faculty or patient versus nurse in the revenue and remuneration context of a non-profit enterprise, it cannot be denied that compensation is related to client payments. Improved compensation normally means higher prices. Rarely is there sufficient room on the expenditure side of the budget to provide higher wages in the absence of a price increase without deferring maintenance, incurring debt, or depriving the enterprise of necessary plant and equipment. Careful management will calculate on an annual basis and communicate to all concerned the ratio of compensation to a given employee group (nurses, for example, or teachers) as a percentage of total fees paid by users of the service the institution provides. The calculation involves a simple fraction.

In the college example, tuition and fees would be in the denominator and faculty compensation would be in the numerator. If a reasonably fair arrangement is already in place, that is, the price is fair and the compensation is reasonable although subject to improvement, then management will want to hold that ratio as constant as possible to safeguard the financial security of the entire enterprise. Hence, adjustments leading to improved compensation (the numerator) must be made with an eye to offsetting adjustments in price (increasing the value of the denominator). If the numerator grows and the denominator stays the same (no price increases) and if there is insufficient growth in other revenue sources like endowment income or external fund raising for current operations, then serious problems will develop elsewhere in the enterprise. The gain-sharing idea is one way of preventing irreversible problems from developing. Gain sharing can enable the institution to stay on the safe side of financial exigency.

Administered Frustration

Management will understandably resent, but must come to expect as normal, employee pressure. A certain pressure to produce, from management to labor, is not unusual. Pressure for pay and for a voice in production decisions is not unexpected from labor to management. When those pressures bear on concealed deficiencies, understandable resentment turns into self-justifying defensiveness that is unworthy of those who are there "to serve and not to be served."

If reciprocal pressures in the workplace are held to normal levels, communication can be constructive and differences will not become entrenched. This can be the case with or without collective bargaining. With or without collective bargaining, labor and management can, in former Secretary of Health, Education and Welfare, John W. Gardner's words, "tolerate extraordinary hardship if they think it is an unalterable part of life's travail. But an administered frustration—unsanctioned by religion or custom or deeply rooted values—is more than the spirit can bear.''*

Administered frustration can force workers to organize. But the collective bargaining process itself can produce administered frustration. Pressure management remains a challenge with or without collective bargaining. Creativity is the best control. And the best application of creativity in this regard is the identification of potential gains and the design of an agreement to share those gains in a way that serves the balanced interests of all parties to the enterprise. If there is no unexpected gain to be shared, the shared commitment of workers and management to the purposes of the service-rendering enterprise will keep the organization together. And the Catholic view would see the organization remaining together as long as the Lord wills it so.

*John W. Gardner, commencement address at Cornell University, Ithaca, NY, quoted in *The Wall Street Journal,* Nov. 26, 1968.

DISCUSSION QUESTIONS

1. What effect should the Catholic character of an institution have on its wages, working conditions, and job security?

2. How does the paternalistic or maternalistic model of employer-employee relations deal with the collective bargaining issue?

3. What does the Catholic character of an institution have to say about collective bargaining in that institution?

4. What is the heart of the remuneration issue in collective bargaining?

5. Of what concern is the survival of the institution in collective bargaining?

6. What must a Catholic institution do when it is incapable of paying a living wage?

7. Is there "Catholic" collective bargaining?

8. What effect does collective bargaining have on institutional communication?

9. To what extent does the presence of a union indicate a failure to communicate by management?

10. What is the effect on the collective bargaining process if negotiators are drawn from the work force or are supplied by the union?

11. Is gain sharing a creative response within the collective bargaining situation?

12. How does gain sharing differ from risk sharing, from the worker's perspective?

13. What degree of openness on the part of management's budgets and records does the gain-sharing concept require?

14. Is this openness an infringement on management's prerogatives?

15. Does the relation of worker compensation to client payments pit the worker against the client?

16. How can "administered frustration" in an institution be avoided via the collective bargaining process?

CONCLUSION

At the center of the consideration of labor-management issues in Catholic health care facilities lies a paradox. The Catholic facility has as its goal the provision of health care, within the millenia-old Catholic tradition of the corporal and spiritual works of mercy. Given its locus in that tradition, how can the division and remuneration of labor within a Catholic facility be a source of contention? Do not the members of the Church community that is the Catholic facility owe each other at least the charity they manifest to the sick, the aged, and the infirm?

Some might call this characterization naive. After all, any health care facility, even a Catholic one, is part of the multibillion dollar American health care system. Health care is big business; health care facilities cannot survive on charity alone. Client, government, and third party payments, not charity, are health care facilities' major sources of income. Why should one be surprised that the health care business, like any business, has its labor problems? Have not Catholic facilities' managers acted like other business managers in fighting off unions? Have not unions ignored these institutions' religious nature in their organizing campaigns?

The authors of this text say differently. They have stressed the Catholic identity of Catholic facilities, and they see existing in this identity a rich tradition of social justice teachings that, if followed, could form the basis of a new reality for Catholic facilities. From this viewpoint, it is not naive to characterize these facilities as individual ecclesial communities, because each one is such a community. Each one is a group of persons, motivated by a common faith or by the concerns of that faith, who have come together to provide physical and spiritual solace and care to the sick, the aged, and the infirm within the tradition of that faith.

A related theme of these essays has been to suggest to the reader that there is a different way to look at things than from the big business vs. big labor perspective. The characterizations of labor-management relations in American history and by the American press is one of conflict and struggle in which the highest interest is self-interest and in which means are justified by ends. The decision makers who read this book must be careful not to make judgments concerning Catholic facilities from this viewpoint. Such a viewpoint implies values and makes value judgments that may be accepted as the common wisdom but that, in fact, are alien to the Catholic tradition.

216

It is from this uniqueness (Catholicity) that Catholic facilities must answer the conflicts of labor and management. If this is not the case, if the answers come not from their Catholic identity but from the common American wisdom, then these institutions will not survive as Catholic ones; worse, they will not deserve to survive. So many forces already push their absorption into generic health care provision, in which one provider is no different than another. It would be tragic if Catholic facilities hastened this trend by their own participation. Rather, Catholic facilities must allow their particular Catholic genius, as it has been variously described by these authors, to provide the answers to labor-management conflicts.

In this way, the Catholic health care community will be a microcosm of the larger Church community. It will exist and grow within the larger communion of the entire People of God. Just as, in the universal Church, leadership exists within the community and is affected by the community, so too, in the health care community, leadership and decision making exists for the community and must be affected by the community. In such a process the important principles of subsidiarity and participation that govern the larger Church community will also be at work within the health care community. Within that community, subsidiarity requires that decisions be made at the most appropriate level, and participation requires that all those affected by the decision have a part in its making. In this way, decisions affecting the health care community's labor-management concerns will reflect the whole community and the Catholic values embodied therein.

This Church perspective must be communicated to those involved in the critical labor-management issues facing Catholic institutions. It must be communicated to administrators, to professional consultants, to attorneys, to workers, and to union representatives. The answers that the Catholic facility will give to labor-management concerns are not managerial answers, nor are they the answers of labor. Rather, they are the answers of the Catholic community that makes up the facility. They are the answers of a community that sees no need for confrontation in its decision making, because it has exercised the ecclesial community values of subsidiarity and participation.

This does not mean that Catholic facilities can or should use their religious identity as a dodge to avoid answering the real conflicts of the real world in a real way. The answers that a shared faith will provide will genuinely respond to these issues because this faith, which has built, staffed, nurtured, and preserved the great Catholic health care facilities, is a faith very much in the world, meeting the world on the cutting edge of life and death, sickness and health, time and eternity, every day.

This collection of essays has attempted to frame the labor and management issues that confront Catholic facilities from a religious—a Catholic—perspective. By so framing the issues, the text is meant to be a guide to informed, intelligent decisions on these issues that are consistent with Catholic tradition and that take their strength from this tradition. There is an old legal saying that whoever frames the issue decides, in effect, how the issue will be answered. Although the authors have framed the issues for the reader, they have not provided any one answer, if in fact any one answer exists. This book, after all, is not meant to be blindly followed; rather, it seeks to assist the reader to participate in policy formulation at any level in the service community. The authors have provided the reader with a means to proceed. How the reader proceeds is his or her decision, but if such a decision relies on the values that make facilities Catholic, the values that this text as a whole has emphasized, there is no wrong way. There are only different reflections of one truth.

APPENDIX
LABOREM EXERCENS
ON HUMAN WORK

Pope John Paul II

Through work man must earn his daily bread[1] and contribute to the continual advance of science and technology and, above all, to elevating unceasingly the cultural and moral level of the society within which he lives in community with those who belong to the same family. And work means any activity by man, whether manual or intellectual, whatever its nature or circumstances; it means any human activity that can and must be recognized as work, in the midst of all the many activities of which man is capable and to which he is predisposed by his very nature, by virtue of humanity itself. Man is made to be in the visible universe an image and likeness of God himelf,[2] and he is placed in it in order to subdue the earth.[3] From the beginning therefore he is called to work. Work is one of the characteristics that distinguish man from the rest of creatures, whose activity for sustaining their lives cannot be called work. Only man is capable of work, and only man works, at the same time by work occupying his existence on earth. Thus work bears a particular mark of man and of humanity, the mark of a person operating within a community of persons. And this mark decides its interior characteristics; in a sense it constitutes its very nature.

I   Introduction
1. Human Work on the 90th Anniversary of *Rerum Novarum*

Since May 15 of the present year was the 90th anniversary of the publication by the great pope of the "social question," Leo XIII, of the decisively important encyclical which begins with the words *rerum novarum,* I wish to devote this document to human work and, even more, to man in the vast context of the reality of work. As I said in the encyclical *Redemptor Hominis,* published at the beginning of my service in the See of St. Peter in Rome, man "is the primary and fundamental way for the church,"[4] precisely because of the inscrutable mystery of redemption in Christ; and so it is necessary to return constantly to this way and to follow it ever anew in the various aspects in which it shows us all the wealth and at the same time all the toil of human existence on earth.

Work is one of these aspects, a perennial and fundamental one, one that is always relevant and constantly demands renewed attention and decisive witness. Because fresh questions and problems are always arising, there are always fresh hopes, but also fresh fears and threats connected with this basic dimension of human existence: Man's life is built up every day from work, from work it derives its specific dignity, but at the same time work contains the unceasing measure of human toil and suffering and also of the harm and injustice which penetrate deeply into social life within individual nations and on the international level. While it is true that man eats the bread produced by the work of his hands[5]— and this means not only the daily bread by which his body keeps alive but also the bread of science and progress, civilization and culture—it is also a perennial truth that he eats this bread by ''the sweat of his face,''[6] that is to say, not only by personal effort and toil, but also in the midst of many tensions, conflicts and crises, which in relationship with the reality of work disturb the life of individual societies and also of all humanity.

We are celebrating the 90th anniversary of the encyclical *Rerum Novarum* on the eve of new developments in technological, economic and political conditions which, according to many experts, will influence the world of work and production no less than the industrial revolution of the last century. There are many factors of a general nature: the widespread introduction of automation into many spheres of production, the increase in the cost of energy and raw materials, the growing realization that the heritage of nature is limited and that it is being intolerably polluted, and the emergence on the political scene of peoples who, after centuries of subjection, are demanding their rightful place among the nations and in international decision making. These new conditions and demands will require a reordering and adjustment of the structures of the modern economy and of the distribution of work. Unfortunately, for millions of skilled workers these changes may perhaps mean unemployment, at least for a time, or the need for retraining. They will very probably involve a reduction or a less rapid increase in material well-being for the more developed countries. But they can also bring relief and hope to the millions who today live in conditions of shameful and unworthy poverty.

It is not for the church to analyze scientifically the consequences that these changes may have on human society. But the church considers it her task always to call attention to the dignity and rights of those who work, to condemn situations in which that dignity and those rights are violated, and to help to guide the above-mentioned changes so as to ensure authentic progress by man and society.

2. In the Organic Development of the Church's Social Action and Teaching

It is certainly true that work as a human issue is at the very center of the "social question" to which, for almost a hundred years since the publication of the above-mentioned encyclical, the church's teaching and the many undertakings connected with her apostolic mission have been especially directed. The present reflections on work are not intended to follow a different line, but rather to be in organic connection with the whole tradition of this teaching and activity. At the same time, however, I am making them, according to the indication in the Gospel, in order to bring out from the heritage of the Gospel "what is new and what is old." [7] Certainly work is part of "what is old"—as old as man and his life on earth. Nevertheless, the general situation of man in the modern world, studied and analyzed in its various aspects of geography, culture and civilization, calls for the discovery of the new meanings of human work. It likewise calls for the formulation of the new tasks that in this sector face each individual, the family, each country, the whole human race and finally the church herself.

During the years that separate us from the publication of the encyclical *Rerum Novarum*, the social question has not ceased to engage the church's attention. Evidence of this are the many documents of the magisterium issued by the popes and by the Second Vatican Council, pronouncements by individual episcopates, and the activity of the various centers of thought and of practical apostolic initiatives, both on the international level and at the level of the local churches. It is difficult to list here in detail all the manifestations of the commitment of the church and of Christians in the social question for they are too numerous. As a result of the council, the main coordinating center in this field is the Pontifical Commission Justice and Peace, which has corresponding bodies within the individual bishops' conferences. The name of this institution is very significant. It indicates that the social question must be dealt with in its whole complex dimension. Commitment to justice must be closely linked with commitment to peace in the modern world. This twofold commitment is certainly supported by the painful experience of the two great world wars which in the course of the last 90 years have convulsed many European countries and, at least partially, countries in other continents. It is supported, especially since World War II, by the permanent threat of a nuclear war and the prospect of the terrible self-destruction that emerges from it.

If we follow the main line of development of the documents of the

221

supreme magisterium of the church, we find in them an explicit confirmation of precisely such a statement of the question. The key position, as regards the question of world peace, is that of John XXIII's encyclical *Pacem in Terris*. However, if one studies the development of the question of social justice, one cannot fail to note that, whereas during the period between *Rerum Novarum* and Pius XI's *Quadragesimo Anno* the church's teaching concentrates mainly on the just solution of the "labor question" within individual nations, in the next period the church's teaching widens its horizon to take in the whole world. The disproportionate distribution of wealth and poverty and the existence of some countries and continents that are developed and of others that are not call for a leveling out and for a search for ways to ensure just development for all. This is the direction of the teaching in John XXIII's encyclical *Mater et Magistra*, in the pastoral constitution *Gaudium et Spes* of the Second Vatican Council and in Paul VI's encyclical *Populorum Progressio*.

This trend of development of the church's teaching and commitment in the social question exactly corresponds to the objective recognition of the state of affairs. While in the past the "class" question was especially highlighted as the center of this issue, in more recent times it is the "world" question that is emphasized. Thus, not only the sphere of class is taken into consideration, but also the world sphere of inequality and injustice and, as a consequence, not only the class dimension, but also the world dimension of the tasks involved in the path toward the achievement of justice in the modern world. A complete analysis of the situation of the world today shows in an even deeper and fuller way the meaning of the previous analysis of social injustices; and it is the meaning that must be given today to efforts to build justice on earth, not concealing thereby unjust structures, but demanding that they be examined and transformed on a more universal scale.

3. The Question of Work, the Key to the Social Question

In the midst of the all these processes—those of the diagnosis of objective social reality and also those of the church's teaching in the sphere of the complex and many-sided social question—the question of human work naturally appears many times. This issue is, in a way, a constant factor both of social life and of the church's teaching. Furthermore, in this teaching attention to the question goes back much further than the last 90 years. In fact the church's social teaching finds its source in sacred scripture, beginning with the Book of Genesis and especially in the Gospel and the writings of the apostles. From the beginning it was part of the church's teaching, her concept of man and life in society, and especially the social morality which she worked out according to the needs of the different ages. This traditional patrimony was then inherited and developed by the teaching of the popes on the modern "social question," beginning with the encyclical *Rerum Novarum*. In this context, study of the question of work, as we have seen, has continually been brought up to date while maintaining that Christian basis of truth which can be called ageless.

While in the present document we return to this question once more—without however any intention of touching on all the topics that concern it—this is not merely in order to gather together and repeat what is already contained in the church's teaching. It is rather in order to highlight—perhaps more than has been done before—the fact that human work is a key, probably the essential key, to the whole social question, if we try to see that question really from the point of view of man's good. And if the solution—or rather the gradual solution—of the social question, which keeps coming up and becomes ever more complex, must be sought in the direction of "making life more human,"[8] then the key, namely human work, acquires fundamental and decisive importance.

II   Work and Man
4. In the Book of Genesis

The church is convinced that work is a fundamental dimension of man's existence on earth. She is confirmed in this conviction by considering the whole heritage of the many sciences devoted to man: anthropology, paleontology, history, sociology, psychology, and so on; they all seem to bear witness to this reality in an irrefutable way. But the source of the church's conviction is above all the revealed word of God, and therefore what is a conviction of the intellect is also a conviction of faith. The reason is that the church—and it is worthwhile stating it at this point—believes in man: She thinks of man and addresses herself to him not only in the light of historical experience, not only with the aid of the many methods of scientific knowledge, but in the first place in the light of the revealed word of the living God. Relating herself to man, she seeks to express the eternal designs and transcendent destiny which the living God, the creator and redeemer, has linked with him.

The church finds in the very first pages of the Book of Genesis the source of her conviction that work is a fundamental dimension of human existence on earth. An analysis of these texts makes us aware that they express—sometimes in an archaic way of manifesting thought—the fundamental truths about man, in the context of the mystery of creation itself. These truths are decisive for man from the very beginning, and at the same time they trace out the main lines of his earthly existence, both in the state of original justice and also after the breaking, caused by sin, of the creator's original covenant with creation in man. When man, who had been created "in the image of God...male and female,"[9] hears the words: "Be fruitful and multiply, and fill the earth and subdue it,"[10] even though these words do not refer directly and explicitly to work, beyond any doubt they indirectly indicate it as an activity for man to carry out in the world. Indeed, they show its very deepest essence. Man is the image of God partly through the mandate received from his creator to subdue, to dominate, the earth. In carrying out this mandate, man, every human being, reflects the very action of the creator of the universe.

Work understood as a "transitive" activity, that is to say, an activity beginning in the human subject and directed toward an external object, presupposes a specific dominion by man over the "the earth," and in its turn it confirms and develops this dominion. It is clear that the term "the earth" of which the biblical text speaks is to be understood in the first place as that fragment of the visible universe that man inhabits. By extension, however, it can be understood as the whole of the visible world insofar as it comes within the range of man's influence and of his striving to satisfy his needs. The expression "subdue the earth" has an immense range. It means all the resources that the earth (and indirectly the visible world) contains and which, through the conscious activity of man, can be discovered and used for his ends. And so these words, placed at the beginning of the Bible, never cease to be relevant. They embrace equally the past ages of civilization and economy, as also the whole of modern reality and future phases of development, which are perhaps already to some extent beginning to take shape, though for the most part they are still almost unknown to man and hidden from him.

While people sometimes speak of periods of "acceleration" in the economic life and civilization of humanity or of individual nations, linking these periods to the progress of science and technology and especially to discoveries which are decisive for social and economic life, at the same time it can be said that none of these phenomena of "acceleration" exceeds the essential content of what was said in that most ancient of biblical texts. As man, through his work, becomes more and more the master of the earth, and as he confirms his dominion over the visible world, again through his work, he nevertheless remains in every case and at every phase of this process within the Creator's original ordering. And this ordering remains necessarily and indissolubly linked with the fact that man was created, as male and female, "in the image of God." This process is, at the same time, universal: It embraces all human beings, every generation, every phase of economic and cultural development, and at the same time it is a process that takes place within each human being, in each conscious human subject. Each and every individual is at the same time embraced by it. Each and every individual, to the proper extent and in an incalculable number of ways, takes part in the giant process whereby man "subdues the earth" through his work.

5. Work in the Objective Sense: Technology

This universality and, at the same time, this multiplicity of the process of "subduing the earth" throw light upon human work, because man's dominion over the earth is achieved in and by means of work. There thus emerges the meaning of work in an objective sense, which finds expression in the various epochs of culture and civilization. Man dominates the earth by the very fact of domesticating animals, rearing them and obtaining from them the food and clothing he needs, and by the fact of being able to extract various natural resources from the earth and the seas. But man "subdues the earth" much more when he begins to cultivate it and then to transform its products, adapting them to his own use. Thus agriculture constitutes through human work a primary field of economic activity and an indispensable factor of production. Industry in its turn will always consist in linking the earth's riches—whether nature's living resources, or the products of agriculture, or the mineral or chemical resources—with man's work, whether physical or intellectual. This is also in a sense true in the sphere of what are called service industries and also in the sphere of research, pure or applied.

In industry and agriculture man's work has today in many cases ceased to be mainly manual for the toil of human hands and muscles is aided by more and more highly perfected machinery. Not only in industry but also in agriculture we are witnessing the transformations made possible by the gradual development of science and technology. Historically speaking this, taken as a whole, has caused great changes in civilization, from the beginning of the "industrial era" to the successive phases of development through new technologies, such as the electronics and the microprocessor technology in recent years.

While it may seem that in the industrial process it is the machine that "works" and man merely supervises it, making it function and keeping it going in various ways, it is also true that for this very reason industrial development provides grounds for reproposing in new ways the question of human work. Both the original industrialization that gave rise to what is called the worker question and the subsequent industrial and post-industrial changes show in an eloquent manner that, even in the age of ever more mechanized ''work,'' the proper subject of work continues to be man.

The development of industry and of the various sectors connected with it, even the most modern electronics technology, especially in the fields of miniaturization, communications and telecommunications and so forth, shows how vast is the role of technology, that ally of work that human thought has produced in the interaction between the subject and object of work (in the widest sense of the word). Understood in this case not as a capacity or aptitude for work, but rather as a whole set of instruments which man uses in his work, technology is undoubtedly man's ally. It facilitates his work, perfects, accelerates and augments it. It leads to an increase in the quantity of things produced by work and in many cases improves their quality. However it is also a fact that in some instances technology can cease to be man's ally and become almost his enemy, as when the mechanization of work ''supplants'' him, taking away all personal satisfaction and the incentive to creativity and responsibility, when it deprives many workers of their previous employment or when, through exalting the machine, it reduces man to the status of its slave.

If the biblical words ''subdue the earth'' addressed to man from the very beginning are understood in the context of the whole modern age, industrial and post-industrial, then they undoubtedly include also a relationship with technology, with the world of machinery which is the fruit of the work of the human intellect and a historical confirmation of man's dominion over nature.

The recent stage of human history, especially that of certain societies, brings a correct affirmation of technology as a basic coefficient of economic progress; but at the same time this affirmation has been accompanied by and continues to be accompanied by essential questions concerning human work in relationship to its subject, which is man. These questions are particularly charged with content and tension of an ethical and social character. They therefore constitute a continual challenge for institutions of many kinds, for states and governments, for systems and international organizations; they also constitute a challenge for the church.

6. Work in the Subjective Sense: Man as the Subject of Work

In order to continue our analysis of work, an analysis linked with the word of the Bible telling man that he is to subdue the earth, we must concentrate our attention on work in the subjective sense, much more than we did on the objective significance, barely touching upon the vast range of problems known intimately and in detail to scholars in various fields and also, according to their specializations, to those who work. If the words of the Book of Genesis to which we refer in this analysis of ours speak of work in the objective sense in an indirect way, they also speak only indirectly of the subject of work; but what they say is very eloquent and is full of great significance.

Man has to subdue the earth and dominate it, because as the "image of God" he is a person, that is to say, a subjective being capable of acting in a planned and rational way, capable of deciding about himself and with a tendency to self-realization. As a person, man is therefore the subject of work. As a person he works, he performs various actions belonging to the work process; independently of their objective content, these actions must all serve to realize his humanity, to fulfill the calling to be a person that is his by reason of his very humanity. The principal truths concerning this theme were recenlty recalled by the Second Vatican Council, in the constitution *Gaudium et Spes,* especially in Chapter 1, which is devoted to man's calling.

And so this "dominion" spoken of in the biblical text being meditated upon here refers not only to the objective dimension of work, but at the same time introduces us to an understanding of its subjective dimension. Understood as a process whereby man and the human race subdue the earth, work corresponds to this basic biblical concept only when throughout the process man manifests himself and confirms himself as the one who "dominates." This dominion, in a certain sense, refers to the subjective dimension even more than to the objective one: This dimension conditions the very ethical nature of work. In fact there is no doubt that human work has an ethical value of its own, which clearly and directly remains linked to the fact that the one who carries it out is a person, a conscious and free subject, that is to say, a subject that decides about himself.

This truth, which in a sense constitutes the fundamental and perennial heart of Christian teaching on human work, has had and continues to have primary significance for the formulation of the important social problems characterizing whole ages.

The ancient world introduced its own typical differentiation of people into classes according to the type of work done. Work which demanded from the worker the exercise of physical strength, the work of muscles and hands, was considered unworthy of free men and was therefore given to slaves. By broadening certain aspects that already belonged to the Old Testament, Christianity brought about a fundamental change of ideas in this field, taking the whole content of the gospel message as its point of departure, especially the fact that the one who, while being God, became like us in all things[11] devoted most of the years of his life on earth to manual work at the carpenter's bench. This circumstance constitutes in itself the most eloquent "gospel of work," showing that the basis for determining the value of human work is not primarily the kind of work being done, but the fact that the one who is doing it is a person. The sources of the dignity of work are to be sought primarily in the subjective dimension, not in the objective one.

Such a concept practically does away with the very basis of the ancient differentiation of people into classes according to the kind of work done. This does not mean that from the objective point of view human work cannot and must not be rated and qualified in any way. It only means that the primary basis of the value of work is man himself, who is its subject. This leads immediately to a very important conclusion of an ethical nature: However true it may be that man is destined for work and called to it, in the first place work is "for man" and not man "for work." Through this conclusion one rightly comes to recognize the pre-eminence of the subjective meaning of work over the objective one. Given this way of understanding things and presupposing that different sorts of work that people do can have greater or lesser objective value, let us try nevertheless to show that each sort is judged above all by the measure of the dignity of the subject of work, that is to say, the person, the individual who carries it out. On the other hand, independent of the work that every man does, and presupposing that this work constitutes a purpose—at times a very demanding one—of his activity, this purpose does not possess a definitive meaning in itself. In fact, in the final analysis it is always man who is the purpose of the work, whatever work it is that is done by man—even if the common scale of values rates it as the merest "service," as the most monotonous, even the most alienating work.

7. A Threat to the Right Order of Values

It is precisely these fundamental affirmations about work that always emerged from the wealth of Christian truth, especially from the very message of the "gospel of work," thus creating the basis for a new way of thinking, judging and acting. In the modern period, from the beginning of the industrial age, the Christian truth about work had to oppose the various trends of materialistic and economistic thought.

For certain supporters of such ideas, work was understood and treated as a sort of "merchandise" that the worker—especially the industrial worker—sells to the employer, who at the same time is the possessor of the capital, that is to say, of all the working tools and means that make production possible. This way of looking at work was widespread especially in the first half of the 19th century. Since then explicit expressions of this sort have almost disappeared and have given way to more human ways of thinking about work and evaluating it. The interaction between the worker and the tools and means of production has given rise to the development of various forms of capitalism—parallel with various forms of collectivism—into which other socioeconomic elements have entered as a consequence of new concrete circumstances, of the activity of workers' associations and public authorities, and of the emergence of large transnational enterprises. Nevertheless, the danger of treating work as a special kind of "mechandise" or as an impersonal "force" needed for production (the expression "work force" is in fact in common use) always exists, especially when the whole way of looking at the question of economics is marked by the premises of materialistic economism.

A systematic opportunity for thinking and evaluating in this way, and in a certain sense a stimulus for doing so, is provided by the quickening process of the development of a onesidely materialistic civilization, which gives prime importance to the objective dimension of work, while the subjective dimension—everything in direct or indirect relationship with the subject of work—remains on a secondary level. In all cases of this sort, in every social situation of this type, there is a confusion or even a reversal of the order laid down from the beginning by the words of the Book of Genesis: Man is treated as an instrument of production,[12] whereas he—he alone, independent of the work he does—ought to be treated as the effective subject of work and its true maker and creator. Precisely this reversal of order, whatever the program or name under which it occurs, should rightly be called "capitalism"—in the sense more fully explained below. Everybody knows that capitalism has a definite historical meaning as a system, an economic and social system, opposed to "socialism" or "communism." But in light of the analysis of the fundamental reality of the whole economic process—first and foremost of the production structure that work is—it should be recognized that the error of early capitalism can be repeated wherever man is in a way treated on the same level as the whole complex of the material means of production, as an instrument and not in accordance with the true dignity of his work—that is to say, where he is not treated as subject and maker, and for this very reason as the true purpose of the whole process of production.

This explains why the analysis of human work in the light of the words concerning man's "dominion" over the earth goes to the very heart of the ethical and social question. This concept should also find a central place in the whole sphere of social and economic policy, both within individual countries and in the wider field of international and intercontinental relationships, particularly with reference to the tensions making themselves felt in the world not only between East and West but also between North and South. Both John XXIII in the encyclical *Mater et Magistra* and Paul VI in the encyclical *Populorum Progressio* gave special attention to these dimensions of the modern ethical and social question.

8. Worker Solidarity

When dealing with human work in the fundamental dimension of its subject, that is to say, the human person doing the work, one must make at least a summary evaluation of developments during the 90 years since *Rerum Novarum* in relation to the subjective dimension of work. Although the subject of work is always the same, that is to say man, nevertheless wide-ranging changes take place in the objective aspect. While one can say that, by reason of its subject, work is one single thing (one and unrepeatable every time) yet when one takes into consideration its objective directions one is forced to admit that there exist many works, many different sorts of work. The development of human civilization brings continual enrichment in this field. But at the same time, one cannot fail to note that in the process of this development not only do new forms of work appear but also others disappear. Even if one accepts that on the whole this is a normal phenomenon, it must still be seen whether certain ethically and socially dangerous irregularities creep in and to what extent.

It was precisely one such wide-ranging anomaly that gave rise in the last century to what has been called "the worker question," sometimes described as "the proletariat question." This question and the problems connected with it gave rise to a just social reaction and caused the impetuous emergence of a great burst of solidarity between workers, first and foremost industrial workers. The call to solidarity and common action addressed to the workers—especially to those engaged in narrowly specialized, monotonous and depersonalized work in industrial plants, when the machine tends to dominate man—was important and eloquent from the point of view of social ethics. It was the reaction against the degradation of man as the subject of work and against the unheard-of accompanying exploitation in the field of wages, working conditions and social security for the worker. This reaction united the working world in a community marked by great solidarity.

Following the lines laid down by the encyclical *Rerum Novarum* and many later documents of the church's magisterium, it must be frankly recognized that the reaction against the system of injustice and harm that cried to heaven for vengeance[13] and that weighed heavily upon workers in that period of rapid industrialization was justified from the point of view of social morality. This state of affairs was favored by the liberal socio-political system, which in accordance with its "economistic" premises, strengthened and safeguarded economic initiative by the possessors of capital alone, but did not pay sufficient attention to the rights of the workers, on the grounds that human work is solely an instrument of production, and that capital is the basis, efficient factor and purpose of production.

From that time, worker solidarity, together with a clearer and more committed realization by others of workers' rights, has in many cases brought about profound changes. Various forms of neocapitalism or collectivism have developed. Various new systems have been thought out. Workers can often share in running businesses and in controlling their productivity, and in fact do so. Through appropriate associations they exercise influence over conditions of work and pay, and also over social legislation. But at the same time various ideological or power systems and new relationships which have arisen at various levels of society have allowed flagrant injustices to persist or have created new ones. On the world level, the development of civilization and of communications has made possible a more complete diagnosis of the living and working conditions of man globally, but it has also revealed other forms of injustice much more extensive than those which in the last century stimulated unity between workers for particular solidarity in the working world. This is true in countries which have completed a certain process of industrial revolution. It is also true in countries where the main working milieu continues to be agriculture or other similar occupations.

Movements of solidarity in the sphere of work—a solidarity that must never mean being closed to dialogue and collaboration with others—can be necessary also with reference to the condition of social groups that were not previously included in such movements, but which in changing social systems and conditions of living are undergoing what is in effect "proletarianization" or which actually already find themselves in a "proletariat" situation, one which, even if not yet given that name, in fact deserves it. This can be true of certain categories or groups of the working "intelligentsia," especially when ever wider access to education and an ever increasing number of people with degrees or diplomas in the fields of their cultural preparation are accompanied by a drop in demand for their labor. This unemployment of intellectuals occurs or increases when the education available is not oriented toward the types of employment or service required by the true needs of society, or when there is less demand for work which requires education, at least professional education, than for manual labor, or when it is less well paid. Of course, education in itself is always valuable and an important enrichment of the human person; but in spite of that, "proletarianization" processes remain possible.

For this reason there must be continued study of the subject of work and of the subject's living conditions. In order to achieve social justice in the various parts of the world, in the various countries and in the relationships between them, there is a need for ever new movements of solidarity of the workers and with the workers. This solidarity must be present whenever it is called for by the social degrading of the subject of work, by exploitation of the workers and by the growing areas of poverty and even hunger. The church is firmly committed to this cause for she considers it her mission, her service, a proof of her fidelity to Christ, so that she can truly be the "church of the poor." And the "poor" appear under various forms; they appear in various places and at various times; in many cases they appear as a result of the violation of the dignity of human work: either because the opportunities for human work are limited as a result of the scourge of unemployment or because a low value is put on work and the rights that flow from it, especially the right to a just wage and to the personal security of the worker and his or her family.

9. Work and Personal Dignity

Remaining within the context of man as the subject of work, it is now appropriate to touch upon, at least in a summary way, certain problems that more closely define the dignity of human work in that they make it possible to characterize more fully its specific moral value. In doing this we must always keep in mind the biblical calling to "subdue the earth,"[14] in which is expressed the will of the Creator that work should enable man to achieve that "dominion" in the visible world that is proper to him.

God's fundamental and original intention with regard to man, whom he created in his image and after his likeness,[15] was not withdrawn or canceled out even when man, having broken the original covenant with God, heard the words: "In the sweat of your face you shall eat bread."[16] These words refer to the sometimes heavy toil that from then onward has accompanied human work; but they do not alter the fact that work is the means whereby man achieves that "dominion" which is proper to him over the visible world, by "subjecting" the earth. Toil is something that is universally known, for it is universally experienced. It is familiar to those doing physical work under sometimes exceptionally laborious conditions. It is familiar not only to agricultural workers, who spend long days working the land, which sometimes "bears thorns and thistles,"[17] but also to those who work in mines and quarries, to steel workers at their blast furnaces, to those who work in builders' yards and in construction work, often in danger of injury or death. It is also familiar to those at an intellectual workbench; to scientists; to those who bear the burden of grave responsibility for decisions that will have a vast impact on society. It is familiar to doctors and nurses, who spend days and nights at their patients' bedside. It is familiar to women, who sometimes without proper recognition on the part of society and even of their own families, bear the daily burden and responsibility for their homes and the upbringing of their children. It is familiar to all workers and, since work is a universal calling, it is familiar to everyone.

And yet in spite of all this toil—perhaps, in a sense, because of it—work is a good thing for man. Even though it bears the mark of a *bonum arduum,* in the terminology of St. Thomas,[18] this does not take away the fact that, as such, it is a good thing for man. It is not only good in the sense that it is useful or something to enjoy; it is also good as being something worthy, that is to say, something that corresponds to man's dignity, that expresses this dignity and increases it. If one wishes to define more clearly the ethical meaning of work, it is this truth that one must particularly keep in mind. Work is a good thing for man—a good thing for his humanity—because through work man not only transforms nature, adapting it to his own needs, but he also achieves fulfillment as a human being and indeed in a sense becomes "more a human being."

Without this consideration it is impossible to understand the meaning of the virtue of industriousness, and more particularly it is impossible to understand why industriousness should be a virtue: For virtue, as a moral habit, is something whereby man becomes good as man.[19] This fact in no way alters our justifiable anxiety that in work, whereby matter gains in nobility, man himself should not experience a lowering of his own dignity.[20] Again, it is well known that it is possible to use work in various ways against man, that it is possible to punish man with the system of forced labor in concentration camps, that work can be made into a means for oppressing man, and that in various ways it is possible to exploit human labor, that is to say, the worker. All this pleads in favor of the moral obligation to link industriousness as a virtue with the social order of work, which will enable man to become in work "more a human being" and not be degraded by it not only because of the wearing out of his physical strength (which, at least up to a certain point, is inevitable), but especially through damage to the dignity and subjectivity that are proper to him.

10. Work and Society: Family and Nation

Having thus confirmed the personal dimension of human work, we must go on to the second sphere of values which is necessarily linked to work. Work constitutes a foundation for the formation of family life, which is a natural right and something that man is called to. These two spheres of values—one linked to work and the other consequent on the family nature of human life—must be properly united and must properly permeate each other. In a way, work is a condition for making it possible to found a family, since the family requires the means of subsistence which man normally gains through work. Work and industriousness also influence the whole process of education in the family, for the very reason that everyone "becomes a human being" through, among other things, work, and becoming a human being is precisely the main purpose of the whole process of education. Obviously, two aspects of work in a sense come into play here: the one making family life and its upkeep possible, and the other making possible the achievement of the purposes of the family, especially education. Nevertheless, these two aspects of work are linked to one another and are mutually complementary in various points.

It must be remembered and affirmed that the family constitutes one of the most important terms of reference for shaping the social and ethical order of human work. The teaching of the church has always devoted special attention to this question, and in the present document we shall have to return to it. In fact, the family is simultaneously a community made possible by work and the first school of work, within the home, for every person.

The third sphere of values that emerges from this point of view—that of the subject of work—concerns the great society to which man belongs on the basis of particular cultural and historical links. This society—even when it has not yet taken on the mature form of a nation—is not only the great "educator" of every man, even though an indirect one (because each individual absorbs within the family the contents and values that go to make up the culture of a given nation); it is also a great historical and social incarnation of the work of all generations. All of this brings it about that man combines his deepest human identity with membership of a nation, and intends his work also to increase the common good developed together with his compatriots, thus realizing that in this way work serves to add to the heritage of the whole human family, of all the people living in the world.

These three spheres are always important for human work in its subjective dimension. And this dimension, that is to say, the concrete reality of the worker, takes precedence over the objective dimension. In the subjective dimension there is realized, first of all, that "dominion" over the world of nature to which man is called from the beginning according to the words of the Book of Genesis. The very process of "subduing the earth," that is to say work, is marked in the course of history and especially in recent centuries by an immense development of technological means. This is an advantageous and positive phenomenon, on condition that the objective dimension of work does not gain the upper hand over the subjective dimension, depriving man of his dignity and inalienable rights or reducing them.

III Conflict Between Labor and Capital in the Present Phase of History

11. Dimensions of the Conflict

The sketch of the basic problems of work outlined above draws inspiration from the texts at the beginning of the Bible and in a sense forms the very framework of the church's teaching, which has remained unchanged throughout the centuries within the context of different historical experiences. However, the experiences preceding and following the publication of the encyclical *Rerum Novarum* form a background that endows that teaching with particular expressiveness and the eloquence of living relevance. In this analysis, work is seen as a great reality with a fundamental influence on the shaping in a human way of the world that the Creator has entrusted to man; it is a reality closely linked with man as the subject of work and with man's rational activity. In the normal course of events this reality fills human life and strongly affects its value and meaning. Even when it is accompanied by toil and effort, work is still something good, and so man develops through love for work. This entirely positive and creative, educational and meritorious character of man's work must be the basis for the judgments and decisions being made today in its regard in spheres that include human rights, as is evidenced by the international declarations on work and the many labor codes prepared either by the competent legislative institutions in the various countries or by organizations devoting their social, or scientific and social, activity to the problems of work. One organization fostering such initiatives on the international level is the International Labor Organization, the oldest specialized agency of the United Nations.

In the following part of these considerations I intend to return in greater detail to these important questions, recalling at least the basic elements of the church's teaching on the matter. I must however first touch on a very important field of questions in which her teaching has taken shape in this latest period, the one marked and in a sense symbolized by the publication of the encyclical *Rerum Novarum*.

Throughout this period, which is by no means yet over, the issue of work has of course been posed on the basis of the great conflict that in the age of and together with industrial development emerged between "capital" and "labor," that is to say between the small but highly influential group of entrepreneurs, owners or holders of the means of production, and the broader multitude of people who lacked these means and who shared in the process of production solely by their labor. The conflict originated in the fact that the workers put their powers at the disposal of the entrepreneurs and these, following the principle of maximum profit, tried to establish the lowest possible wages for the work done by the employees. In addition there were other elements of exploitation connected with the lack of safety at work and of safeguards regarding the health and living conditions of the workers and their families.

This conflict, interpreted by some as a socioeconomic class conflict, found expression in the ideological conflict between liberalism, understood as the ideology of capitalism, and Marxism, understood as the ideology of scientific socialism and communism, which professes to act as the spokesman for the working class and the worldwide proletariat.

Thus the real conflict between labor and capital was transformed into a systematic class struggle conducted not only by ideological means, but also and chiefly by political means. We are familiar with the history of this conflict and with the demands of both sides. The Marxist program, based on the philosophy of Marx and Engels, sees in class struggle the only way to eliminate class injustices in society and to eliminate the classes themselves. Putting this program into practice presupposes the collectivization of the means of production so that through the transfer of these means from private hands to the collectivity human labor will be preserved from exploitation.

This is the goal of the struggle carried on by political as well as ideological means. In accordance with the principle of "the dictatorship of the proletariat," the groups that as political parties follow the guidance of Marxist ideology aim by the use of various kinds of influence, including revolutionary pressure, to win a monopoly of power in each society in order to introduce the collectivist system into it by eliminating private ownership of the means of production. According to the principal ideologists and leaders of this broad international movement, the purpose of this program of action is to achieve the social revolution and to introduce socialism and finally the communist system throughout the world.

As we touch on this extremely important field of issues, which constitute not only a theory but a whole fabric of socioeconomic, political and international life in our age, we cannot go into the details nor is this necessary for they are known both from the vast literature on the subject and by experience. Instead we must leave the context of these issues and go back to the fundamental issue of human work, which is the main subject of the considerations in this document. It is clear indeed that this issue, which is of such importance for man—it constitutes one of the fundamental dimensions of his earthly existence and of his vocation—can also be explained only by taking into account the full context of the contemporary situation.

12. The Priority of Labor

The structure of the present-day situation is deeply marked by many conflicts caused by man, and the technological means produced by human work play a primary role in it. We should also consider here the prospect of worldwide catastrophe in the case of a nuclear war, which would have almost unimaginable possibilities of destruction. In view of this situation we must first of all recall a principle that has always been taught by the church: the principle of the priority of labor over capital. This principle directly concerns the process of production: In this process labor is always a primary efficient cause, while capital, the whole collection of means of production, remains a mere instrument or instrumental cause. This principle is an evident truth that emerges from the whole of man's historical experience.

When we read in the first chapter of the Bible that man is to subdue the earth, we know that these words refer to all the resources contained in the visible world and placed at man's disposal. However, these resources can serve man only through work. From the beginning there is also linked with work the question of ownership, for the only means that man has for causing the resources hidden in nature to serve himself and others is his work. And to be able through his work to make these resources bear fruit, man takes over ownership of small parts of the various riches of nature: those beneath the ground, those in the seas, on land or in space. He takes over all these things by making them his workbench. He takes them over through work and for work.

The same principle applies in the successive phases of this process, in which the first phase always remains the relationship of man with the resources and riches of nature. The whole of the effort to acquire knowledge with the aim of discovering these riches and specifying the various ways in which they can be used by man and for man teaches us that everything that comes from man throughout the whole process of economic production, whether labor or the whole collection of means of production and the technology connected with these means (meaning the capability to use them in work), presupposes these riches and resources of the visible world, riches and resources that man finds and does not create. In a sense man finds them already prepared, ready for him to discover them and to use them correctly in the productive process. In every phase of the development of his work man comes up against the leading role of the gift made by ''nature,'' that is to say, in the final analysis, by the Creator. At the beginning of man's work is the mystery of creation. This affirmation, already indicated as my starting point, is the guiding thread of this document and will be further developed in the last part of these reflections.

Further consideration of this question should confirm our conviction of the priority of human labor over what in the course of time we have grown accustomed to calling capital. Since the concept of capital includes not only the natural resources placed at man's disposal, but also the whole collection of means by which man appropriates natural resources and transforms them in accordance with his needs (and thus in a sense humanizes them), it must immediately be noted that all these means are the result of the historical heritage of human labor. All the means of production, from the most primitive to the ultramodern ones—it is man that has gradually developed them: man's experience and intellect. In this way there have appeared not only the simplest instruments for cultivating the earth, but also through adequate progress in science and technology the more modern and complex ones: machines, factories, laboratories and computers. Thus everything that is at the service of work, everything that in the present state of technology constitutes its ever more highly perfected "instrument," is the result of work.

This gigantic and powerful instrument—the whole collection of means of production that in a sense are considered synonymous with "capital"—is the result of work and bears the signs of human labor. At the present stage of technological advance, when man, who is the subject of work, wishes to make use of this collection of modern instruments, the means of production, he must first assimilate cognitively the result of the work of the people who invented those instruments, who planned them, built them and perfected them, and who continue to do so. Capacity for work—that is to say, for sharing efficiently in the modern production process—demands greater and greater preparation and, before all else, proper training. Obviously it remains clear that every human being sharing in the production process, even if he or she is only doing the kind of work for which no special training or qualifications are required, is the real efficient subject in this production process, while the whole collection of instruments, no matter how perfect they may be in themselves, are only a mere instrument subordinate to human labor.

This truth, which is part of the abiding heritage of the church's teaching, must always be emphasized with reference to the question of the labor system and with regard to the whole socioeconomic system. We must emphasize and give prominence to the primacy of man in the production process, the primacy of man over things. Everything contained in the concept of capital in the strict sense is only a collection of things. Man, as the subject of work and independent of the work he does—man alone is a person. This truth has important and decisive consequences.

13. Economism and Materialism

In the light of the above truth we see clearly, first of all, that capital cannot be separated from labor; in no way can labor be opposed to capital or capital to labor, and still less can the actual people behind these concepts be opposed to each other, as will be explained later. A labor system can be right, in the sense of being in conformity with the very essence of the issue and in the sense of being intrinsically true and also morally legitimate, if in its very basis it overcomes the opposition between labor and capital through an effort at being shaped in accordance with the principle put forward above: the principle of the substantial and real priority of labor, of the subjectivity of human labor and its effective participation in the whole production process, independent of the nature of the services provided by the worker.

Opposition between labor and capital does not spring from the structure of the production process or from the structure of the economic process. In general the latter process demonstrates that labor and what we are accustomed to call capital are intermingled; it shows that they are inseparably linked. Working at any workbench, whether a relatively primitive or an ultramodern one, a man can easily see that through his work he enters into two inheritances: the inheritance of what is given to the whole of humanity in the resources of nature and the inheritance of what others have already developed on the basis of those resources, primarily by developing technology, that is to say, by producing a whole collection of increasingly perfect instruments for work. In working, man also "enters into the labor of others."[21] Guided both by our intelligence and by the faith that draws light from the word of God, we have no difficulty in accepting this image of the sphere and process of man's labor. It is a consistent image, one that is humanistic as well as theological. In it man is the master of the creatures placed at his disposal in the visible world. If some dependence is discovered in the work process, it is dependence on the Giver of all the resources of creation and also on other human beings, those to whose work and initiative we owe the perfected and increased possibilities of our own work. All that we can say of everything in the production process which constitutes a whole collection of "things," the instruments, the capital, is that it conditions man's work; we cannot assert that it constitutes as it were an impersonal "subject" putting man and man's work into a position of dependence.

This consistent image, in which the principle of the primacy of person over things is strictly preserved, was broken up in human thought, sometimes after a long period of incubation in practical living. The break occurred in such a way that labor was separated from capital and set in opposition to it, and capital was set in opposition to labor, as though they were two impersonal forces, two production factors juxtaposed in the same "economistic" perspective. This way of stating the issue contained a fundamental error, what we can call the error of economism, that of considering human labor solely according to its economic purpose. This fundamental error of thought can and must be called an error of materialism, in that economism directly or indirectly includes a conviction of the primacy and superiority of the material, and directly or indirectly places the spiritual and the personal (man's activity, moral values and such matters) in a position of subordination to material reality. This is still not theoretical materialism in the full sense of the term, but it is certainly practical materialism, a materialism judged capable of satisfying man's needs not so much on the grounds of premises derived from materialist theory as on the grounds of a particular way of evaluating things and so on the grounds of a certain hierarchy of goods based on the greater immediate attractiveness of what is material.

The error of thinking in the categories of economism went hand in hand with the formation of a materialist philosophy, as this philosophy developed from the most elementary and common phase (also called common materialism, because it professes to reduce spiritual reality to a superfluous phenomenon) to the phase of what is called dialectical materialism. However, within the framework of the present consideration, it seems that economism had a decisive importance for the fundamental issue of human work, in particular for the separation of labor and capital and for setting them up in opposition as two production factors viewed in the above-mentioned economistic perspective; and it seems that economism influenced this nonhumanistic way of stating the issue before the materialist philosophical system did. Nevertheless it is obvious that materialism, including its dialectical form, is incapable of providing sufficient and definitive bases for thinking about human work, in order that the primacy of man over the capital instrument, the primacy of the person over things, may find in it adequate and irrefutable confirmation and support. In dialectical materialism too man is not first and foremost the subject of work and the efficient cause of the production process, but continues to be understood and treated, in dependence on what is material, as a kind of "resultant" of the economic or production relations prevailing at a given period.

Obviously the antinomy between labor and capital under consideration here—the antinomy in which labor was separated from capital and set up in opposition to it, in a certain sense on the ontic level as if it were just an element like any other in the economic process—did not originate merely in the philosophy and economic theories of the 18th century; rather it originated in the whole of the economic and social practice of that time, the time of the birth and rapid development of industrialization, in which what was mainly seen was the possibility of vastly increasing material wealth, means, while the end, that is to say man, who should be served by the means, was ignored. It was this practical error that struck a blow first and foremost against human labor, against the working man, and caused the ethically just social reaction already spoken of above. The same error, which is now part of history and which was connected with the period of primitive capitalism and liberalism, can nevertheless be repeated in other circumstances of time and place if people's thinking starts from the same theoretical or practical premises. The only chance there seems to be for radically overcoming this error is through adequate changes both in theory and in practice, changes in line with the definite conviction of the primacy of the person over things and of human labor over capital as a whole collection of means of production.

14. Work and Ownership

The historical process briefly presented here has certainly gone beyond its initial phase, but it is still taking place and indeed is spreading in the relationships between nations and continents. It needs to be specified further from another point of view. It is obvious that when we speak of opposition between labor and capital, we are not dealing only with abstract concepts or "impersonal forces" operating in economic production. Behind both concepts there are people, living, actual people: On the one side are those who do the work without being the owners of the means of production, and on the other side those who act as entrepreneurs and who own these means or represent the owners. Thus the issue of ownership or property enters from the beginning into the whole of this difficult historical process. The encyclical *Rerum Novarum,* which has the social question as its theme, stresses this issue also, recalling and confirming the church's teaching on ownership, on the right to private property even when it is a question of the means of production. The encyclical *Mater et Magistra* did the same.

The above principle, as it was then stated and as it is still taught by the church, diverges radically from the program of collectivism as proclaimed by Marxism and put into practice in various countries in the decades following the time of Leo XIII's encyclical. At the same time it differs from the program of capitalism practiced by liberalism and by the political systems inspired by it. In the latter case, the difference consists in the way the right to ownership or property is understood. Christian tradition has never upheld this right as absolute and untouchable. On the contrary, it has always understood this right within the broader context of the right common to all to use the goods of the whole of creation: The right to private property is subordinated to the right to common use, to the fact that goods are meant for everyone.

Furthermore, in the church's teaching, ownership has never been understood in a way that could constitute grounds for social conflict in labor. As mentioned above, property is acquired first of all through work in order that it may serve work. This concerns in a special way ownership of the means of production. Isolating these means as a separate property in order to set it up in the form of "capital" in opposition to "labor" —and even to practice exploitation of labor—is contrary to the very nature of these means and their possession. They cannot be possessed against labor, they cannot even be possessed for possession's sake, because the only legitimate title to their possession—whether in the form of private ownership or in the form of public or collective ownership—is that they should serve labor and thus by serving labor that they should make possible the achievement of the first principle of this order, namely the universal destination of goods and the right to common use of them. From this point of view, therefore, in consideration of human labor and of common access to the goods meant for man, one cannot exclude the socialization, in suitable conditions, of certain means of production. In the course of the decades since the publication of the encyclical *Rerum Novarum,* the church's teaching has always recalled all these principles, going back to the arguments formulated in a much older tradition, for example, the well-known arguments of the *Summa Theologiae* of St. Thomas Aquinas.[22]

In the present document, which has human work as its main theme, it is right to confirm all the effort with which the church's teaching has striven and continues to strive always to ensure the priority of work and thereby man's character as a subject in social life and especially in the dynamic structure of the whole economic process. From this point of view the position of "rigid" capitalism continues to remain unacceptable, namely the position that defends the exclusive right to private ownership of the means of production as an untouchable "dogma" of economic life. The principle of respect for work demands that this right should undergo a constructive revision both in theory and in practice. If it is true that capital, as the whole of the means of production, is at the same time the product of the work of generations, it is equally true that capital is being unceasingly created through the work done with the help of all these means of production, and these means can be seen as a great workbench at which the present generation of workers is working day after day. Obviously we are dealing here with different kinds of work, not only so-called manual labor, but also the many forms of intellectual work, including white-collar work and management.

In the light of the above, the many proposals put forward by experts in Catholic social teaching and by the highest magisterium of the church take on special significance:[23] proposals for joint ownership of the means of work, sharing by the workers in the management and-or profits of businesses, so-called shareholding by labor, etc. Whether these various proposals can or cannot be applied concretely, it is clear that recognition of the proper position of labor and the worker in the production process demands various adaptations in the sphere of the right to ownership of the means of production. This is so not only in view of older situations but also, first and foremost, in view of the whole of the situation and the problems in the second half of the present century with regard to the so-called Third World and the various new independent countries that have arisen, especially in Africa but elsewhere as well, in place of the colonial territories of the past.

Therefore, while the position of "rigid" capitalism must undergo continual revision in order to be reformed from the point of view of human rights, both human rights in the widest sense and those linked with man's work, it must be stated that from the same point of view these many deeply desired reforms cannot be achieved by an *a priori* elimination of private ownership of the means of production. For it must be noted that merely taking these means of production (capital) out of the hands of their private owners is not enough to ensure their satisfactory socialization. They cease to be the property of a certain social group, namely the private owners, and become the property of organized society, coming under the administration and direct control of another group of people, namely those who, though not owning them, from the fact of exercising power in society manage them on the level of the whole national or the local economy.

This group in authority may carry out its task satisfactorily from the point of view of the priority of labor; but it may also carry it out badly by claiming for itself a monopoly of the administration and disposal of the means of production and not refraining even from offending basic human rights. Thus, merely converting the means of production into state property in the collectivist systems is by no means equivalent to "socializing" that property. We can speak of socializing only when the subject character of society is ensured, that is to say, when on the basis of his work each person is fully entitled to consider himself a part owner of the great workbench at which he is working with everyone else. A way toward that goal could be found by associating labor with the ownership of capital, as far as possible, and by producing a wide range of intermediate bodies with economic, social and cultural purposes; they would be bodies enjoying real autonomy with regard to the public powers, pursuing their specific aims in honest collaboration with each other and in subordination to the demands of the common good, and they would be living communities both in form and in substance in the sense that the members of each body would be looked upon and treated as persons and encouraged to take an active part in the life of the body.[24]

15. The "Personalist" Argument

Thus the principle of the priority of labor over capital is a postulate of the order of social morality. It has key importance both in the system built on the principle of private ownership of the means of production and also in the systems in which private ownership of these means has been limited even in a radical way. Labor is in a sense inseparable from capital; in no way does it accept the antinomy, that is to say, the separation and opposition with regard to the means of production that has weighed upon human life in recent centuries as a result of merely economic premises. When man works, using all the means of production, he also wishes the fruit of this work to be used by himself and others, and he wishes to be able to take part in the very work process as a sharer in responsibility and creativity at the workbench to which he applies himself.

From this spring certain specific rights of workers, corresponding to the obligation of work. They will be discussed later. But here it must be emphasized in general terms that the person who works desires not only due remuneration for his work; he also wishes that within the production process provision be made for him to be able to know that in his work, even on something that is owned in common, he is working "for himself." This awareness is extinguished within him in a system of excessive bureaucratic centralization, which makes the worker feel that he is just a cog in a huge machine moved from above, that he is for more reasons than one a mere production instrument rather than a true subject of work with an initiative of his own. The church's teaching has always expressed the strong and deep conviction that man's work concerns not only the economy but also, and especially, personal values. The economic system itself and the production process benefit precisely when these personal values are fully respected. In the mind of St. Thomas Aquinas,[25] this is the principal reason in favor of private ownership of the means of production. While we accept that for certain well-founded reasons exceptions can be made to the principle of private ownership—in our own time we even see that the system of "socialized ownership" has been introduced—nevertheless the personalist argument still holds good both on the level of principles and on the practical level. If it is to be rational and fruitful, any socialization of the means of production must take this argument into consideration. Every effort must be made to ensure that in this kind of system also the human person can preserve his awareness of working "for himself." If this is not done, incalculable damage is inevitably done throughout the economic process, not only economic damage but first and foremost damage to man.

IV   Rights of Workers
16. Within the Broad Context of Human Rights

While work, in all its many senses, is an obligation, that is to say a duty, it is also a source of rights on the part of the worker. These rights must be examined in the broad context of human rights as a whole, which are connatural with man and many of which are proclaimed by various international organizations and increasingly guaranteed by the individual states for their citizens. Respect for this broad range of human rights constitutes the fundamental condition for peace in the modern world: peace both within individual countries and societies and in international relations, as the church's magisterium has several times noted, especially since the encyclical *Pacem in Terris*. The human rights that flow from work are part of the broader context of those fundamental rights of the person.

However, within this context they have a specific character corresponding to the specific nature of human work as outlined above. It is in keeping with this character that we must view them. Work is, as has been said, an obligation, that is to say, a duty, on the part of man. This is true in all the many meanings of the word. Man must work both because the Creator has commanded it and because of his own humanity, which requires work in order to be maintained and developed. Man must work out of regard for others, especially his own family, but also for the society he belongs to, the country of which he is a child and the whole human family of which he is a member, since he is the heir to the work of generations and at the same time a sharer in building the future of those who will come after him in the succession of history. All this constitutes the moral obligation of work, understood in its wide sense. When we have to consider the moral rights corresponding to this obligation of every person with regard to work, we must always keep before our eyes the whole vast range of points of reference in which the labor of every working subject is manifested.

For when we speak of the obligation of work and of the rights of the worker that correspond to this obligation, we think in the first place of the relationship between the employer, direct or indirect, and the worker.

The distinction between the direct and the indirect employer is seen to be very important when one considers both the way in which labor is actually organized and the possibility of the formation of just or unjust relationships in the field of labor.

Since the direct employer is the person or institution with whom the worker enters directly into a work contract in accordance with definite conditions, we must understand as the indirect employer many different factors, other than the direct employer, that exercise a determining influence on the shaping both of the work contract and consequently of just or unjust relationships in the field of human labor.

17. Direct and Indirect Employer

The concept of indirect employer includes both persons and institutions of various kinds and also collective labor contracts and the principles of conduct which are laid down by these persons and institutions and which determine the whole socioeconomic system or are its result. The concept of "indirect employer" thus refers to many different elements. The responsibility of the indirect employer differs from that of the direct employer—the term itself indicates that the responsibility is less direct—but it remains a true responsibility: The indirect employer substantially determines one or other facet of the labor relationship, thus conditioning the conduct of the direct employer when the latter determines in concrete terms the actual work contract and labor relations. This is not to absolve the direct employer from his own responsibility, but only to draw attention to the whole network of influences that condition his conduct. When it is a question of establishing an ethically correct labor policy, all these influences must be kept in mind. A policy is correct when the objective rights of the worker are fully respected.

The concept of indirect employer is applicable to every society and in the first place to the state. For it is the state that must conduct a just labor policy. However, it is common knowledge that in the present system of economic relations in the world there are numerous links between individual states, links that find expression, for instance, in the import and export process, that is to say, in the mutual exchange of economic goods, whether raw materials, semimanufactured goods or finished industrial products. These links also create mutual dependence, and as a result it would be difficult to speak in the case of any state, even the economically most powerful, of complete self-sufficiency or autarky.

Such a system of mutual dependence is in itself normal. However it can easily become an occasion for various forms of exploitation or injustice and as a result influence the labor policy of individual states; and finally it can influence the individual worker who is the proper subject of labor. For instance the highly industrialized countries, and even more the businesses that direct on a large scale the means of industrial production (the companies referred to as multinational or transnational), fix the highest possible prices for their products, while trying at the same time to fix the lowest possible prices for raw materials or semimanufactured goods. This is one of the causes of an ever increasing disproportion between national incomes. The gap between most of the richest countries and the poorest ones is not diminishing or being stabilized, but is increasing more and more to the detriment, obviously, of the poor countries. Evidently this must have an effect on local labor policy and on the worker's situation in the economically disadvantaged societies. Finding himself in a system thus conditioned, the direct employer fixes working conditions below the objective requirements of the workers, especially if he himself wishes to obtain the highest possible profits from the business which he runs (or from the businesses which he runs, in the case of a situation of ''socialized'' ownership of the means of production).

It is easy to see that this framework of forms of dependence linked with the concept of the indirect employer is enormously extensive and complicated. It is determined, in a sense, by all the elements that are decisive for economic life within a given society and state, but also by much wider links and forms of dependence. The attainment of the worker's rights cannot however be doomed to be merely a result of economic systems which on a larger or smaller scale are guided chiefly by the criterion of maximum profit. On the contrary, it is respect for the objective rights of the worker—every kind of worker: manual or intellectual, industrial or agricultural, etc.—that must constitute the adequate and fundamental criterion for shaping the whole economy, both on the level of the individual society and state and within the whole of the world economic policy and of the systems of international relationships that derive from it.

Influence in this direction should be exercised by all the international organizations whose concern it is, beginning with the United Nations. It appears that the International Labor Organization and the Food and Agriculture Organization of the United Nations and other bodies too have fresh contributions to offer on this point in particular. Within the individual states there are ministries or public departments and also various social institutions set up for this purpose. All of this effectively indicates the importance of the indirect employer—as has been said above—in achieving full respect for the worker's rights, since the rights of the human person are the key element in the whole of the social moral order.

18. The Employment Issue

When we consider the rights of workers in relation to the "indirect employer," that is to say, all the agents at the national and international level that are responsible for the whole orientation of labor policy, we must first direct our attention to a fundamental issue: the question of finding work or, in other words, the issue of suitable employment for all who are capable of it. The opposite of a just and right situation in this field is unemployment, that is to say, the lack of work for those who are capable of it. It can be a question of general unemployment or of unemployment in certain sectors of work. The role of the agents included under the title of indirect employer is to act against unemployment, which in all cases is an evil and which, when it reaches a certain level, can become a real social disaster. It is particularly painful when it especially affects young people, who after appropriate cultural, technical and professional preparation fail to find work and see their sincere wish to work and their readiness to take on their own responsibility for the economic and social development of the community sadly frustrated. The obligation to provide unemployment benefits, that is to say, the duty to make suitable grants indispensable for the subsistence of unemployed workers and their families, is a duty springing from the fundamental principle of the moral order in this sphere, namely the principle of the common use of goods or, to put it in another and still simpler way, the right to life and subsistence.

In order to meet the danger of unemployment and to ensure employment for all, the agents defined here as "indirect employer" must make provision for overall planning with regard to the different kinds of work by which not only the economic life, but also the cultural life of a given society is shaped; they must also give attention to organizing that work in a correct and rational way. In the final analysis this overall concern weighs on the shoulders of the state, but it cannot mean one-sided centralization by the public authorities. Instead, what is in question is a just and rational coordination, within the framework of which the initiative of individuals, free groups and local work centers and complexes must be safeguarded, keeping in mind what has been said above with regard to the subject character of human labor.

The fact of the mutual dependence of societies and states and the need to collaborate in various areas mean that, while preserving the sovereign rights of each society and state in the field of planning and organizing labor in its own society, action in this important area must also be taken in the dimension of international collaboration by means of the necessary treaties and agreements. Here too the criterion for these pacts and agreements must more and more be the criterion of human work considered as a fundamental right of all human beings, work which gives similar rights to all those who work in such a way that the living standard of the workers in the different societies will less and less show those disturbing differences which are unjust and are apt to provoke even violent reactions. The international organizations have an enormous part to play in this area. They must let themselves be guided by an exact diagnosis of the complex situations and of the influence exercised by natural, historical, civil and other such circumstances. They must also be more highly operative with regard to plans for action jointly decided on, that is to say, they must be more effective in carrying them out.

In this direction, it is possible to actuate a plan for universal and proportionate progress by all in accordance with the guidelines of Paul VI's encyclical *Populorum Progressio*. It must be stressed that the constitutive element in this progress and also the most adequate way to verify it in a spirit of justice and peace, which the church proclaims and for which she does not cease to pray to the Father of all individuals and of all peoples, is the continual reappraisal of man's work, both in the aspect of its objective finality and in the aspect of the dignity of the subject of all work, that is to say, man. The progress in question must be made through man and for man and it must produce its fruit in man. A test of this progress will be the increasingly mature recognition of the purpose of work and increasingly universal respect for the rights inherent in work in conformity with the dignity of man, the subject of work.

Rational planning and the proper organization of human labor in keeping with individual societies and states should also facilitate the discovery of the right proportions between the different kinds of employment: work on the land, in industry, in the various services, white-collar work and scientific or artistic work, in accordance with the capacities of individuals and for the common good of each society and of the whole of mankind. The organization of human life in accordance with the many possibilities of labor should be matched by a suitable system of instruction and education aimed first of all at developing mature human beings, but also aimed at preparing people specifically for assuming to good advantage an appropriate place in the vast and socially differentiated world of work.

As we view the whole human family throughout the world, we cannot fail to be struck by a disconcerting fact of immense proportions: the fact that while conspicuous natural resources remain unused there are huge numbers of people who are unemployed or underemployed and countless multitudes of people suffering from hunger. This is a fact that without any doubt demonstrates that both within the individual political communities and in their relationships on the continental and world levels there is something wrong with the organization of work and employment, precisely at the most critical and socially most important points.

19. Wages and Other Social Benefits

After outlining the important role that concern for providing employment for all workers plays in safeguarding respect for the inalienable rights of man in view of his work, it is worthwhile taking a closer look at these rights, which in the final analysis are formed within the relationship between worker and direct employer. All that has been said above on the subject of the indirect employer is aimed at defining these relationships more exactly, by showing the many forms of conditioning within which these relationships are indirectly formed. This consideration does not however have a purely descriptive purpose; it is not a brief treatise on economics or politics. It is a matter of highlighting the deontological and moral aspect. The key problem of social ethics in this case is that of just remuneration for work done. In the context of the present there is no more important way for securing a just relationship between the worker and the employer than that constituted by remuneration for work. Whether the work is done in a system of private ownership of the means of production or in a system where ownership has undergone a certain ''socialization,'' the relationship between the employer (first and foremost the direct employer) and the worker is resolved on the basis of the wage, that is, through just remuneration of the work done.

It should also be noted that the justice of a socioeconomic system and, in each case, its just functioning, deserve in the final analysis to be evaluated by the way in which man's work is properly remunerated in the system. Here we return once more to the first principle of the whole ethical and social order, namely the principle of the common use of goods. In every system, regardless of the fundamental relationships within it between capital and labor, wages, that is to say remuneration for work, are still a practical means whereby the vast majority of people can have access to those goods which are intended for common use: both the goods of nature and manufactured goods. Both kinds of goods become accessible to the worker through the wage which he receives as remuneration for his work. Hence in every case a just wage is the concrete means of verifying the justice of the whole socioeconomic system and, in any case, of checking that it is functioning justly. It is not the only means of checking, but it is a particularly important one and in a sense the key means.

This means of checking concerns above all the family. Just remuneration for the work of an adult who is responsible for a family means remuneration which will suffice for establishing and properly maintaining a family and for providing security for its future. Such remuneration can be given either through what is called a family wage—that is, a single salary given to the head of the family for his work, sufficient for the needs of the family without the other spouse having to take up gainful employment outside the home—or through other social measures such as family allowances or grants to mothers devoting themselves exclusively to their families. These grants should correspond to the actual needs, that is, to the number of dependents for as long as they are not in a position to assume proper responsibility for their own lives.

Experience confirms that there must be a social re-evaluation of the mother's role, of the toil connected with it and of the need that children have for care, love and affection in order that they may develop into responsible, morally and religiously mature and psychologically stable persons. It will redound to the credit of society to make it possible for a mother—without inhibiting her freedom, without psychological or practical discrimination, and without penalizing her as compared with other women—to devote herself to taking care of her children and educating them in accordance with their needs, which vary with age. Having to abandon these tasks in order to take up paid work outside the home is wrong from the point of view of the good of society and of the family when it contradicts or hinders these primary goals of the mission of a mother.[26]

In this context it should be emphasized that on a more general level the whole labor process must be organized and adapted in such a way as to respect the requirements of the person and his or her forms of life, above all life in the home, taking into account the individual's age and sex. It is a fact that in many societies women work in nearly every sector of life. But it is fitting that they should be able to fulfill their tasks in accordance with their own nature, without being discriminated against and without being excluded from jobs for which they are capable, but also without lack of respect for their family aspirations and for their specific role in contributing, together with men, to the good of society. The true advancement of women requires that labor should be structured in such a way that women do not have to pay for their advancement by abandoning what is specific to them and at the expense of the family, in which women as mothers have an irreplaceable role.

Besides wages, various social benefits intended to ensure the life and health of workers and their families play a part here. The expenses involved in health care, especially in the case of accidents at work, demand that medical assistance should be easily available for workers and that as far as possible it should be cheap or even free of charge. Another sector regarding benefits is the sector associated with the right to rest. In the first place this involves a regular weekly rest comprising at least Sunday and also a longer period of rest, namely the holiday or vacation taken once a year or possibly in several shorter periods during the year. A third sector concerns the right to a pension and to insurance for old age and in case of accidents at work. Within the sphere of these principal rights there develops a whole system of particular rights which, together with remuneration for work, determine the correct relationship between worker and employer. Among these rights there should never be overlooked the right to a working environment and to manufacturing processes which are not harmful to the workers' physical health or to their moral integrity.

20. Importance of Unions

All these rights, together with the need for the workers themselves to secure them, give rise to yet another right: the right of association, that is, to form associations for the purpose of defending the vital interests of those employed in the various professions. These associations are called labor or trade unions. The vital interests of the workers are to a certain extent common for all of them; at the same time, however, each type of work, each profession, has its own specific character which should find a particular reflection in these organizations.

In a sense, unions go back to the medieval guilds of artisans, insofar as those organizations brought together people belonging to the same craft and thus on the basis of their work. However unions differ from the guilds on this essential point: The modern unions grew up from the struggle of the workers—workers in general but especially the industrial workers—to protect their just rights vis-a-vis the entrepreneurs and the owners of the means of production. Their task is to defend the existential interests of workers in all sectors in which their rights are concerned. The experience of history teaches that organizations of this type are an indispensable element of social life, especially in modern industrialized societies. Obviously this does not mean that only industrial workers can set up associations of this type. Representatives of every profession can use them to ensure their own rights. Thus there are unions of agricultural workers and of white-collar workers; there are also employers' associations. All, as has been said above, are further divided into groups or subgroups according to particular professional specializations.

Catholic social teaching does not hold that unions are no more than a reflection of the ''class'' structure of society and that they are a mouthpiece for a class struggle which inevitably governs social life. They are indeed a mouthpiece for the struggle for social justice, for the just rights of working people in accordance with their individual professions. However, this struggle should be seen as a normal endeavor ''for'' the just good: In the present case, for the good which corresponds to the needs and merits of working people associated by profession; but it is not a struggle ''against'' others. Even if in controversial questions the struggle takes on a character of opposition toward others, this is because it aims at the good of social justice, not for the sake of ''struggle'' or in order to eliminate the opponent. It is characteristic of work that it first and foremost unites people. In this consists its social power: the power to build a community. In the final analysis, both those who work and those who manage the means of production or who own them must in some way be united in this community. In the light of this fundamental structure of all work—in the light of the fact that, in the final analysis, labor and capital are indispensable components of the process of production in any social system—it is clear that even if it is because of their work needs that people unite to secure their rights, their union remains a constructive factor of social order and solidarity, and it is impossible to ignore it.

Just efforts to secure the rights of workers who are united by the same profession should always take into account the limitations imposed by the general economic situation of the country. Union demands cannot be turned into a kind of group or class ''egoism,'' although they can and should also aim at correcting—with a view to the common good of the whole of society—everything defective in the system of ownership of the means of production or in the way these are managed. Social and socioeconomic life is certainly like a system of "connected vessels," and every social activity directed toward safeguarding the rights of particular groups should adapt itself to this system.

In this sense, union activity undoubtedly enters the field of politics, understood as prudent concern for the common good. However, the role of unions is not to "play politics" in the sense that the expression is commonly understood today. Unions do not have the character of political parties struggling for power; they should not be subjected to the decision of political parties or have too close links with them. In fact, in such a situation they easily lose contact with their specific role, which is to secure the just rights of workers within the framework of the common good of the whole of society; instead they become an instrument used for other purposes.

Speaking of the protection of the just rights of workers according to their individual professions, we must of course always keep in mind that which determines the subjective character of work in each profession, but at the same time, indeed before all else, we must keep in mind that which conditions the specific dignity of the subject of the work. The activity of union organizations opens up many possibilities in this respect, including their efforts to instruct and educate the workers and to foster their self-education. Praise is due to the work of the schools, what are known as workers' or people's universities and the training programs and courses which have developed and are still developing this field of activity. It is always to be hoped that, thanks to the work of their unions, workers will not only have more, but above all be more: in other words that they will realize their humanity more fully in every respect.

One method used by unions in pursuing the just rights of their members is the strike or work stoppage, as a kind of ultimatum to the competent bodies, especially the employers. This method is recognized by Catholic social teaching as legitimate in the proper conditions and within just limits. In this connection workers should be assured the right to strike, without being subjected to personal penal sanctions for taking part in a strike. While admitting that it is a legitimate means, we must at the same time emphasize that a strike remains, in a sense, an extreme means. It must not be abused; it must not be abused especially for "political" purposes. Furthermore, it must never be forgotten that when essential community services are in question, they must in every case be ensured, if necessary by means of appropriate legislation. Abuse of the strike weapon can lead to the paralysis of the whole of socioeconomic life, and this is contrary to the requirements of the common good of society, which also corresponds to the properly understood nature of work itself.

21. Dignity of Agricultural Work

All that has been said thus far on the dignity of work, on the objective and subjective dimension of human work, can be directly applied to the question of agricultural work and to the situation of the person who cultivates the earth by toiling in the fields. This is a vast sector of work on our planet, a sector not restricted to one or other continent nor limited to the societies which have already attained a certain level of development and progress. The world of agriculture, which provides society with the goods it needs for its daily sustenance, is of fundamental importance. The conditions of the rural population and of agricultural work vary from place to place, and the social position of agricultural workers differs from country to country. This depends not only on the level of development of agricultural technology but also, and perhaps more, on the recognition of the just rights of agricultural workers and, finally, on the level of awareness regarding the social ethics of work.

Agricultural work involves considerable difficulties, including unremitting and sometimes exhausting physical effort and a lack of appreciation on the part of society, to the point of making agricultural people feel that they are social outcasts and of speeding up the phenomenon of their mass exodus from the countryside to the cities and unfortunately to still more dehumanizing living conditions. Added to this are the lack of adequate professional training and of proper equipment, the spread of a certain indvidualism and also objectively unjust situations. In certain developing countries, millions of people are forced to cultivate the land belonging to others and are exploited by the big landowners, without any hope of ever being able to gain possession of even a small piece of land of their own. There is a lack of forms of legal protection for the agricultural workers themselves and for their families in case of old age, sickness or unemployment. Long days of hard physical work are paid miserably. Land which could be cultivated is left abandoned by the owners. Legal titles to possession of a small portion of land that someone has personally cultivated for years are disregarded or left defenseless against the "land hunger" of more powerful individuals or groups. But even in the economically developed countries, where scientific research, technological achievements and state policy have brought agriculture to a very advanced level, the right to work can be infringed when the farm workers are denied the possibility of sharing in decisions concerning their services, or when they are denied the right to free association with a view to their just advancement socially, culturally and economically.

In many situations radical and urgent changes are therefore needed in order to restore to agriculture—and to rural people—its just value as the basis for a healthy economy, within the social community's development as a whole. Thus it is necessary to proclaim and promote the dignity of work, of all work, but especially of agricultural work in which man so eloquently "subdues" the earth he has received as a gift from God and affirms his "dominion" in the visible world.

22. The Disabled Person and Work

Recently national communities and international organizations have turned their attention to another question connected with work, one full of implications: the question of disabled people. They too are fully human subjects with corresponding innate, sacred and inviolable rights and, in spite of the limitations and sufferings affecting their bodies and faculties, they point up more clearly the dignity and greatness of man. Since disabled people are subjects with all their rights, they should be helped to participate in the life of society in all its aspects and at all the levels accessible to their capacities. The disabled person is one of us and participates fully in the same humanity that we possess. It would be radically unworthy of man and a denial of our common humanity to admit to the life of the community, and thus admit to work, only those who are fully functional. To do so would be to practice a serious form of discrimination, that of the strong and healthy against the weak and sick. Work in the objective sense should be subordinated in this circumstance too to the dignity of man, to the subject of work and not to economic advantage.

The various bodies involved in the world of labor, both the direct and the indirect employer, should therefore, by means of effective and appropriate measures, foster the right of disabled people to professional training and work so that they can be given a productive activity suited to them. Many practical problems arise at this point, as well as legal and economic ones; but the community, that is to say, the public authorities, associations and intermediate groups, business enterprises and the disabled themselves should pool their ideas and resources so as to attain this goal that must not be shirked: that disabled people may be offered work according to their capabilities, for this is demanded by their dignity as persons and as subjects of work. Each community will be able to set up suitable structures for finding or creating jobs for such people both in the usual public or private enterprises, by offering them ordinary or suitably adapted jobs, and in what are called ''protected'' enterprises and surroundings.

Careful attention must be devoted to the physical and psychological working conditions of disabled people—as for all workers—to their just remuneration, to the possibility of their promotion and to the elimination of various obstacles. Without hiding the fact that this is a complex and difficult task, it is to be hoped that a correct concept of labor in the subjective sense will produce a situation which will make it possible for disabled people to feel that they are not cut off from the working world or dependent upon society, but that they are full-scale subjects of work, useful, respected for their human dignity and called to contribute to the progress and welfare of their families and of the community according to their particular capacities.

23. Work and the Emigration Question

Finally, we must say at least a few words on the subject of emigration in search of work. This is an age-old phenomenon which nevertheless continues to be repeated and is still today very widespread as a result of the complexities of modern life. Man has the right to leave his native land for various motives—and also the right to return—in order to seek better conditions of life in another country. This fact is certainly not without difficulties of various kinds. Above all it generally constitutes a loss for the country which is left behind. It is the departure of a person who is also a member of a great community united by history, tradition and culture; and that person must begin life in the midst of another society united by a different culture and very often by a different language. In this case, it is the loss of a subject of work, whose efforts of mind and body could contribute to the common good of his own country, but these efforts, this contribution, are instead offered to another society which in a sense has less right to them than the person's country of origin.

Nevertheless, even if emigration is in some aspects an evil, in certain circumstances it is, as the phrase goes, a necessary evil. Everything should be done—and certainly much is being done to this end—to prevent this material evil from causing greater moral harm; indeed every possible effort should be made to ensure that it may bring benefit to the emigrant's personal, family and social life, both for the country to which he goes and the country which he leaves. In this area much depends on just legislation, in particular with regard to the rights of workers. It is obvious that the question of just legislation enters into the context of the present considerations, especially from the point of view of these rights.

The most important thing is that the person working away from his native land, whether as a permanent emigrant or as a seasonal worker, should not be placed at a disadvantage in comparison with the other workers in that society in the matter of working rights. Emigration in search of work must in no way become an opportunity for financial or social exploitation. As regards the work relationship, the same criteria should be applied to immigrant workers as to all other workers in the society concerned. The value of work should be measured by the same standard and not according to the difference in nationality, religion or race. For even greater reason the situation of constraint in which the emigrant may find himself should not be exploited. All these circumstances should categorically give way, after special qualifications have of course been taken into consideration, to the fundamental value of work, which is bound up with the dignity of the human person. Once more the fundamental principle must be repeated: The hierarchy of values and the profound meaning of work itself require that capital should be at the service of labor and not labor at the service of capital.

V   Elements for a Spirituality of Work

24. A Particular Task for the Church

It is right to devote the last part of these reflections about human work on the occasion of the 90th anniversary of the encyclical *Rerum Novarum* to the spirituality of work in the Christian sense. Since work in its subjective aspect is always a personal action, an *actus personae,* it follows that the whole person, body and spirit, participates in it, whether it is manual or intellectual work. It is also to the whole person that the word of the living God is directed, the evangelical message of salvation in which we find many points which concern human work and which throw particular light on it. These points need to be properly assimilated: An inner effort on the part of the human spirit, guided by faith, hope and charity, is needed in order that through these points the work of the individual human being may be given the meaning which it has in the eyes of God and by means of which work enters into the salvation process on a par with the other ordinary yet particularly important components of its texture.

The church considers it her duty to speak out on work from the viewpoint of its human value and of the moral order to which it belongs, and she sees this as one of her important tasks within the service that she renders to the evangelical message as a whole. At the same time she sees it as her particular duty to form a spirituality of work which will help all people to come closer, through work, to God, the creator and redeemer, to participate in his salvific plan for man and the world and to deepen their friendship with Christ in their lives by accepting, through faith, a living participation in his threefold mission as priest, prophet and king, as the Second Vatican Council so eloquently teaches.

25. Work as a Sharing in the Activity of the Creator

As the Second Vatican Council says, "Throughout the course of the centuries, men have labored to better the circumstances of their lives through a monumental amount of individual and collective effort. To believers, this point is settled: Considered in itself, such human activity accords with God's will. For man, created to God's image, received a mandate to subject to himself the earth and all that it contains, and to govern the world with justice and holiness; a mandate to relate himself and the totality of things to him who was to be acknowledged as the Lord and Creator of all. Thus, by the subjection of all things to man, the name of God would be wonderful in all the earth."[27]

The word of God's revelation is profoundly marked by the fundamental truth that man, created in the image of God, shares by his work in the activity of the Creator and that, within the limits of his own human capabilities, man in a sense continues to develop that activity and perfects it as he advances further and further in the discovery of the resources and values contained in the whole of creation. We find this truth at the very beginning of sacred scripture in the Book of Genesis, where the creation activity itself is presented in the form of "work" done by God during "six days,"[28] "resting" on the seventh day.[29] Besides, the last book of sacred scripture echoes the same respect for what God has done through his creative "work" when it proclaims: "Great and wonderful are your deeds, O Lord God the Almighty";[30] this is similar to the Book of Genesis, which concludes the description of each day of creation with the statement: "And God saw that it was good."[31]

This description of creation, which we find in the very first chapter of the Book of Genesis, is also in a sense the first "gospel of work." For it shows what the dignity of work consists of: It teaches that man ought to imitate God, his creator, in working, because man alone has the unique characteristic of likeness to God. Man ought to imitate God both in working and also in resting, since God himself wished to present his own creative activity under the form of work and rest. This activity by God in the world always continues, as the words of Christ attest: "My father is working still";[32] he works with creative power by sustaining in existence the world that he called into being from nothing, and he works with salvific power in the hearts of those whom from the beginning he has destined for "rest"[33] in union with himself in his "Father's house."[34] Therefore man's work too not only requires a rest every "seventh day,"[35] but also cannot consist in the mere exercise of human strength in external action; it must leave room for man to prepare himself, by becoming more and more what in the will of God he ought to be, for the "rest" that the Lord reserves for his servants and friends.[36]

Awareness that man's work is a participation in God's activity ought to permeate, as the council teaches, even "the most ordinary everyday activities. For, while providing the substance of life for themselves and their families, men and women are performing their activities in a way which appropriately benefits society. They can justly consider that by their labor they are unfolding the Creator's work, consulting the advantages of their brothers and sisters, and contributing by their personal industry to the realization in history of the divine plan."[37]

This Christian spirituality of work should be a heritage shared by all. Especially in the modern age, the spirituality of work should show the maturity called for by the tensions and restlessness of mind and heart. "Far from thinking that works produced by man's own talent and energy are in opposition to God's power, and that the rational creature exists as a kind of rival to the Creator, Christians are convinced that the triumphs of the human race are a sign of God's greatness and the flowering of his own mysterious design. For the greater man's power becomes, the farther his individual and community responsibility extends . . . People are not deterred by the Christian message from building up the world or impelled to neglect the welfare of their fellows. They are, rather, more stringently bound to do these very things."[38]

The knowledge that by means of work man shares in the work of creation constitutes the most profound motive for undertaking it in various sectors. "The faithful, therefore," we read in the constitution *Lumen Gentium,* "must learn the deepest meaning and the value of all creation, and its orientation to the praise of God. Even by their secular activity they must assist one another to live holier lives. In this way the world will be permeated by the spirit of Christ and more effectively achieve its purpose in justice, charity and peace . . . Therefore, by their competence in secular fields and by their personal activity, elevated from within by the grace of Christ, let them work vigorously so that by human labor, technical skill and civil culture, created goods may be perfected according to the design of the Creator and the light of his word."[39]

26. Christ, the Man of Work

The truth that by means of work man participates in the activity of God himself, his creator, was given particular prominence by Jesus Christ—the Jesus at whom many of his first listeners in Nazareth "were astonished, saying, 'Where did this man get all this? What is the wisdom given to him? . . . Is not this the carpenter?' "[40] For Jesus not only proclaimed but first and foremost fulfilled by his deeds the "gospel," the word of eternal wisdom that had been entrusted to him. Therefore, this was also "the gospel of work," because he who proclaimed it was himself a man of work, a craftsman like Joseph of Nazareth.[41] And if we do not find in his words a special command to work—but rather on one occasion a prohibition against too much anxiety about work and life[42]—at the same time the eloquence of the life of Christ is unequivocal: He belongs to the "working world," he has appreciation and respect for human work. It can indeed be said that he looks with love upon human work and the different forms that it takes, seeing in each one of these forms a particular facet of man's likeness with God, the creator and Father. Is it not he who says: "My Father is the vinedresser,"[43] and in various ways puts into his teaching the fundamental truth about work which is already expressed in the whole tradition of the Old Testament, beginning with the Book of Genesis?

The books of the Old Testament contain many references to human work and to the individual professions exercised by man: for example, the doctor,[44] the pharmacist,[45] the craftsman or artist,[46] the blacksmith[47] —we could apply these words to today's foundry workers—the potter,[48] the farmer,[49] the scholar,[50] the sailor,[51] the builder,[52] the musician,[53] the shepherd[54] and the fisherman.[55] The words of praise for the work of women are well known.[56] In his parables on the kingdom of God, Jesus Christ constantly refers to human work: that of the shepherd,[57] the farmer,[58] the doctor,[59] the sower,[60] the householder,[61] the servant,[62] the steward,[63] the fisherman,[64] the merchant,[65] the laborer.[66] He also speaks of the various forms of women's work.[67] He compares the apostolate to the manual work of harvesters[68] or fisherman.[69] He refers to the work of scholars too.[70]

This teaching of Christ on work, based on the example of his life during his years in Nazareth, finds a particularly lively echo in the teaching of the apostle Paul. Paul boasts of working at his trade (he was probably a tentmaker),[71] and thanks to that work he was able even as an apostle to earn his own bread.[72] "With toil and labor we worked night and day, that we might not burden any of you."[73] Hence his instructions, in the form of exhortation and command, on the subject of work: "Now such persons we command and exhort in the Lord Jesus Christ to do their work in quietness and to earn their own living," he writes to the Thessalonians.[74] In fact, noting that some "are living in idleness... not doing any work,"[75] the apostle does not hesitate to say in the same context: "If any one will not work, let him not eat."[76] In another passage he encourages his readers: "Whatever your task, work heartily, as serving the Lord and not men, knowing that from the Lord you will receive the inheritance as your reward."[77]

The teachings of the "apostle of the gentiles" obviously have key importance for the morality and spirituality of human work. They are an important complement to the great though discreet gospel of work that we find in the life and parables of Christ, in what Jesus "did and taught."[78].

On the basis of these illuminations emanating from the source himself, the church has always proclaimed what we find expressed in modern terms in the teaching of the Second Vatican Council: "Just as human activity proceeds from man, so it is ordered toward man. For when a man works he not only alters things and society, he develops himself as well. He learns much, he cultivates his resources, he goes outside of himself and beyond himself. Rightly understood, this kind of growth is of greater value than any external riches which can be garnered... Hence, the norm of human activity is this: that in accord with the divine plan and will, it should harmonize with the genuine good of the human race and allow people as individuals and as members of society to pursue their total vocation and fulfill it."[79]

Such a vision of the values of human work, or in other words such a spirituality of work, fully explains what we read in the same section of the council's pastoral constitution with regard to the right meaning of progress: "A person is more precious for what he is than for what he has. Similarly, all that people do to obtain greater justice, wider brotherhood and a more humane ordering of social relationships has greater worth than technical advances. For these advances can supply the material for human progress, but of themselves alone they can never actually bring it about."[80]

This teaching on the question of progress and development—a subject that dominates present-day thought—can be understood only as the fruit of a tested spirituality of human work; and it is only on the basis of such a spirituality that it can be realized and put into practice. This is the teaching and also the program that has its roots in "the gospel of work."

27. Human Work in the Light of the Cross and the Resurrection of Christ

There is yet another aspect of human work, an essential dimension of it, that is profoundly imbued with the spirituality based on the Gospel. All work, whether manual or intellectual, is inevitably linked with toil. The Book of Genesis expresses it in a truly penetrating manner: The original blessing of work contained in the very mystery of creation and connected with man's elevation as the image of God is contrasted with the curse that sin brought with it: "Cursed is the ground because of you; in toil you shall eat of it all the days of your life."[81] This toil connected with work marks the way of human life on earth and constitutes an announcement of death: "In the sweat of your face you shall eat bread till you return to the ground, for out of it you were taken."[82] Almost as an echo of these words, the author of one of the wisdom books says: "Then I considered all that my hands had done and the toil I had spent in doing it."[83] There is no one on earth who could not apply these words to himself.

In a sense, the final word of the Gospel on this matter as on others is found in the paschal mystery of Jesus Christ. It is here that we must seek an answer to these problems so important for the spirituality of human work. The paschal mystery contains the cross of the Christ and his obedience unto death, which the apostle contrasts with the disobedience which from the beginning has burdened man's history on earth.[84] It also contains the elevation of Christ, who by means of death on a cross returns to his disciples in the resurrection with the power of the Holy Spirit.

Sweat and toil, which work necessarily involves in the present condition of the human race, present the Christian and everyone who is called to follow Christ with the possibility of sharing lovingly in the work that Christ came to do.[85] This work of salvation came about through suffering and death on a cross. By enduring the toil of work in union with Christ crucified for us, man in a way collaborates with the Son of God for the redemption of humanity. He shows himself a true disciple of Christ by carrying the cross in his turn every day[86] in the activity that he is called upon to perform.

Christ, "undergong death itself for all of us sinners, taught us by example that we too must shoulder that cross which the world and the flesh inflict upon those who pursue peace and justice"; but also, at the same time, "appointed Lord by his resurrection and given all authority in heaven and on earth, Christ is now at work in people's hearts through the power of his Spirit...He animates, purifies and strengthens those noble longings too by which the human family strives to make its life more human and to render the whole earth submissive to this goal."[87]

The Christian finds in human work a small part of the cross of Christ and accepts it in the same spirit of redemption in which Christ accepted his cross for us. In work, thanks to the light that penetrates us from the resurrection of Christ, we always find a glimmer of new life, of the new good, as if it were an announcement of "the new heavens and the new earth"[88] in which man and the world participate precisely through the toil that goes with work. Through toil—and never without it. On the one hand this confirms the indispensability of the cross in the spirituality of human work; on the other hand the cross which this toil constitutes reveals a new good springing from work itself, from work understood in depth and in all its aspects and never apart from work.

Is this new good—the fruit of human work—already a small part of that "new earth" where justice dwells?[89] If it is true that the many forms of toil that go with man's work are a small part of the cross of Christ, what is the relationship of this new good to the resurrection of Christ? The council seeks to reply to this question also, drawing light from the very sources of the revealed word: "Therefore, while we are warned that it profits a man nothing if he gains the whole world and loses himself (cf. Lk. 9:25), the expectation of a new earth must not weaken but rather stimulate our concern for cultivating this one. For here grows the body of a new human family, a body which even now is able to give some kind of foreshadowing of the new age. Earthly progress must be carefully distinguished from the growth of Christ's kingdom. Nevertheless, to the extent that the former can contribute to the better ordering of human society, it is of vital concern to the kingdom of God."[90]

In these present reflections devoted to human work we have tried to emphasize everything that seemed essential to it, since it is through man's labor that not only "the fruits of our activity," but also "human dignity, brotherhood and freedom" must increase on earth.[91] Let the Christian who listens to the word of the living God, uniting work with prayer, know the place that his work has not only in earthly progress, but also in the development of the kingdom of God, to which we are all called through the power of the Holy Spirit and through the word of the Gospel.

In concluding these reflections, I gladly impart the apostolic blessing to all of you, venerable brothers and beloved sons and daughters.

I prepared this document for publication last May 15, on the 90th anniversary of the encyclical *Rerum Novarum,* but it is only after my stay in the hospital that I have been able to revise it definitively.

Given at Castelgandolfo, the 14th day of September, the feast of the triumph of the cross, in the year 1981, the third of the pontificate.

1. Cf. Ps. 127 (128):2; cf. also Gn. 3:17-19; Prv. 10:22; Ex. 1:8-14; Jer. 22:13.
2. Cf. Gn. 1:26.
3. Cf. Gn. 1:28.
4. Encyclical *Redemptor Hominis,* 14.
5. Cf. Ps. 127(128):2.
6. Gn. 3:19.
7. Cf. Mt. 13:52.
8. Second Vatican Council, Pastoral Constitution on the Church in the Modern World, *Gaudium et Spes,* 38.
9. Gn. 1:27.
10. Gn. 1:28.
11. Cf. Heb. 2:17; Phil 2:5-8.
12. Cf. Pope Pius XI, encyclical *Quadragesimo Anno:* AAS 23 (1931), p. 221.
13. Dt. 24:15; Jas. 5:4; and also Gn. 4:10.
14. Cf. Gn. 1:28.
15. Cf. Gn. 1:26-27.
16. Gn. 3:19.
17. Heb. 6:8; cf. Gn. 3:18.
18. Cf. *Summa Th.,* I-II, q. 40, a. 1, c.; I-II, q. 34, a. 2, ad 1.
19. *Ibid.*
20. Cf. *Quadragesimo Anno:* AAS 23 (1931) pp. 221-222.
21. Cf. Jn. 4:38.
22. On the right to property see *Summa Th.,* II-II, q. 66, arts. 2 and 6; *De Regimine Principum,* Book 1, Chapters 15 and 17. On the social function of property see *Summa Th.,* II-II, q. 134, art. 1, ad 3.
23. Cf. *Quadragesimo Anno:* AAS 23 (1931) p. 199; Second Vatican Council, *Gaudium et Spes,* 68.
24. Cf. Pope John XXIII, encyclical *Mater et Magistra:* AAS 53 (1961), p. 419.
25. Cf. *Summa Th.,* II-II, q. 65, a. 2.
26. *Gaudium et Spes,* 67.
27. *Ibid.,* 34.
28. Cf. Gn. 2:2; Ex. 20:8, 11; Dt. 5:12-14.
29. Cf. Gn. 2:3.
30. Rv. 15:3.
31. Gn. 1:4, 10, 12, 18, 21, 25, 31.
32. Jn. 5:17.
33. Cf. Heb. 4:1, 9-10.
34. Jn. 14:2.
35. Cf. Dt. 5:12-14; Ex. 20:8-12.
36. Cf. Mt. 25:21.
38. *Ibid.*
39. Second Vatican Council, Dogmatic Constitution on the Church *Lumen Gentium,* 36.

40. Mk. 6:2-3.
41. Cf. Mt. 13:55.
42. Cf. Mt. 6:25-34.
43. Jn. 15:1.
44. Cf. Sir. 38:1-3.
45. Cf. *Ibid.*, 38:4-8.
46. Cf. Ex. 31:1-5; Sir. 38:27.
47. Cf. Gn. 4:22; Is. 44:12.
48. Cf. Jer. 18:3-4; Sir. 38:29-30.
49. Cf. Gn. 9:20; Is. 5:1-2.
50. Cf. Eccl. 12:9-12; Sir. 39:1-8.
51. Cf. Ps. 107(108):23-30:Wis. 14:2-3a.
52. Cf. Gn. 11:3; 2 Kgs. 12:12-13; 22:5-6.
53. Cf. Gn. 4:21.
54. Cf. Gn. 4:2; 37:3; Ex. 3:1; 1 Sm. 16:11; *et passim.*
55. Cf. Ez. 47:10.
56. Cf. Prv. 31:15-27.
57. E.g., Jn. 10:1-16.
58. Cf. Mk. 12:1-12.
59. Cf. Lk. 4:23.
60. Cf. Mk. 4:1-9.
61. Cf. Mt. 13:52.
62. Cf. Mt. 24:45; Lk. 12:42-48.
63. Cf. Lk. 16:1-8.
64. Cf. Mt. 13:47-50.
65. Cf. Mt. 13:45-46.
66. Cf. Mt. 20:1-16.
67. Cf. Mt. 13:33; Lk. 15:8-9.
68. Cf. Mt. 9:37; Jn. 4:35-38.
69. Cf. Mt. 4:19.
70. Cf. Mt. 13:52.
71. Cf. Acts. 18:3.
72. *Ibid.*, 20:34-35.
73. 2 Thes. 3:8. St. Paul recognizes that missionaries have a right to their keep: 1 Cor. 9:6-14; Gal. 6:6; 2 Thes. 3:9; cf. Lk. 10:7.
74. 2 Thes. 3:12.
75. *Ibid.*, 3:11.
76. *Ibid.*, 3:10.
77. Col. 3:23-24.
78. Cf. Acts 1:1.
79. *Gaudium et Spes*, 35.
80. *Ibid.*
81. Gn. 3:17.
82. *Ibid.*, 3:19.

83. Eccl. 2:11.
84. Cf. Rom. 5:19.
85. Cf. Jn. 17:4.
86. Cf. Lk. 9:23.
87. *Gaudium et Spes,* 38.
88. Cf. 2 Pt. 3:13; Rv. 21:1.
89. Cf. 2 Pt. 3:13.
90. *Gaudium et Spes,* 39.
91. *Ibid.*

INDEX